All The People

NEA's Legacy of Inclusion and Its Minority Presidents

Al-Tony Gilmore

National Education Association, Washington, D.C.

Library of Congress Cataloging-in-Publication Data

Gilmore, Al-Tony.
  All the people : the National Education Association's legacy of inclusion and its
minority presidents / Al-Tony Gilmore.
      p. cm.
  Includes bibliographical references and index.
  ISBN 978-0-8106-0000-3 (alk. paper)
  1. National Education Association of the United States--History. 2. National
Education Association of the United States--Officials and employees. 3. Teachers'
unions--United States--History. I. Title.
  LB2844.53.U6G55 2008
  370.6073--dc22
                              2008036574

To the National Education Association's

Leadership Training and Development Programs

Contents

Preface..iii

Introduction 1

The Origins of the Legacy of Inclusion, 1857-1966................................3

Braulio Alonso: 1967-1968 – The Teacher Revolution,
    the Urban Movement, and the Merger 59

Elizabeth (Libby) Duncan Koontz: 1968-1969 – Human and Civil
    Rights, Decentralization, and Black Power 85

James Alexander Harris: 1974-1975 – Project Urban Neglect and
    the Constitutional Convention Transition 121

Mary Hatwood Futrell: 1983-1989 – The Education Reform
    Movement and the Rise of Presidential Identity 151

Reginald (Reg) Weaver: 2002-2008 – No Child Left Behind,
    Great Public Schools, and Team NEA 195

Epilogue...233

Notes 237

Index 263

Preface

The list of those who assisted in the research, writing, and conceptual development of this book is considerably longer than the acknowledgements suggest. Though I have criss-crossed the country many times over the years, giving presentations and talking with members about various aspects of the National Education Association's history with minorities, the actual idea for this project was the brainchild of John I. Wilson, NEA's Executive Director. When he first approached me about a book-length study of NEA's minority presidents, my initial instinct was to decline his request politely. I was almost certain that he had grossly underestimated the amount of work involved for a six-month sabbatical leave, but I was equally impressed by his resolve that it was a worthy pursuit, by his matching commitment to provide the resources, and by his confidence in me to deliver a quality product and meet a tight deadline.

I pondered over his idea for several weeks, and the more I thought about it, the more it became appealing to me for several reasons, some professional and some purely personal, but all challenging. Being a historian, I thought about the opportunity this project would allow me to share the contributions made to NEA by so many remarkable individuals, largely unknown to the current generation of NEA members and staff, as well as the American public. And then, like a bolt of lightning out of nowhere, it struck me that future generations should also know about these individuals and NEA's long journey into becoming the nation's leading racially inclusive organization of its size and significance. My preliminary research confirmed my decision to proceed with a full-length book when it disclosed how relatively little has been researched or written about the presidents in NEA's rich and illustrious history. Thus, I became fully engaged and energized in my search for the many pieces of the puzzle required to tell the story.

Other factors pushed me in the direction of writing the book. I distinctly recall several conversations I had with those who had attended my presentations in 2006, when NEA was celebrating the 40th Anniversary of the NEA/ATA merger, which made me more sensitive to the fragility of organizational memory. I had worked on two projects that resulted in a DVD on NEA's legacy of inclusion and an exhibit based on that theme for the 2006 Representative Assembly (RA) in Orlando. Far exceeding expectations, the responses to both were exceptional. Over 8,000 RA delegates visited the exhibit and countless others viewed the DVD, but what stunned me even more than the initial interest were those who approached me indicating that they were unaware that NEA had once maintained segregated state affiliates, and an even larger number who knew nothing about Braulio Alonso, Libby Koontz, and James Harris, all central figures in NEA's legacy of racial inclusion, and each an architect of the modern culture of NEA. I hope that this book will contribute toward reducing the frequency of those types of questions and improve our understanding of the long history of the minority contribution to NEA.

On the personal side of the coin, a number of the personalities now less well known than they were 25 years ago—J. Rupert Picott, Sam Ethridge, Ruby King, Vivian Bowser, Eugene Dryer, John Lucas, Sr., Walter Ridley, Horace Tate, Ruth Cage, Boyd Bosma, Jackie Gilmore, Mary Bishop, and Lillie Carswell—were all close friends who mentored me into the world of NEA culture. In fact, a number of my former teachers, including Hudson Barksdale, Ellen C. Watson, and C.C. Woodson, were leading figures in the Palmetto Education Association and the American Teachers Association, and they played pivotal roles in the respective mergers of the South Carolina Education Association and of NEA and ATA. To each I owe a debt of profound gratitude for sharing with me memories and documentation of minorities in NEA, some of which guided my intellectual curiosity, and many of which appear for the first time in this book.

For those who consented to my requests for interviews, I am appreciative of their time and efforts in recalling events that provided facts, texture, and context to the narrative. Among those who spent hours recording their thoughts with me were Bob Chanin, George Fischer, Lolita Dozier, Sandra Lamb, Ann Davis, Linda Pondexter-Chesterfield, Eugene Dryer, Chuck Williams, James Harris,

Mary Hatwood Futrell, Harold Webb, Lauri Wynn, Craig Phillips, Stan Johnson, Eleanor Coleman, Lois Edinger, Joe Reed, Keith Geiger, and Reg Weaver. I am especially thankful for those who welcomed me into their homes and extended warm and gracious hospitality: Craig Phillips, E. B. Palmer, Helen Bain, Don Morrison, and Braulio Alonso.

Olivia Gattis, of the NEA Archives, has unparalleled knowledge of organizational elements and was essential in the identification of photographs and key records and publications. Branita Griffin Henson and Lynn Coffin both gave their skills to the many layers of work required to transition a concept to a manuscript and then on to publication. For book layout and design, Kelly Cedeño was exceptional and delivered beyond expectations. Vanessa Nugent was also helpful with issues around production scheduling and permissions.

The late Walter Hill, Senior Archivist with the National Archives, and Richard Blackett, Distinguished Professor of History at Vanderbilt University, helped me greatly in my research on the elusive Robert Campbell, NEA's black founding father and its first minority member. The Bethesda, Maryland Public Library and the American University Library were gracious to allow me on-going desk space and assistance in securing secondary source materials. Of course, my colleagues, who value scholarly writing and the rigors of intellectual inquiry and who encouraged me along the way by asking all of the appropriate questions and probing my answers, led to the inclusion of important facts, many of which may have escaped my scrutiny. They include, but are not limited to: Nelson Canton, Sabrina Holcomb, Kevin Kumashiro, Maurice Joseph, Therman Evans, Bouy Te, Derrick Johnson, Al Mance, Ron Henderson, Mike McPherson, Bob Kim, David Sheridan, Britt Whiting, Reuben Porter, Dorothy Harrell, Tamara Hamilton, Pat Wright, Genevieve Phelps, Richard Verdugo, Pamela Rios-Mobley, and Doug Walker. Other colleagues who contributed in one way or another were Jim Hristakos, Sabrina Williams, Teresa Kelly, Robert Eagan, Bill Raabe, Steven Sluchansky, Mike Edwards, Lorenzo David, Marsha Blackburn, Nesa Chappelle, Everett Lucas, Margaret Laney, Evon Mazyck and Michael Rollocks.

Monique Bailey, my administrative assistant, typed the manuscript. Only she understands and has the skills to decipher the idiosyncrasies of my handwriting.

Monique brought the eye of a neutral observer and a fresh perspective to the review process, the value of which cannot be discounted. In what ultimately became a triangle of paper movement, Mary Claycomb, my editor, adroitly managed the flow of every draft and revision of the manuscript. My good fortune was the knowledge of the Association she brought to the project and her appreciation of American history. A consummate professional, she meticulously guided the manuscript into production, and because of her unparalleled attention to detail, this book profits. To both Monique and Mary I express deep respect and gratitude.

I have discussed and tested much of this work in various settings provided by NEA's Ethnic Minority Affairs Committee (EMAC), the planning committees of the Regional Minority Leadership Training Seminars, state and local NEA affiliates, and NEA's ethnic minority caucuses. It has been those NEA constituent groups that have provided venues for the sharing of the Association's history with countless members. By experience, as well as foresight, they understand philosopher George Santayana's warning of a century ago, that "Those who cannot remember the past are condemned to repeat it." It has been with those groups, that I have learned the value and significance of memory—both theirs and my own—in corroborating and enhancing events of the past. Without their trust and long support of my work, I do not believe any of this would have been possible.

Finally, thanks to Beryl and Jack, my wife and son, both lawyers, for augmenting my historical understanding of the many court cases cited in this book with the foundations of the legal arguments on which the decisions were based. And to Genevieve, my daughter, a public communications specialist, for her uncompensated research and design assistance, I am also grateful. Together, they endured the long evening hours spent on this book, which rightfully belongs to them. For their personal sacrifices, I can only promise to make it up.

Despite the assistance provided me by those I acknowledge and many others, the reader may encounter errors. If such there be, I take full responsibility for them.

Al-Tony Gilmore, Ph.D.

Introduction

Mary Hatwood Futrell, president of the National Education Association (NEA) from 1983 to 1989, astutely described NEA as an organization "with a soul." The simplicity and precision of that statement captures the essence of a broad range of thoughts and feelings about the Association. For Futrell, "soul" becomes a metaphor explaining the Association's programs and policies promoting human and civil rights; its demonstrated commitment to social justice; the remarkable number of minorities, women, and those of different sexual orientation and varying beliefs participating in the leadership of its local, state, and national organization; and the stable race and ethnic diversity of its staff members. At once, NEA is an idea and organization firmly interlocked to embrace inclusion and democracy. And, the pleasure of it all for Mary Futrell in the 1980s was that NEA had come to personify her own deeply held core values and convictions. The expression of her belief may have been novel, but she was then, and is now, not alone in holding it.

Soul, in the political context of NEA, is a derivative of the will of governance. Having a deliberative governing body elected by its membership, the Association has always been at any given point in time whatever its Board of Directors and the delegates to its Representative Assembly deemed it to be. In the search for the origins of the Association's soul, it seems logical to point to the 1966 merger of NEA with the black American Teachers Association (ATA). Others might attribute NEA's inclusive soul to the Civil Rights Movement's impact on the collective consciousness of its members, and the evidence persuasively suggests that recognition of those two events is essential to an appreciation of the culture of the dynamic, modern NEA. The soul of NEA, however, has been much longer in the making, and a closer scrutiny and probing of its past reveals that the Association's instincts for equality, fairness, and the promotion of the American ideal can be traced back to its purpose and the composition of its membership at its conception, more than a century before either the merger or the Civil Rights Movement.

Any penetrating search for the soul of the National Education Association must begin with its founders in the summer of 1857. At the base of the organization's family tree are two white women and a black man, all three of whom signed the first constitution as charter members. When those three individuals assembled with 40 other largely liberal and progressive-minded educators to found an organization first named the National Teachers' Association (NTA), there was nothing ordinary about their participation. The inclusive composition of this motley group was as anachronistic as the vision they crafted for the new organization was bold and inspiring.

The Origins of the Legacy of Inclusion, 1857-1966

T he year 1857 was typical of the preceding mid-century decades: the South cultivated cotton, defended slavery, enjoyed an agricultural economy, and discussed secession, while the North cultivated wheat, questioned slavery, rejected the concept of secession, and promoted manufacture and trade. The coexistence of slave and free states dominated political discourse in both regions, with neither willing to concede dominance to the other. Illiteracy and poverty were rampant in both regions. Although the principle of maintaining tax-supported schools had been established in the North and was gaining a foothold in the South, the distribution of schools and educational services favored those residing in cities and small towns measurably more than those living in rural areas and isolated villages. The greater concentration of schools in areas having larger populations gave decided advantages to residents of the North for access to education. Still, in both regions, the children of professionals, skilled artisans, and others of stable financial means were more likely to have sustained enrollment in schools.[1]

No publicly-funded schools in the South enrolled free blacks, and laws and customs forbade any teaching of slaves. Northern black families treasured educational opportunities and either formed private, independent schools, or enrolled their children in schools receptive to integrated education. Between those two options, some communities designated funds for schools established entirely for black education. The quality of instruction and adequacy of resources in both scenarios varied greatly, but for all that was lacking, these schools gave rise to black teachers. It was a fortunate beginning that characterized the black education landscape in 1857. The next decade would bring the emancipation of slaves and an explosion in the need for black teachers and others to provide education for black children and adults.[2]

The peculiar institution of slavery had flourished for over two hundred years before 1857, holding more than four million black men, women, and children in a perpetual system of involuntary servitude. It required complete subjugation of slaves to owners, many of whom meted out harsh discipline to those who, wittingly or unwittingly, did not obey their commands or live by their rules. The enslaved were without legal recourse, and punishment of those who resisted that social arrangement was swift and brutal. Slave-owners reaped handsome profits from the commerce of slavery; in Virginia in 1857, for example, 35 slaves sold for an average of $700 each on the Richmond market. By contrast, white women other than bond-servants had always been free, many actually benefiting from the wealth, status, and prestige of their slaveholding spouses or family members. Yet in both North and South, they were restricted to a limited range of occupations; denied equal pay for equal work; systematically excluded from membership in "men's" organizations; subject to property-holding restrictions; and were still some 60 years removed from obtaining the basic right to vote.[3]

That same year, in the infamous Dred Scott decision handed down by the U.S. Supreme Court, Chief Justice Roger B. Taney echoed the sentiments of the slaveholding states and many Americans in free states when he offered his chilling legal opinion, which reverberated throughout America. "A black man," wrote Taney from his post as leader of the nation's highest tribunal, "has no rights which a white man is bound to respect." Drawing on the traditions of Europe for precedent, he asserted that blacks for more than a century had "been regarded as beings of an inferior order, and altogether, unfit to associate with the white race, either in social or political relations."[4] The crushing decision in effect denied the legal consideration of blacks as citizens and affirmed their status as property; forbade them from initiating lawsuits in the courts; and tilted the delicate balance between free and slave states by allowing slavery into the territories. Indeed, it fueled the debate over the merits of slave labor versus free labor, and moved the nation closer to the precipice of war.

That was the national context in which two white women and one black man signed the constitution of the new National Teachers' Association. Little is known about the women, Miss Agnes W. Beecher and Mrs. Hannah DeWolfe Conrad, both of whom came from Dayton, Ohio, where they taught at the Cooper Institute, which was headed between 1857 and 1861 by Mrs. Conrad's husband, who also attended the NTA meeting and signed the charter.[5]

A bit more is known about Robert Campbell, a free "quadroon" who, despite his light skin, identified black. He was born in 1829 in Jamaica to a mulatto mother and a Scottish father. Because his father and maternal grandfather were both white and because of his fair complexion, he was classified by Jamaican law as "colored," which meant that he belonged to a group to which the Enfranchisement Law of 1834 extended voting rights. His strong identification with blacks can also be attributed to his maternal grandmother who was of pure African blood. According to the 1844 census, the Jamaican population was divided among 293,128 blacks, 68,529 coloreds, and 15,776 whites. Governmental concern to maintain a peaceful balance of power enabled the coloreds to make considerable progress in the island's political, social, and economic life, and to take advantage of the increasing educational opportunities that opened up to them after emancipation.[6]

By 1840, Campbell had become a printer's apprentice, and by the end of the decade he had entered the new government Normal School, founded in 1847 to meet the demand for trained teachers. By that time, however, the Jamaican economy was near collapse, faced with a decline in demand for its sugar as a result of the removal by the British government of preferential prices for West Indian sugar on the British market. By 1853, he had migrated with his wife and family to Central America and from there to New York City, where, to his dismay, he found that he was no longer "colored" but black. Jamaican class structure meant nothing in America. According to one scholar's description of the shock Jamaicans experienced when they came to America during this period, they underwent an "American racial baptism by fire."[7]

After working as a printer in New York, Campbell moved to Philadelphia in 1855, where he joined the faculty at the Quaker-operated Institute for

Colored Youth (also known as the Institute for Colored Children) as assistant principal. At a salary of $400 per year, he taught natural sciences, geography, elementary algebra, and Latin. He also taught evening classes, giving a series of lectures open to the public. From a meagerly attended 12 lectures in 1856, his schedule increased to 17 in 1857, and enrollment in the series, promoted by "leading men among the colored people," also increased. By the spring of 1857, he had become well-known in Philadelphia among a small and elite group of educated blacks.[8]

When Campbell arrived in Philadelphia slavery had been abolished in Pennsylvania through a gradual emancipation process that began with a state abolition law passed in 1780, the first in the nation. Free blacks had also been encouraged by the Better Regulation Act of 1826, which granted them the right to testify in courts of law. Racism in the 1850s, however, continued to run deep in Philadelphia, and blacks were far from being accepted as citizens equal with whites. In fact, the city was in reality two cities—one for blacks and one for whites—and the atmosphere was divided and hostile. There had been six major race riots in the city between 1829 and 1850, and the casualty rate for blacks had run high, with many being beaten, maimed, and killed. Black schools, churches, and homes were burned, and segregation flourished in churches and schools, and on public transportation. Largely because of these difficult conditions, schools such as the Institute for Colored Youth were founded, along with other all-black institutions and organizations. Denied access to classes at the Franklin Institute to continue his own scientific education, Campbell sought every opportunity to challenge the dual system, which may have been a primary reason for his attending the founding meeting of NTA. His personal crusade to integrate Philadelphia's institutions of higher education and its cultural and intellectual infrastructure would make him a revered figure among those of his race.[9]

His mere presence at the first meeting introduced him to the other founders of the organization that was to become NEA and reminded them of the principles of fairness, equality, and the spirit of justice as embodied in the NTA constitution, when it embraced "all the people." The decision to allow him to be a founding father was NTA's first and most profound statement of its position on race, and, in retrospect, it was one of the organization's finest moments—one which cannot be erased, and one that belongs to the ages. It was a beginning place from which forward progress could be measured.

The announcement of the meeting appeared in many journals that year, soliciting "practical teachers" to assemble in Philadelphia, to form a national association. Being a member of the state teachers' association in Pennsylvania, Campbell must have had confidence that there would be no membership restrictions based on race when he noticed that the "call" had been issued over the signatures of the presidents of ten state teachers' associations, all except one being free states. The summer of 1857 also was one of announcements of other professional meetings such as the Association for the Advancement of Education, the American Association for the Advancement of Science, and the American Institute of Instruction—none of which counted blacks among its members.[10] Because the "new" meeting for teachers was to take place in Philadelphia, he must have been curious about what prospects it held for his race.

Thomas Valentine and Daniel Hager, presidents of the teachers' associations of New York and Massachusetts, both free states, were responsible for issuing the call. Avoiding any references to race, the announcement cast a net large enough to include "all practicing teachers in the North and South, the East and West,

> "who are willing to unite in a general effort to promote the
> general welfare of our country by concentrating the wisdom
> and power of numerous minds, and distributing among all the
> accumulated experiences of all; who are ready to devote their
> energies and their means to advance the dignity, respectability
> and usefulness of their calling; and who, in fine, believe that
> the time has come when the teachers of the nation should
> gather into one great educational brotherhood."[11]

However intriguing the call may have been, had it been issued with identical wording by anyone from a slaveholding state, neither Campbell nor any other black educator would have misunderstood the regional coding of the message—whites only. And had the announced location of the meeting been in a slaveholding state, no reasonable black educator would have entertained the preposterous suggestion of traveling into the South and placing his or her own personal freedom in peril. Fortunately, Philadelphia, the city of Campbell's residence, was chosen for the first meeting.

Forty-three educators—three from slaveholding states—responded to the call, actively participated, and expressed their faith in the organization by becoming charter members. They represented 15 states and the District of Columbia. Attendance was smaller than had been anticipated and generally uneven from one session to the next, though the local newspapers reported that, overall, upwards of 100 persons were present. Aside from Campbell, there is no indication that other blacks attended, but the press reported "a good attendance of ladies." Not much is known about Campbell's participation at the first meeting beyond his signing as a charter member. The *Philadelphia Press*, however, did notice him and observed that "a quadroon from the Island of Jamaica, introduced himself to the convention," and "desired to take part in the proceedings."[12]

The convention lasted only one day, with President Thomas Valentine noting that it was "not large in point of numbers." It was not an auspicious beginning, but the size of the group did not deter attendees from going forward with the work required to form a stable organization. On that single day, they worked with dispatch, writing a preamble to the constitution, which has survived over the years, and is as relevant today as when first written. Captured in a single sentence was the purpose of the organization that was to become NEA: "To elevate the character and advance the interests of the profession of teaching, and to promote the course of popular education in the United States, we, whose names are subjoined, agree to adopt the following constitution. . . "

Still, the fleeting one-day gathering, coupled with the sparse attendance, bothered the editor of the *Pennsylvania School Journal*. "Where," he asked, "were the many hundreds of teachers of Philadelphia?"[13] No one knows the answer to the query, but one Philadelphia teacher from the "colored schools" attended, participated, and is forever enshrined as a founding father, and NEA's first black member and leader. Of parallel importance from an organizational perspective, whether owing to calculating and methodical design or simply through circumstance and sheer coincidence, by bridging the race and gender divide, the Association unveiled itself to the public as a democratic and progressive organization. From day one, by virtue of its promising inclusive and diverse membership and the conspicuous absence of race-restrictive language in its call and constitution, the new organization introduced itself with a vision of hope, and the ambition of greatness for educators in America. Now under the umbrella of one organization, there was a single-voice bully pulpit for teachers and the increasing number of schools in which they were employed. That one voice would be a democratic amalgam of the teachers' associations of 15 states—and soon more— that existed in the then 31 states of the Union.

The true test for any organization often has less to do with its enabling documents and lofty and inspiriting statements of intention than with the real-life and real-time positions of its leaders and membership. The match between the words of the new National Teachers' Association, and the actions and positions of its leaders soon became seamless. By the second meeting in Cincinnati, Ohio, in 1858, the fledging teacher group embraced universal education, resolving that it was the responsibility of states to provide the resources for full and free education for all youths within their jurisdiction. No exceptions were noted for free blacks, and even though the implication for enslaved youths may lend itself to speculation bordering on the incredulous, *all* youths were to be eligible. That same year, a conference on women's issues was sponsored by NTA to address general discrepancies in the teaching profession and in society.[14] Within a few years, women would be "formally" admitted to membership, marking the culmination of a nine-year discussion around women's membership which began with founding mothers Beecher and Conrad, who had been denied official membership in 1857, though—with inexplicable inconsistency— they had been granted charter membership status.

The initial meeting in Philadelphia was heralded by the press as the unfolding of a new era in American education. On perhaps no issue was this more pronounced than in the speeches, addresses, and proclamations on race given by NTA's early leaders. Not only did they argue vehemently against the institution of slavery and insist on universal education, but they also made clear that the term "all youths" was to include blacks and other minorities. Northern and antislavery members clearly dominated the young Association, and though the membership included some southerners, the pro-slavery stance of the South prior to the Civil War failed to find support in the new organization, nor did it accept the arguments of black inferiority that continued to be raised in that region after the war.[15]

Robert Campbell and other blacks who attended early conventions must have been impressed by the organization's posture on race, but to what extent was not recorded and, therefore, is not known. If having his name affixed to the constitution means that Campbell was influential and one whose opinions were solicited and valued by his co-founder colleagues, the implication is not corroborated by the proceedings of the first meeting or by subsequent documents. Yet, as we have seen, he stood out from the others, so much so, in fact, that a local newspaper reported that he "announced himself to the body" and was welcomed without reservations.[16] Though Campbell's name does not appear in the record of the proceedings, it should be noted that the names of other attendees are also absent from the recorded dialogue. What is known is that he did not attend any other NTA meetings. It is highly unlikely that his silence was motivated by any acrimony or displeasure with the goals of the organization, since, to the contrary, the new association reached out to him as an equal, signaling that race would not preclude his membership. Campbell was simply a bright and alert individual whose curiosity, which led him to NTA in the first place, was soon to lead him in pursuit of other promising ventures for his race. By 1858, he had left teaching and was emerging as a leading figure in the Pan African Movement, a repatriation initiative that had allied itself with the American Colonization Society, which had spearheaded the Back-to-Africa Movement. Joining forces under the direction of Martin Delaney, the most widely known emigrationist, he traveled extensively, lecturing and soliciting funds for the purpose of emigrating free blacks back to Africa to establish a colony on the African continent. In a word, the movement faltered after experiencing marginal success, ultimately failing for two reasons: the argument of the northern abolitionists that slavery would become even more firmly entrenched in America if free blacks abandoned the antislavery crusade; and, once the Civil War began in 1861, the encouragement and recruitment of free black men to join the Union Army and contribute to ending slavery.[17] Though the movement was largely unsuccessful, it was not because Campbell gave up on it. Being one of its leading proponents, he was convinced that Africa was a better alternative for his race than America. After making several trips to Africa in the hope of securing an infrastructure receptive to blacks moving back to Africa, in 1861 he took his family to settle in Lagos, Nigeria, and began to publish there the first English language newspaper, *The Anglo African*. He also wrote a book on his travels to Africa, entitled *A Pilgrimage to My Motherland*. Campbell lived in Lagos until his death in 1884.[18] Historically, he is remembered for his contributions as a leading African emigrationist, rather than as a founder of NEA.

The Association's loss of Campbell to his other interests in no way caused any shift in the organization's goal of universal education for all youth; its staunch criticism of slavery; and its post-Civil War emphasis on the training of black teachers for the multitudes of blacks recently freed from bondage. In fact, those issues soon began to flourish as established priorities and bedrock principles among the NTA leaders. The irony, however, is that for close to a century, while those issues gained a foothold in the organization, no single black personality would reach the level of brief acclaim achieved by Campbell.

A period of growth – 1865 to 1912

The National Teachers' Association changed its name to the National Educational Association in 1870, thus expanding its view of education as an institution and educators as careerists. In 1906, the Association was incorporated by an Act of Congress as the National Education Association.

All of NEA's convention proceedings between 1885 and 1912 were augmented by information on the delegates, including the names of the colleges they attended and their places of employment. In no instance were they identified by race. By cross-referencing names with black colleges, however, it can be determined that NEA appealed to black teachers—men and women—who attended the annual conventions in all of the years for which information is provided. And to advance this line of reasoning one step further, if practice precedes record-keeping, then blacks must have been attending the annual conventions before such documentation was introduced. The reasons may be obvious. The philosophy of the organization was well aligned with black educational interests—the lack of racial restrictions on membership would have been inviting; the frequent selection of prominent black speakers to address the conventions, and the annual sessions, reports, and discussions focusing on black education—all are persuasive reasons for the strong appeal to black educators. Moreover, with the conventions often being hosted in cities with large black teacher populations, local black attendance would almost certainly have peaked when the meetings could be reached easily and inexpensively.

Prior to 1868, all of NTA's annual conventions were held outside of the South, and only seven times in its first 100 years was a convention held in that region. But even when the Association chose a southern location, black education issues and black speakers were included on the agenda. The sum of NEA's outreach efforts to black educators was impressive, and the organization's message did not go unheard. The appeal of NEA to black educators, however, continued to lose ground to the emphasis black teachers in both North and South were giving to forming their own local and state teachers' associations; and what they sought to accomplish on their own made their black organizations more attractive than the original local and state associations dominated by white members, in which alienation and rejection were common, or than those in the South where membership was still restricted to whites. NEA, though admirable for not allowing race to enter into membership eligibility, was a national organization whose progressive behaviors were not necessarily modeled at the local level nor, for that matter, enforceable where there might be resistance. Black teachers understood that most pragmatic decisions on black education were made by officials at the local and state levels. Also, and not to be underestimated, the salaries of black teachers made it more economically efficient for them to be active in meetings that did not require long-distance travel. The early focus of black educators was on their immediate communities, and attending the annual meetings of NEA was a luxury most could not afford. After the Civil War it became increasingly clear to many that black teachers were best situated to address the needs of their schools and the students they taught.[19]

*****

During the latter half of the 19th century, recognition of a value in black teachers instructing black students was expressed over and over again by NEA leaders during annual conventions. It is possible that this position may have contributed inadvertently to the isolation of African American educators that persisted into the mid-20th century. During the Civil War, NTA had sided with the Union, and the castigation of those who denied education to blacks continued well after the war. At the 1865 convention in Harrisburg, Pennsylvania, Past President Andrew J. Rickoff, citing the closing of black schools in Columbia, Tennessee, and the infliction of 25 lashes on "an old gray-haired preacher" for teaching former slaves to read, blasted the South for its hostility to the education of blacks.[20] President-elect J. P. Wickersham also spoke scathingly to the delegates, choosing as his theme, "Education as an Element of Reconstruction." To the consternation of white southerners in attendance, he blamed slavery as the cause of the war and rejected contentions of the conflict of economic interests and federalism versus states' rights, in favor of an argument rooted in "the antagonism between free and slave labor." He urged the training of teachers for blacks and poor whites—both victims of slavery—as a preventive measure against the reestablishment of slavery. Reserving most of his anger for the former slave-owners, he questioned the efficacy of too quickly restoring their property and citizenship. If both were revoked, "some," he surmised, "will leave the country—the more the better." Former slave-owners, he suggested, must be dealt with "as Western farmers do the stumps in the clearings: work around them, and let them rot out." Unable to restrain his hatred of the defeated "tyrannical aristocracy," he hoped for a penalty that would require some to "atone for their crimes on the scaffold."[21]

Shifting to the freedmen, Wickersham spoke at length about education being a prerequisite to enable them to exercise the responsibilities of citizenship, and he warned that the formidable task of educating "four millions of people scattered over nine hundred thousand square miles of territory, even in the rudiments of learning, will require an army of superintendents and teachers, and complicated educational machinery." White teachers who, of course, were in far greater supply than black teachers, were encouraged to assume roles in educating the freedmen. But black teachers trained in the "Normal schools adapted to the purpose," were to eventually assume their share of the workload. They would be willing to live among their pupils; they would understand their wants and enjoy their sympathy; and they could do vastly more for them than white teachers, though better qualified. "These colored teachers should instruct the people wherever they can find them, adults as well as children, on the plantations, in camps or cabins, or meeting houses. . . . A people so eager to learn must be taught; and it will be found the best policy is to teach them by employing mainly teachers of their own race."[22]

Following Wickersham's address, Alexander Crummell was introduced to the assembly, thus becoming the first black to have the honor of addressing the convention. The theologian-scholar's experiences in merging the spread of education and Christianity had helped him build a national reputation. A native of Boston and a graduate of Cambridge University, he served as a professor at Liberia College in Africa. In 1865, at age 46, he belonged to that generation of Americans whose perspectives spanned two radically different worlds divided by the turmoil of the Civil War.[23] When the tall, proud, dark-complexioned speaker reached the podium, a deafening silence engulfed the room. "There was a nigger in our midst," recalled one observer. "What shall we do," he wondered, "refuse him a hearing because he is a lower-order being?" All of the convention stood still—some in disbelief, others in awe, but all intrigued—as Crummell, a man of pure African descent, began a mesmerizing address in an elegant and scholarly voice, shattering every stereotype attributed to his race.[24]

Basking in the wake of the 13th, 14th, and 15th Amendments, Crummell opened with a salute to those who assisted his race in rising from "degradation and benightedness" to "manhood and citizenship." He exhorted the convention attendees to understand that freedmen could only fulfill their duties and obligations as citizens through developing schools and teachers willing to train them. "Colored men," he said, echoing Wickersham, "are without doubt, the best agents for this end. Teachers raised up from among themselves, men who know their minds, men who have a common feeling and sympathy with them, these are the men best adapted to instruct, to elevate, and to lead them." He closed with a reminder to American blacks that their teaching responsibilities should not be limited to America, but should be extended to the African continent where the need for education was equally great. When his speech drew to a close, the audience responded with a sustained ovation, and many of those cheering and applauding may have first heard there the message that black educators were destined to play a role in spreading education and democracy in the nation. [25] NEA's conventions of the 19th century are noted as well for the regularity of reports and sessions on Indian, Mexican, and Chinese education.

*****

Generally regarded as NEA's first "major" assembly, the 1884 convention in Madison, Wisconsin was described as "the greatest educational show on earth." Attended by between 5,000 and 6,000 educators, it surpassed every convention that had preceded it. Exhibits of educational materials first appeared there; distinguished educators from throughout the nation attended; every state in the union was represented; the convention gave special consideration to "the Problems of Blacks and Indians"; and a special event billed as a Women's Evening was inaugurated to appease women whose attendance in Madison was noted as slightly exceeding that of men. The person credited for this celebrated meeting was Thomas W. Bicknell, who had won the NEA presidency on the promise of his promotional skills for staging large meetings. Unprecedented in the planning of NEA conventions were the week-after-week advertisements for the meeting carried in publications targeted to the education community. It lived up to expectations, and the size and grandeur of the event dominated the reports filed by the press. Those in attendance marveled as if it were a Barnum and Bailey circus, and Edgar Wesley, in his book *NEA: The First Hundred Years*, called it "The Greatest Educational Show on Earth."[26] Bicknell had delivered superbly, and for education stakeholders, NEA's annual convention soon became education's premier annual event. All of this was prelude to the introduction of the convention's keynote speaker, Booker T. Washington, principal of Tuskegee Institute in Alabama, whose selection as a speaker may have come as a surprise to many attendees. Virtually unknown outside of Alabama, Washington had founded his school only three years earlier. In that short time, however, he had crafted a message on black education and post-war reconciliation that appealed particularly to northern philanthropists and white southerners. The latter group had not had much influence in NEA, and Bicknell was committed to making them feel welcome and to improving their participation in the Association's conventions. His design was to make NEA truly national in more than just its name. He was unwilling, however, to placate southerners with concessions on unequal treatment of black convention members. Bicknell's determination met a stern test when he faced a race relations crisis. Upon learning that three black delegates to the Madison convention had been denied rooms at a local boarding house, he threatened to move the convention to another city unless all members were treated fairly. He prevailed, and the black delegates were provided accommodations. It was a daring move, risking the cordial relations he sincerely wanted with southern members, but the courage he displayed on civil rights was the talk of the convention, and unrestricted lodging for all its members became a trademark of NEA. It was the first, but not the last time NEA would have to take a stand to ensure non-discriminatory hotel accommodations for all of its members.[27]

Since Reconstruction had been overthrown and white rule restored in the South, the conditions of blacks had deteriorated, the political progress they had achieved had all but disappeared, and the promises made to them by the U.S. government immediately after the war had not been fulfilled. With former slaveholders regaining control of southern government, the rights secured for blacks under the 13th, 14th, and 15th Amendments were being virtually ignored by 1885: it was exactly as J. P. Wickersham had warned at the convention some twenty years earlier. In this post-Reconstruction atmosphere, the message of the young Booker T. Washington assuaged the fears of white southerners in that it defined a subservient role for blacks in the "New South." Maintaining that black progress should be invested in industrial, rather than liberal arts education; marginalizing the importance of black suffrage; and confirming by accepting the disturbing trend toward social segregation of the races, the theme of Washington's speech was one that would dominate policies on black education and life well into the next century.

In a speech laced with humor, he called on blacks to display goodwill and deference toward whites in matters suggesting equality. Expressing no animosity toward the violent overthrow of Reconstruction and the resulting denial of basic rights to blacks throughout the South, he chastised black "so called leaders, who are as a rule ignorant, immoral preachers or selfish politicians." After vividly describing the dismal rural environments where many southern blacks resided, he lampooned traditional and classical education for blacks, favoring teachers with skills in industrial arts. Speaking of the South of his own experience, he continued:

> "They need teachers with not only trained heads and hearts, but with trained hands. Schoolhouses are needed in every township and county. . . .The present wrecks of log cabins and bush harbors, where many of the schools are now taught, must be replaced…. Add to this a teacher who can scarcely write his name, and who is as weak mentally as morally, and you then have a faint idea of the educational condition of many parts of the South."[28]

Turning his attention to Tuskegee, he spoke proudly of his school having "a farm of five hundred acres, carpenter's shop, printing office, blacksmith's shop, and brick yard for boys, and a sewing department, laundry, flower gardening, and practical housekeeping for girls," all designed to secure places for blacks in the nation's economy. Washington brought his speech to a close with a plea to the audience to have faith in the leadership he sought to provide, which would ultimately remove "poverty and ignorance" from his race and diminish prejudice among whites. This address resonated with the audience, fascinated the press, and catapulted him into national prominence. Having heard from the young black educator, who would leave Madison as a noted rising star and continue to refine his theme, the convention roared with approval of his first major address.[29] Washington would go on to become the most powerful black man of his generation.

Following Washington's address, Bicknell next introduced a former confederate soldier, Robert Bingham, to speak to the audience about the "New South." Conditions for blacks in the South, Bingham argued, were strenuous, but not nearly as deplorable as northerners believed. Like Washington, he gave examples of black mechanics, carpenters, bricklayers, painters, and common laborers working "together in the greatest harmony at the same wages for the same kind of work," something he claimed that "could hardly have occurred in New England...Michigan or Wisconsin" or any other northern state. He boasted of the development and work of the recently founded black colleges in training teachers, and of prominent white physicians training "a class of colored medical students" at Shaw University in North Carolina. The New South, according to Bingham, accepted its defeat in the war, and he emphasized the fact that it "advanced the civilization of this country." Still, "the two races in the South must BE DEALT WITH SEPARATELY," because blacks, he argued, were innately inferior to whites, though with time and patience the gaps in achievement and progress would be closed, though not enough ever to contemplate integration. Patronizing and paternalistic with apology, he continued:

> "Compare the negro as he is in the South today—the quiet,
> peaceable, industrious citizen, the labor of whose hands
> produces six million bales of cotton annually—compare him,
> I say, with what he was one hundred years ago; compare him

with what his cannibal savage kindred are now in Africa;
compare the Southern negro who has received nothing but the
ballot from the United States Government, and who produces
six million bales of cotton annually—compare him, I say, with
the American Indian, whom the United States Government
has had in its special charge for one hundred years, and on
whom millions have been spent, and who produces absolutely
nothing. Make these comparisons and ask yourselves if any
savage race has ever shown such development in so short a
time."[30]

Washington and Bingham, one black, one white, both southerners, gave
their analyses to a receptive NEA audience, with neither coming close to
articulating the vision of the nation enshrined in the U.S. Constitution, or
in the hopes and dreams of all who believed in the doctrine that all men are
created equal. In retrospect, "the greatest educational show on earth," was a
moment that will not be counted among the best in NEA's illustrious history.

Between 1884 and the turn of the century, the NEA conventions provided
reports, discussions, and presentations on the educational status of blacks
and other minorities but failed to monitor or pay attention to the rising
local and state laws aimed at segregating the races. No one questioned
W. H. Bartholomew of Kentucky, when in 1886, he spoke glowingly of
segregated schools with the caveat "that the salaries of whites and the
salaries of the colored—those discharging equal responsibility—are exactly
the same."[31] That black schools and black teachers were best equipped for the
delivery of black education services seems to have been a consensus. Some
of the experiences of blacks at conventions during this period, and those
commented on by speakers, suggest that NEA was remarkably silent on or
oblivious to the random acts of discrimination in the daily lives of blacks
and other minorities. They provide pithy glimpses of the emergence of the
segregation patterns that would become law in the *Plessy v. Ferguson* decision
of 1896, and remain an intractable barrier to American democracy until the
Brown v. Board of Education decision of 1954.

Throughout the late 19th century NEA members continued to hear differing views on the treatment of African Americans. In 1884, the Reverend A. D. Mayo addressed the convention on the pernicious effects of segregation in the southern states. Citing the experience of R. T. Greener, a black Harvard graduate who traveled south on the trains, he spoke out against the shame of a society which demanded that this "cultured gentleman [be] four times ordered out of first-class cars." Mayo continued, "and it is to his credit that in each case he refused to go."[32] Interestingly, a contrary view was expressed subsequently by Booker T. Washington several months before the *Plessy v. Fergusson* decision was handed down. Speaking again at the 1896 convention, Washington bragged to NEA about the power of wealth to overcome segregation. "The black man," he quipped, "who spends $10,000 a year in freight charges with one of the southern railroads can select his own seat in the railroad coaches, or else a Pullman palace car will be put on for his special accommodation."[33] The frivolity of that statement on segregation was secondary only to the silence of the convention participants who failed to challenge that exaggerated example of segregated transportation. It glossed over the shame blacks had to endure and incorrectly envisioned a South that would make distinctions in segregation based on income. Even Joseph C. Price, the noted black North Carolina educator and the founder of Livingstone College, could not bring himself to the point of questioning segregation as a viable system of race relations. Speaking to the 1890 convention, he praised "this great Association" for never failing "to encompass the whole country in its patriotic vision. It is itself national. During all these years of struggles," he saluted NEA, "your annual trumpet tone has reverberated throughout the land, calling for national aid to education."[34]

Hence, although NEA was far from a perfect organization on race issues, black education leaders were impressed by it, and even the venerable Kelly Miller of Howard University and other prominent black educators were moved to join NEA. Aside from its cornerstone vision of "universal free education for all youth," a tradition of progressive leadership on the race question; discussions on black education at its annual conventions; and its ban on race-restrictive membership in the national organization, NEA appealed to blacks because it would not tolerate assertions that the race was uneducable, and because it did not have a closed mind on liberal arts as a viable alternative to industrial education for black students. Further, NEA refused to ignore or allow itself to become oblivious to the fact that the nation had a race problem affecting education, and NEA remained open to providing a platform for all proposed solutions. For late 19th century America, that predisposition qualified the organization as progressive, though not radical by any definition. A widely held opinion during that period about the "dangers" of educating blacks was never endorsed by National Educational Association leaders. Some individuals influential in national political and social sectors, however, believed that only industrial education designed for manual-labor occupations was acceptable as schooling for blacks. According to one white official, "The argument often advanced that book-learning carries a negro (sic) to the penitentiary" was accurate. Problems would result, he stated, if blacks were given a more advanced education. "[I]f his faculties of ambition and desire are stimulated along lines in which they cannot obtain their legitimate gratification, [a black] has been educated out of harmony with the requirements of his life and his inevitable circumstances will suffer from his abnormal inclinations and aspirations." That popular view was not exceptional, though it was one that Association leaders were loath to promote. NEA never climbed aboard the bandwagon of white supremacy as demonstrated by the general moderation of the tone of its convention discussions on black and minority education issues and concerns.[35]

NEA's 19th century convention sessions on "Negro Education" underscored the campaign for universal education with exalted testimonies on education's civilizing effects, which discouraged any extended discussions about the educability of blacks. One example offered by W. B. Powell, at an 1890 session, is noteworthy for the contentious trilogy it exposed: white fear of and paranoia about personal interactions with groups of uneducated blacks; the faith and optimism in what education could accomplish; and the casual suspension of the civil liberties of a whole race of people under the guise of public safety. Powell, a member from Washington, D.C., recounted a recent remark made by a District of Columbia Commissioner of Education, William B. Webb, at a black graduation exercise in the nation's capital.

> "Twenty-five years ago colored men were not allowed upon the streets of the city of Washington after sundown without passes. Twenty-five years ago, I myself, as Superintendent of Metropolitan Police, issued passes permitting colored persons to be found on the streets after sundown in the city of Washington. Tonight I am permitted, and I assure you it is no small pleasure to me, to give young colored people, not unlikely the sons and daughters of those to whom I issued passes twenty-five years ago, certificates showing that you have completed a course of instruction, including that of high school, provided for the young people of the District of Columbia, white and colored alike."[36]

In the realm of higher education, nothing was more impressive—even stunning—in the period between the Civil War and the turn of the century, than the number of Historically Black Colleges and Universities (HBCUs) founded. Where none existed before the war, more than 50 had been established by the early 1900s and were offering credentials ranging from secondary school diplomas to higher education certificates and degrees. A select few offered training in the professional fields of medicine, dentistry, pharmacy, and law. But for those fortunate enough to attend HBCUs, no training was more in demand than that of preparing teachers. Graduates were in high demand and some were recruited by entire communities to teach where no formal schooling had previously existed.[37]

The need for black teachers was colossal and so massively disproportionate to the supply that many teachers were admitted to the classrooms without proper preparation, and a sizable number lacked any college or normal school training. To a slightly lesser, but still significant, extent this early pattern of entry into the teaching profession was paralleled in white communities, particularly in rural areas, and in small towns and villages. The concept of free universal public education for all youth and accountable standards for teacher training were ideas whose currency had yet to reach most small communities with black schools. Although some schools enjoyed public funding, others were supported by churches and northern philanthropists, and a few were private, requiring parents to pay from their personal resources. Regardless of where the schools were established, however, observers noted that they were generally oversubscribed in student enrollment.[38] And while white missionaries assumed active roles in teaching black students and even larger roles in administering HBCUs, NEA leaders conceded the point, and frequently offered the audience of its convention, to those who thought black teachers were better prepared than whites to educate black students effectively. "The teacher and the taught must possess a common consciousness, a mutual affinity, as a condition of proper intellectual and moral growth," said J. H. Phillips in a speech to the annual meeting in 1897. "A white teacher and negro (sic) class will never realize the ideal school," he concluded, because "a teacher cannot appeal to the inner life of the pupil, and the craving consciousness of the child finds no responsive chord in the teacher."[39] He then summarized his argument for employing "Negro teachers in Negro schools" with the following points:

1. The educational development of the Negro must be from within, and by the race itself, and not solely through extraneous agencies.

2. The intellectual and moral dependence of the race should not be perpetuated. The Negro needs to be stimulated to independent activity.

3. As teacher of his race, the Negro occupies a position of trust and honor, which he needs to quicken his sense of responsibility, and to furnish him the incentives and the means for race elevation.

4. The teacher and the pupil must possess a common consciousness, whose historic processes have common elements, resulting in common intuitions. The teacher must embody in his character the race epochs and processes represented in the child.

5. The instinct of race identity renders impossible the realization of an ideal relation between the white teacher and the Negro pupil. The teacher and the child must be coordinated.[40]

Phillips was a white southerner, but his opinions were shared by numerous black educators and convention speakers, though most were loath to reject the usefulness of white teachers to the same degree. Given the severe shortage of black teachers during this period, black leaders and communities engaged in the common practice of lowering standards, often accepting those with mediocre abilities, who nonetheless professed a desire to improve the education of the race. Often the line between ability and desire became blurred and students were the recipients of the consequences. Teachers were at a premium, and allowances were made regularly for shortcomings, particularly when the alternative was a schoolroom without a teacher.[41]

Black teachers responded to the challenge, accepting positions in the schools of cities, towns, villages, hamlets, and distant rural areas, wherever there was a need. In all these locations status and prestige were bestowed on them. Teaching became a sacred duty and the work, though largely secular, was revered as providential among those they served. Assuming the roles of agents in the spreading of literacy and lifting of the veils of ignorance, they were placed on pedestals, respected by young and old alike and sought out for advice and guidance on issues from the mundane to the complex. They were architects in the building of educated and informed black communities, often building bridges of goodwill with well-meaning whites and serving as buffers between hostile communities. Their influence reverberated well beyond pedagogy. These educators were mirrors of black hope and aspiration, and their talents were projected on students, most of whom were without prior exposure to the daily restraint of the classroom and the rigors of discipline required for learning. The mere presence of the teachers cultivated the prospect of countless possibilities in the minds of those they taught, and was reassuring to appreciative parents desiring improved lives for their children. The value placed on acquiring an education became paramount and was associated with the goals sought by all: racial progress, economic stability, the sustenance of cohesive families, and the exercise of the responsibilities of citizenship. "Thou shalt seek learning" became the eleventh commandment, and like the impossibility of un-ringing a bell, once learning had occurred it could not be taken away.

*****

Even as it became increasingly clear that black teachers were in the best position to address the needs of their schools and the students under their tutelage, they understood that most pragmatic decisions on black education were made by officials at the local and state levels. Also, and not to be underestimated, the salaries of black teachers made it more economically efficient for them to be active in meetings that did not require long-distance travel. Consequently, the early focus of black educators was generously devoted to their immediate communities, and the building blocks for unity were first laid at the local level before spreading elsewhere. White teachers, however, proved highly capable of educating blacks and were welcomed into black communities, though their advocacy for black education lacked the same passion or sense of racial pride that their black counterparts exhibited.

Unfortunately, the respect and esteem accorded black teachers who taught black students—rarely did any teach white students—was not usually matched by the working conditions and learning environments in which they taught. Whether their meager salaries were publicly or privately funded, many were destined to spend their days in desolate one-room schools in isolated rural locations, working with inadequate resources and in substandard facilities. No dedication or training could have prepared them for the daily life of a teacher. Success was predicated upon faith, perseverance, and the transformative power of education to change lives and society. Not unaware of the conditions under which these educators labored, NEA continued to make the case that publicly funded schools for black youth would ensure an educated citizenry benefiting both races. But the southern black teachers were generally removed by geographical circumstances from the information flow of NEA and were not permitted to participate in the segregated local and state teachers' associations. Almost singularly focused on improving their immediate working conditions and their abilities to improve the lives of their students, they were moved to form their own teacher organizations.[42]

The sense of self-pride, the comfort and security of protective shelter, and the contagious feeling of unity and brotherhood generated by black organizations could not find equivalent expression in predominantly white organizations. In the confines of their own institutions, black teachers knew that their leadership skills could be refined and exercised on the issues they determined to be most important. Further, the decision-making process in a black organization was relieved of the suspicious presence of whites, allowing for free and more candid expressions of ideas without fear of retribution. Moreover, within their own associations there were fewer distractions from those without affinity for the nuances of black culture, and the personal day-to-day trials and tribulations of black life. Infinitely more than any other reason, however, the desire to control their own destinies led them to develop and nurture their own independent organizations. This did not mean blacks were adverse to collaborating with white associations on concerns mutually essential to progress; and it did not prohibit them from pursuing opportunities to work in both their own institutions and those of others. Over time, with the overthrow of Reconstruction, which was followed immediately by the withdrawal of the federal troops from the South in 1877; the resurrection of the white South; and the introduction of suppressive Black Codes and Jim Crow laws designed to limit black progress and regulate interactions between the races, the black teachers' associations became even more of a sanctuary from an increasingly oppressive world divided by racial segregation.[43] In many ways, these teacher organizations found counterparts in the one-race composition of black churches, schools, social groups, and other such institutions, in the sense that they constituted a firewall that gave blacks some protection against the effects of exclusionary racial policies and white-supremacy ideology.

The concept of the black teacher organization had taken root as early as 1861, when 23 black Ohio teachers met in Springfield to form the Ohio Colored Teachers Association, becoming the nation's first organization of its type.

Over three days, a constitution was adopted, officers elected, and sessions conducted in which discussions took place on enrollment, attendance, course offerings, and salaries. A widely circulated publication, "Address to the Friends of Colored Schools," was based on the proceedings. Distributed to blacks throughout the state as well as to sympathetic and trusted white officials who had influence over black schools, its message on schooling mirrored that of NEA, though differing in a decisive way. It spoke more directly to black people, outlining the role of parents in visiting schools and exercising concern with regard to the "mental development" of their children. Education was to be the highest priority of the race; every parent was to understand that education "exceeded any legacy that a parent could leave a child." Black parents and communities were to be proactive, involved, and protective of educational opportunities by agitating for improved schools. On education issues in the communities, passivity was not tolerated because the progress of the race was contingent upon developing an educated citizenry.[44]

The pioneering Ohio association evolved as a vehicle for group expression, and a cauldron for developing black education leaders. All of its officers and members belonged to the race, and, while this would not prohibit coalitions with others, it allowed for the development of black leaders and discussions of black education in a way that could not be matched by predominately white teacher groups. For example, by 1866, women were officially admitted to NEA, and three years later, Emily Rice was chosen to be its vice president. Although white women, to be sure, were subject to gender discrimination, they were white, and their routes to Association leadership were far more accessible than were those available to blacks. No blacks, during the late 19th century—men or women—could aspire to elected or appointed positions of leadership in the Association, and none would hold any office at the national, state, or local levels of NEA for several generations to come. Still, NEA kept the discussion on the table about the need to educate blacks and other minorities with public funds, at a time when white supremacy and Social Darwinism questioned the wisdom of efforts to educate blacks, often proclaiming them unworthy for any pursuit beyond menial labor.

When NEA espoused the position that women teachers' salaries were to be equal to those of men when performing the same duties, and that the "gender conduct" provisions of their contracts be eliminated, the inequities in black teachers' salaries—for both men and women—were omitted from that discussion.[45] Taking matters into their own hands, in 1886, the North Carolina State Teachers Association for Negroes raised the stakes, presenting demands to the state legislature for the establishment of uniform requirements and salaries for teachers of both races.[46] It would be more than sixty years, however, before equal salaries for black teachers would win approval in U.S. courts, though the obscure origins of the equitable salary discussions are to be found in the efforts of early black teachers' groups, and not in the endeavors of NEA.

Following the Civil War, black teachers' organizations spread throughout the South and other regions of the country like grassfires driven by strong winds. The Kentucky Negro Education Association, Georgia Negro Teachers Association, Florida State Teachers Association, Alabama State Teachers Association, Association of Teachers of Negro Youth of Arkansas, and other organizations of black educators were examples of what had been established in every southern state by 1900.[47] As Thelma Perry explained, in her *History of the American Teachers Association*, black teachers' associations seemed best to define their purpose, maintain active members, and thrive in areas where segregation was most rigid. The concept of "separate but equal" had not yet been broadly condemned, but the egregious common practice of "separate and flagrantly unequal" in the schools occupied most of the energies of their members.[48] Southerners across-the-board, they soon discovered, had no intention of being fair and equitable in the distribution of public resources. And though blacks comprised a large percentage of the populations of southern states, without the ballot they found effecting change a formidable task. It was the implementation of the 1896 *Plessy v. Ferguson* decision, rather than the decision itself, that irritated black educators who strenuously objected to the blatant discrepancies in education for blacks and whites. The conditions under which they worked were often deplorable and uniformly inferior to those in which white educators worked, and by forming teachers' organizations they sought change and improvement, while developing within those organizations spokespersons who could lead the charge.

The growing independence of black teachers – 1900-1940

By the time J. R. E. Lee, Director of the Academic Department of Tuskegee Institute, issued a call in 1904 for the founding of a national black teachers' organization, the groundwork for membership had already been laid at the local and state levels.[49]   First called the National Association of Colored Teachers (NACT), in NEA it found a ready model of a national organization of teachers. At that time NEA had already demonstrated what a national union of teachers might accomplish, though its focus was not always specific to the experiences of black teachers. NEA had also earned respect as a fair organization whose doors were open at the national level to members of all races, though its doors at the local and state levels often remained closed to blacks. It had never encouraged integration of the southern teachers' associations or of the public schools and, interestingly, had received no internal or external pressure to do so. When the brilliant W. E. B. Du Bois of Atlanta University predicted in 1903 that the problem of the twentieth century would be "the problem of the color-line," neither NEA nor NACT entertained integration as an antidote for the problem. The egalitarian promises of Reconstruction had faded to a distant memory, and Americans were reduced to preparing themselves for a world of two nations: one white and one black.

Holding its first meeting in Nashville, Tennessee in 1904, NACT elected J. R. E. Lee as its first president, and a constitution was adopted. The organization provided black teachers a forum to share experiences and ideas, and it offered them opportunities to discuss problems and propose solutions. Establishing more and better equipped schools, preparing and compensating teachers, addressing inequities in school funding, and assisting students in attending college were the priorities agreed upon. Early on, a decision was made to change the name of the organization to one more descriptive of its membership—many of whom were white—and it came to be more accurately named the National Association of Teachers in Colored Schools (NATCS).[50]

Booker T. Washington, by then the most politically powerful black person in America, endorsed NATCS, and his approval gave it instant credibility as it worked diligently to build a strong membership base. The competition for organization membership and allegiance among blacks was strong, and other black uplift organizations were vying for the support and membership of blacks whose impoverished financial conditions limited the number of dues-sustained organizations they could join. But NATCS held its own despite the low salaries of its members. "Consider a male teacher," wrote Thelma Perry, "who earned barely enough to house and feed his wife and children, plus perhaps a widowed, ailing parent in the home. He and members of his family must try to dress neatly, support the church, the lodge, charitable and racial uplift organizations, the local and state teachers group, as well as the national association. He must include gifts, medical bills, and innumerable incidentals." Perry concluded, "It becomes obvious that these Negro teachers were sincerely committed to the idea of a professional organization as a constructive educational force, or they would not have made the sacrifices that active membership in such a group required."[51]

Traveling to the out-of-town meetings of NATCS strained family budgets, but in increasing numbers members came to its annual meetings, and the HBCUs, with their vacant summer dormitories available as inexpensive housing, became favorite meeting places. Those sites proved to be even more logical choices in 1907 when the NATCS merged with the umbrella group for HBCUs, the National Association of Land Grant College Presidents. During the early 1900s, NEA maintained its membership of black educators, and it continued to invite black speakers to its annual conventions. But where NEA spent *some* time on black education issues, NATCS devoted *all* of its time to those issues. Some blacks, including the more prominent educators such as administrators, college presidents, and professors, who had sufficient time and resources, maintained membership in both organizations. The remarkable growth of NATCS, however, was a result of its appeal to southern black rank-and-file educators.[52]

Richard R. Wright who followed Lee in 1907as president of NATCS, had affiliations with both groups. Having founded Ware High School in Augusta,

Georgia, the first publicly funded school for blacks in the state, as president of the Georgia State Industrial College, he is credited with having issued the call for the first convention of black teachers in his state. A well-known educator, Wright was also an NEA member, and at the 1900 convention in Charleston, South Carolina, he participated in an NEA panel discussion. He was the first black to warn NEA that dual segregated school systems isolated blacks, denied black and white teachers the opportunity for collaboration, and "prevented the white people from knowing anything of our social life."[53] Unlike other organizations at the time, only NEA would not have censored those remarks, considered anathema to the southern way of life. Wright knew that the culture of NEA did not embargo open and vigorous debate on all issues, and for that reason he was proud of his membership, and offered no apologies for his sharp criticism and rebuke of the doctrine of separate but equal. Not only were Wright's remarks unusual for an NEA convention, but they were exceptional for any black leader speaking in the South during this period, which historian Rayford Logan describes as the "nadir" for black life in America.[54]

Until the death of Booker T. Washington in 1915, all of the NATCS presidents were disciples of his industrial arts education philosophy and depended on him for support, advice, and direction. John Hope, Morehouse College president, became the exception in 1916 when he headed NATCS. A Phi Beta Kappa graduate of Brown University, he was the only southern black educator who dared to challenge Washington's "obsequiousness around white people and his apparent catering to them."[55] Hope and his close friend Du Bois, an influential duo, formed the vanguard of critics of Washington's diminished appreciation of black suffrage, and his overemphasis on the virtues of industrial education and social separation of the races. Following Hope's lead and that of later NATCS presidents, college instructors gradually became an influential part of the membership that supported the movement toward more liberal, rather than technical college programs, and with their help, the pendulum of organizational emphasis swung from industrial to liberal arts education.

To fully comprehend NATCS, the stature of those selected to be its leaders, and the quality of its annual conventions, one needs to review the achievements of those presidents and the blue-ribbon black scholars who gave presentations at those annual meetings. Suffice it to say that virtually every notable black personality in America appeared on its programs. By the mid-1920s it had no rival on black education issues, and had become in black America what NEA was in white America. Its prestigious leadership and programs also explain why the association grew to become the nation's largest black professional organization, and why its annual meetings, followed intensively by the black press, became the place to be for all black educators. One standard that might be used to measure the distinction of the NATCS leadership is the number of NATCS officers who received NAACP's esteemed Spingarn Medal, instituted in 1914, and awarded annually since then for the highest achievement by a black American. Four of the first 21 recipients were former presidents of NATCS—Mordecai Johnson, William Taylor Williams, Mary McLeod Bethune, and John Hope. The impact of these powerful national figures on black education, along with the influence of lesser known but equally important state and local teacher leaders, was immeasurable. The excellence, courage, compassion, and sense of purpose they exemplified validated the worth of the teaching profession.

The strange career of Jim Crow created a system that grudgingly came to accept schooling for black students, provided it did not conflict with the southern economy or contest segregated race arrangements, and was conducted in facilities inferior to those provided for whites. But because whites teaching blacks was generally frowned upon, black teachers had to be "trusted" to teach in black schools and to follow the rules set forth by whites. Any transgression against those rules that caught the attention of whites could result in immediate job termination. Thus, black teachers joined black communities in teaching students to "survive" rather than to "accept" or "internalize" the system, taking advantage of every opportunity that allowed for progress and racial uplift.[56] The local, state, and NATCS meetings were safe harbors for the sharing and trading of techniques designed to exact more from Jim Crow than southerners intended. NEA—though ahead of the curve on civil rights and black education—could never be expected to accommodate or fully comprehend the agendas of black teachers, making it considerably less attractive to them than NATCS. The alternative organizations for smaller populations of black professionals that also grew steadily under Jim Crow included the National Bar Association, the National Medical Association, the National Business League, and the Association for the Study of Negro Life and History.[57]

For the entire period of its existence, 1903 to 1966, the potential membership pool of NATCS expanded annually, benefiting from the majority of black college students preparing for the teaching profession. Those career-decisions were practical by-products of the stringent restrictions imposed by segregation on black employment in business, industry, government, and other professions. A re-creative cycle occurred when teachers often became the sole professional role models in their communities, encouraging students to attend college and return as teachers. Schools of education became flagship departments at the HBCUs, attracting substantially more than their share of both the resources and the best and brightest students.

Not every black college student, to be sure, elected an education major. Social work, business, religion and, to a lesser extent, medicine, pharmacy, and dentistry, were among degree options. But where teacher graduates could count on employment, those graduating from schools of law, engineering, architecture, and related professions found few, if any, employment opportunities in their fields of study. Opening their own businesses to serve the race became the rule more than the exception. Black banks, insurance companies, construction firms, and real estate businesses did offer employment, but their small numbers could not absorb the annual supply of graduates seeking employment in those areas. After long periods of frustration in seeking employment, some transitioned to teaching, while others succumbed to jobs at the post office, operating elevators, and doing other work considerably below the level of their talents and education. Those with Ph.D.s could expect teaching and administrative positions at HBCUs, though they need not bother applying for positions at white institutions of higher education because, until the 1940s, none would consider hiring black professors and administrators, and it was not until the 1960s that they would begin actively recruiting black scholars.

*****

In the mid-1920s, two NATCS leaders, H. Councill Trenholm of Alabama and W. A. Robinson of North Carolina, took the lead in exploring a potential collaborative relationship with NEA. All signs indicated that NEA might be amenable to such a partnership. Since the founding of NATCS, NEA had elected a woman president; formally endorsed women's suffrage; passed a resolution supporting equal pay for equal work; backed the new child welfare movement; and maintained its non-discriminatory policy on membership at the national level. NATCS respected NEA for its courage, prestige, and size—170,000 members in 1925. But respect was a two-way street, with NATCS hoping its mission and credibility were sufficient to approach NEA for assistance in advancing several concerns requiring more clout than it could leverage alone. NATCS officials believed the time was ripe for new relationships.[58]

All of the things that cemented NATCS' position as the leading organization of its kind, had not been enough to persuade the Southern Association of Schools and Colleges (SASC) to evaluate and accredit black schools. The net effect was that in the region of the country where the majority of blacks attended school, students were forced to graduate from non-accredited schools, and without certification from an accredited school, acceptance by many colleges was impossible. None of that mattered to white southerners whose educational policies were intended to keep blacks functionally, if not outright, illiterate. Controlling black education, the white governors and legislators generally appointed a white state school board, which selected a white state school superintendent. Together, the state board and white legislative delegations then selected white county school boards, which, in turn, named white trustees for each local school district. Blacks were never factored into the decision-making levels, and there were virtually no supervision, standards, or concern for the quality of the education blacks received. Maintaining poor schools guaranteed the promotion of white supremacy as a national system of race relations. While supremacy was dominant and demanding, the educational philosophy of supremacists divided them into two groups: those who were opposed or indifferent to offering any education to blacks, and those who insisted that the "right kind" of education was the best mechanism for adapting blacks to segregation and work in manual jobs. At the time, there were 10 million blacks in southern schools, only 166 of which were accredited. When directly approaching the accrediting agency, Trenholm and Robinson encountered stiff resistance. Had all things been equitable in the distribution of school resources, as in "separate but equal," the condition would not have existed. And for SASC to have forayed into the business of evaluating black schools, no deal could have been brokered without making the vast funding discrepancies transparent. Not only would such a disclosure embarrass the states having SASC member schools, but any reasonable remedy would have necessitated increased southern funding for black education. NATCS countered with an appeal to NEA for assistance on the accrediting issue and other concerns. Under the leadership of Mary McSkimmon, a Joint Committee of the two organizations was appointed to study problems of black schools. Moving cautiously and deliberately, this interracial committee began negotiations with SASC, which eventually began the process of accrediting black schools.[59]

Other issues on the table for the Joint Committee included the treatment of blacks in textbooks; increasing the number of students preparing for acceptance to medical, dental, and nursing schools; and having access to more federal funds for equalizing opportunities. Neither NATCS nor NEA openly advocated for the desegregation of southern schools, nor were they ambiguous about the unrealized promises of separate but equal education. Both organizations soon realized that all that could be accomplished by the committee could not be done in a single year. The NEA-appointed chair of the committee, N. C. Newbold, agreed. Priding himself on his knowledge of black education issues and his friendships with blacks, Newbold, though white, was director of Negro Education in North Carolina.[60] No other southern state at that time had more liberal white educators or HBCUs. Still, liberal southerners in the 1920s, '30s, and '40s were, by and large, unable to connect the dots between equity, justice, democracy, and integration. Newbold was from that progressive tradition and brought his enlightened views on race to the committee. Black people "form a component part of our population [who] are eager to bear their full part of the responsibilities of other American citizens," he said. Whatever differences existed between the races, he reasoned, had nothing to do with the potential to achieve, or the inalienable rights of all Americans. In a summary statement to the annual convention, now called the Representative Assembly, (RA), he pointed out that blacks were, "just as human, just as anxious to enjoy the privileges of life, liberty, and the pursuit of happiness" as whites.[61] From 1926 to 1945, Newbold was a steady and stabilizing force on the Joint Committee, whose contributions gave it credibility and made many white members pause—if only for a moment—to reflect on the continuing racial disparities in public education.

The Joint Committee quietly and without fanfare made progress, and all the solutions it pursued were easily defensible for NEA. It had not asked for equal salaries or integrated schools, either of which might have proved too risky to maintain the cohesiveness of the coalition. In 1928, NEA's RA was encouraged enough by the work and camaraderie of the committee to make it permanent, and to provide a regular budget appropriation for its meetings. It soon began to conduct surveys, prepare kits on race relations for use in teacher-training institutions, and report on the negative portrayals of blacks in textbooks with suggestions for their revision.[62] For NEA members, it was a committee charged with valuable and informative work; for NATCS it was all of that and much more: it legitimized and brought NATCS priorities to a much wider stage and larger audience. For both organizations, it was a major interracial experiment, and one that produced results. The concerns of progressive elements within NEA could not have been affirmed more clearly, though no one seemed to notice how white the RA had become. A year later, in 1929, Robert R. Moton, president of Tuskegee Institute, was to remind NEA of segregation issues when, in a convention speech, he made an observation that questioned NEA's commitment to organizational fairness.

"I am somewhat embarrassed this morning but I don't want
to embarrass you. This platform and this auditorium are
not lacking in character and dignity. I think they are lacking
somewhat in color. I shall not attempt to add anything in the
way of dignity or character, or of inspiration or information,
but I am perfectly sure I will bring more color than any other
speaker of the morning."[63]

Economic hardship imposed on teachers by the Great Depression in the early
1930s also caused the Association to drift on racial problems. In 1937, Edwin
Embree, President of the Rosenwald Fund, brought the segregation issue to
the forefront of NEA when he publicly announced that he was withdrawing
from the NEA convention in New Orleans because of discrimination against
its black members. His decision to leave was based on a rule which stated,
"Negro visitors and delegates in the city audience will have to occupy a
designated section of the gallery reserved for them." It went on to indicate
that black delegates and visitors "cannot use the passenger elevators, but
must use the service elevators." Adding more insult and humiliation,
Embree cited the rule that governed attendance at all other places in the city
where NEA would conduct meetings, "Those of the Negro race who attend
must take places at the rear of the meeting hall."   NEA, seemingly, had taken
a step backward since 1884 when it threatened to move the convention to
another city if the hotels in Madison, Wisconsin would not provide rooms for
black members. Embree left the convention, but the publicity surrounding
his departure would soon force NEA to revisit its convention policies and
strengthen the non-restrictive rulings for its black members.[64]

Two years later, in 1939, NATCS adopted a new and more modern name,
the American Teachers Association (ATA). The term "colored" had given
way to the "New Negro" concepts of racial pride evolving from the Harlem
Renaissance of the 1920s. Many of the leading personalities from that
literary and cultural movement appeared on ATA programs and spoke at its
meetings. As the Joint Committee became more institutionalized, and the
members more relaxed and comfortable working together, both NEA and
ATA developed an understanding of what they had in common. Soon they

began sharing cultural and intellectual ideas, agreeing to exchange speakers and cooperate in efforts for federal legislation and other mutual goals. Another internal NEA entity, the Committee on Equal Opportunity, had made a resolution in 1935 that "Teachers should not be discriminated against because of race, color, belief, residence, economics, or marital status."[65] ATA members and leaders were coming to understand that over and above the Joint Committee, in NEA it had a partnership with an organization willing to challenge the status quo. Consider that in 1937, the NEA Research Department documented what *every* ATA member already knew, when it reported a 252.2 percent difference in pupil expenditures between southern white and black schools. The same ongoing database, provided information on the salary differences of black and white teachers, which would later be used by Thurgood Marshall and Charles Houston of the National Association for the Advancement of Colored People (NAACP) when preparing arguments for equal salary and school integration cases in the courts.[66]

The Joint Committee's stature and influence within NEA grew steadily over the years, and by the early 1940s, it had become the "soul" of NEA. By far, the person most deserving of admiration for that progress was H. Councill Trenholm, who became the most dedicated, persistent, courageous, and determined person in the entire history of ATA. The son of a legendary teacher, Trenholm completed his secondary education in Tuscumbia, Alabama at Trenholm High School, named after his father. After completing his education at Morehouse and the University of Chicago, he joined the faculty of the State Normal School, of which his father was president. Later, the son was appointed president and guided the institution to become a fully accredited four-year degree-granting college. At the unusually early age of 32, he was elected president of NATCS, after serving as president of the Alabama State Teachers Association (ASTA). His contemporaries insisted that during his term as ASTA president, through his personality and extraordinary passion for black teachers, he made his state association the "backbone" of the ATA.[67] He was dynamic and powerful enough to be admired by his peers, and shrewd and political enough to be respected by whites. All of his skills and determination, and the leadership needs of ATA, converged into a perfect marriage of ability and opportunity.

Nothing was more critical for the early work of the Joint Committee than the careful selection of those chosen to serve on it. NEA and ATA selected their own members, and, as was characteristic of the era, both organizations appointed members whose positions and educational backgrounds were considered superior to those of classroom teachers. NEA's selections over the years included school superintendents from large southern cities, college professors, principals, and state education officials. ATA representatives, on the other hand, were almost exclusively college presidents, administrators, and white-appointed local black public school supervisors. But ATA had other subtle, unwritten qualifications and requirements, all predicated on two things: conceding that NEA was the power organization, and believing that black educators bore the burden of proof of their worth to the relationship.

The Joint Committee also impaneled many subcommittees over the years, charging them with investigating designated topics and concerns. They, too, were interracial in composition and blue-ribbon in credentials, always pushing, persuading, and cajoling the Association to embrace, protect, and advance the educational interests of black students and teachers. NEA carefully selected level-headed, fair-minded, highly-respected, and well-informed representatives to the committee. ATA abided by the same criteria—and went even farther in selecting its committee members. Well-groomed appearance, dignified manner, command of the language, mental dexterity, and restrained temperament were all premium attributes in ATA's view. Advancing ATA's agenda and impressing committee colleagues were inseparable goals, each being dependent on the other.

The images projected by ATA's Joint Committee members and leaders were relatively standard for black leaders and professionals, though so much of what made them unique was not to be found on résumés. Even blacks without education portfolios—farmers, cooks, maintenance workers, domestics, and low-level industry workers—admired those same traits, hoping that their children would follow in the footsteps of those who manifested them. What the ATA Joint Committee members exemplified at NEA is what black teachers showcased in their classrooms through appearance on a daily basis, changing the perspectives and outlook of their students in ways not easily covered in a lesson plan or taught from a textbook.

Prior to World War II, the struggle against black inequalities emphasized leveling the playing field through improvement of separate segregated facilities, and a more balanced sharing of public resources. Most race advancement organizations and institutions strategized for better opportunities, with infrequent challenges to restrictive covenants, and to segregated labor unions, public facilities, and transportation. But there was also a contentious southern mix of grassroots radicals, labor activists, newspaper editors, black workers, educators, clergy, and intellectuals calling for a complete dismantling of the South's racial segregation.[68] More frequently in the 1930s than in earlier decades, the concept of segregation came under intense scrutiny as the Great Depression pushed poor blacks to the brink of destitution. Distribution of public resources made separate but equal even more of a farce, and fairness in allocating public funds for black teachers and students went from bad to worse. This did not go unnoticed by NEA. "Social justice," argued a Michigan school superintendent at an RA during that period, "demands that the needs of Negro pupils and teachers be given equitable consideration along with all other groups."[69] The Joint Committee went beyond proclamations, appointing a sub-committee to study the effect of racism and the Great Depression "on Negroes, Japanese, Chinese, and Mexicans in California."[70] In incremental steps, NEA was becoming more aggressive in fighting the day-to-day discrimination in schools and society.

*****

Outside of NEA new strategies were being explored that would ultimately dismantle the legal foundation of segregation in American society. Charles Hamilton Houston, Dean of Howard University's Law School and head of the NAACP's Legal Defense Fund, remembered being counseled by his

Harvard law professor Felix Frankfurter that the constitutional basis of *Plessy v. Ferguson* was vulnerable because a sound legal argument could be made that it violated the equal protection clause of the 14th Amendment. Houston and his law classmate William Hastie, also black—two of Harvard's most capable students—never forgot that advice from Frankfurter, a wise sage who would go on to become a U.S. Supreme Court Justice.[71] At Howard, Houston initiated courses in civil rights law, and several of his students, including Thurgood Marshall, became the nation's leading lawyers in that new field. Together with other attorneys who had been trained at Howard, Houston and Hastie became the chief architects of the legal challenge to segregation. They decided that of all the segregated institutions in American life, public schools were those which would be challenged. ATA members strongly identified with NAACP, and assisted with locating "model" plaintiffs willing to engage in litigation that sought to overthrow segregation. Among all black professionals, no group had a higher percentage of NAACP members than teachers, who suffered more daily indignities from segregation than perhaps all the others together. The humiliation was even more painful and complex for the teachers because their students were co-victims. The welfare of both was linked to NAACP and the goals of ATA.

Houston and Marshall decided to begin the legal campaign by seeking admission of blacks to segregated institutions of higher education. Cases paving the way were *Hocutt v. North Carolina* in 1934; *Murray v. Maryland* in 1936; and *Gaines v. Missouri* in 1937. The contention in all three cases was that the premise of separate but equal was being violated because graduate and professional programs offered at white institutions were unavailable at the HBCUs in those respective states. The Hocutt case, brilliantly argued by Hastie, while proceeding favorably for the plaintiff, was lost because James Shepard, president of the North Carolina College for Negroes, under pressure from the governor, would not release Hocutt's undergraduate transcript to the University of North Carolina. Outmaneuvered politically if not legally in that case, Houston and Marshall next brought the Murray case, litigated by Marshall, which was won when the Maryland Court of Appeals ordered the University of Maryland to admit Donald Murray, an honors graduate of

Amherst College to its Law School. In the Gaines case, also prepared by Marshall and Houston, the U.S. Supreme Court ruled that Lloyd Gaines be admitted to the University of Missouri's Law School, and that Missouri's offer to pay his tuition to a school outside of the state would be in denial of equal protection laws. Winning two out of three of these highly publicized cases marked a turning point in civil rights litigation. Revealing that the system of segregation was not impenetrable, the courts now would be the battlegrounds in the struggle to achieve democracy and equal opportunity for all of the people.[72]

The results of those three cases generated excitement and hope in black communities, inspired ATA, and motivated the Joint Committee to take inventory of NEA's policies regarding race and its segregated southern affiliates. But none of those cases struck home with ATA and the Joint Committee more than *Gibbs v. Board of Education* in Montgomery County, Maryland. In that landmark decision, the U.S. Supreme Court declared that setting unequal salaries for black and white teachers was unconstitutional. The decision formed the basis for a series of NAACP-initiated lawsuits to eliminate teacher wage differentials based on race. Organizationally, the energy ATA exerted for the equal salary cases was more abundant than that of NEA, which, incidentally, had collected more data on black teacher salaries than any other organization, though its findings had never been published. To the credit of NEA, however, it did allow NAACP access to that salary data, which was crucial in preparing the court arguments. Buoyed by the decisions rendered by the courts, NAACP's Legal Defense and Education Fund had marshaled its resources by 1939 in an all-out war against segregation, and began mobilizing the nation's best legal talent to battle racial bias and discrimination.[73] ATA aided NAACP's effort in two important ways: earmarking for the Legal Defense Fund a contribution of 10 cents from each membership dollar, and urging members to join NAACP in order to assist with the goal of eliminating racial inequalities in public education.[74]

ATA's ongoing campaign of encouraging its members to join NAACP experienced success because of the specific cases involving public education and salary equalization. Southern government officials took note of the

relationship of black teachers to NAACP, viewing it as a threat to segregation.
In Alabama, black teachers had to sign loyalty oaths and pledge not to
support school desegregation. In South Carolina, prospective employees'
answers to questions on teacher applications and in interviews determined
their employability. To teach in South Carolina, black teacher applicants
either lied or answered truthfully to loaded questions such as:

> Do you favor integration of the races in schools?

> Do you feel you would be happy in an integrated school
> system, knowing that parents and students do not favor this
> system?

> Do you feel that an integrated school system would better fit
> the colored for their life's work?

> Do you feel that parents of your school know that no public
> schools will be operated if they are integrated?[75]

The Palmetto Education Association, ATA's South Carolina affiliate, was
asked for its membership lists to cross reference with those of NAACP, after
members of the state legislature claimed that all of the 7,500 teachers in black
schools belonged to NAACP. Teacher membership in NAACP was forbidden
by state statutes, making the contributions through ATA membership all the
more attractive as a way of circumventing the intimidating restrictions.

*****

When America entered World War II immediately after the Japanese bombing
of Pearl Harbor on December 7, 1941, "a date which shall live in infamy,"
separate but equal had been applied "infamously" for 45 years. NAACP,
ATA, and black America demonstrated patriotism and resolve by declaring a
war on two fronts: abroad and at home. The popular "Double V" campaign
galvanized strength for the defeat of both international fascism and domestic
discrimination. The concept of a double victory was cultivated into a rallying
cry, and the Double V logo was found nationwide on buttons, posters,
bumper stickers, in clubs, at dances, and in ATA publications and those of
other black organizations.[76] Also with America's entry into the war, Japanese

Americans suffered indignities unparalleled since slavery. In the heat and excitement following Japan's attack on Pearl Harbor, more than 110,000 loyal and law-abiding Japanese Americans were placed in the "protective custody" of their own government in internment camps surrounded by barbed wire fences, and guarded by armed troops. America largely ignored this atrocity, but NEA did not, and an article in the *NEA Journal* in 1943, entitled "What Makes an American?" questioned the government for gross violation of all of the constitutional protections of Americans of Japanese ancestry. NEA's patriotism was fundamental to the war effort, though it was troubled by the compromise of the basic rights of those held against their will in the internment camps.[77]

During the war, the Association, continuing to be alert to injustices practiced against teachers, came to the defense of three in Muskogee, Oklahoma who were dismissed from their jobs in 1943 without warning or the opportunity for a hearing. They had criticized the local school board's mismanagement and led a drive to unseat some board members in a 1942 election. When one of the teachers, Kate Frank, fought back in court, NEA—led by President Donald Dushane—intervened to defend them. The successful legal defense mounted by NEA was the beginning of the Kate Frank/Dushane Fund for Teacher Rights, which became a multimillion-dollar fund and the leading resource for fighting threats to the civil, human, constitutional, and professional rights of educators.[78]

NEA—like all of America—declared its unanimity with the war effort. The influence of the sentiments of the "Double V" campaign on the Joint Committee is evident in the words of its national defense sub-committee encouraging "fair and adequate treatment and use of Negroes in all phases of service in war and peace."[79]

For NEA, the irony of domestic racial policy during a war to free the world from tyranny was an embarrassment that required reconciliation. In 1943, NEA passed a resolution promising to refrain from convening meetings in any city in which hotels and other facilities failed "to make provisions without discrimination for the housing, feeding, seating at the convention, and general welfare of all delegates and teachers, regardless of race, color or creed."[80] Resulting from the Edwin Embree incident of 1937, this resolution followed NEA's reexamination of its conference policies with regard to race. No major national organization had ever taken such an action. ATA leaders and members could not have been prouder of their relationship with NEA, and the black press took notice, saluting NEA's powerful stand for racial fairness.[81] By comparison, the American Federation of Labor (AFL) was lambasted by the black press when, at its 1941 convention, it rejected a resolution introduced by A. Philip Randolph, president of its affiliate, the Brotherhood of Sleeping Car Porters, requesting that a committee study evidence of discrimination against blacks in the union. Where none of NEA's racial laundry had been exempt from public washing by the Joint Committee, the AFL would not entertain this resolution brought forward by the most powerful member of its largest black affiliate.[82]

Blacks performed gallantly in the war, though they routinely faced discrimination in military assignments. The most notable example of exemption from discriminatory and demeaning assignments was that of the all-black 332nd Fighter Group, known as the Tuskegee Airmen, whose widely publicized aviation exploits laid to rest any doubts about the abilities of blacks to excel in the most demanding of military arenas. When the veterans returned from the war, changes were taking place, making America a much different country from the one they had left. Jackie Robinson integrated major league baseball; the U.S. Supreme Court prohibited segregation on interstate bus travel; and that Court also ruled that all-white political primaries were unconstitutional. President Harry S. Truman appointed a national interracial Committee on Civil Rights to investigate racial injustices and signed an Executive Order to end discrimination in the armed forces. The U.S. Supreme Court struck down restrictive housing covenants.[83]

****

NEA was not to keep itself apart from change, but, rather, attacked its most irritating structural problem—the segregated southern affiliates. In 1947, it affiliated 18 of ATA's education associations in the southern and border states and the District of Columbia. Later, in 1949, it went a step farther, allowing those black affiliates to send delegates to the RA in the same proportion to their memberships as that of the white state affiliates. Although from NEA's earliest years blacks had participated as individual members attending the convention, this innovation gave evidence of the value to NEA of its local associations and their black and white members.[84] By 1949, the Joint Committee observed 36 black delegates at the RA, a representation made possible by "an increasing number of local Negro units of classroom teachers." And in 1951, members of ATA were given delegate representation in the RA in proportion to their state membership. In the legal climate that prevailed before the 1954 ruling in the case of *Brown v. Board of Education of Topeka, Kansas*, no other major national organization had responded so creatively to integrating itself.[85] That same year, another milestone was reached at NEA when John W. Davis, president of West Virginia State College and a former ATA president, was appointed to lead the Commission on the Defense of Democracy through Education, thus becoming the first of his race to chair an NEA commission.[86] Internally, his appointment broke new ground in race relations, and it was reported in the black press. Excluding black members of the Joint Committee, Davis' was the most visible presence of a black person in NEA, and his appointment was not met with any significant resentment from southern members.

Integration was painful in society, and it was painful in the Association. Resistance to it, both openly and surreptitiously, was not uncommon in the 1950s and '60s, and there were ugly incidents to prove it. Two examples are worthy of note. One occurred when an NEA Committee to Select a Conference site for the RA had a memory lapse in 1950 about the 1943 resolution promising that NEA would not hold meetings in locations where hotels and other facilities practiced racial discrimination. The committee had selected St. Louis, a city notorious for its segregated facilities, and the decision was troubling to black members, particularly because the Joint Committee had questioned the suitability of that city. The NEA Board debated the issue but retreated from the 1943 resolution when it voted to uphold the selection committee's decision. It was a setback that was further aggravated when Willard Givens, the executive secretary, promised the Joint Committee that black delegates in St. Louis would "have *practically* all privileges of other members except the privilege of staying in the first-class hotels and eating as individuals."[87] After St. Louis, NEA learned that no apology would ever be acceptable to the offended black delegates, and it was the last time such a breach of promise about a convention city would be allowed to occur.

Later, in the 1960s, Horace Tate challenged the Georgia Association of Educators (GAE) for misrepresenting the votes cast in his bid for a seat on the NEA Board. Some were skeptical of Tate's claim, but Braulio Alonso, NEA president, appointed a committee headed by John H. Lucas, a black member of the Board, to investigate the charges. Lucas' team conducted a thorough investigation, which ultimately led to the NEA Board voting to give Tate a seat for three terms (nine years). To its credit, the Board had shown the capacity to correct Association injustices, which in this instance had occurred at the state level. Years later, Don Morrison, the NEA president who recommended the Board's action, had a conversation with Tate. "He was still angry and fuming," recalled Morrison. "He told me if the Board had seated him during Alonso's term—several years before he was actually seated—he would likely have been NEA's first black president."[88] Indeed, he may very well have been, because his credentials outside of NEA pointed to his leadership capabilities. He went on to serve on the Atlanta school board, to run a creditable race for mayor of Atlanta, to be elected to the Georgia state senate, to be appointed as service-chair of the state Democratic party, and to be the first black to be appointed executive director of a merged affiliate, GAE.[89] ATA members took careful note of NEA's sanctioning of dual affiliates and the separate but equal formula devised for participation at the RA. Never since Robert Campbell had become a founding father in 1857, had there been a brighter moment for black participation in the Association. Now, beyond the Joint Committee, greater involvement at the decision-making level and an increase of leadership positions were real possibilities. In retrospect, NEA had never ignored black education issues, consistently engaging black speakers, establishing the Joint Committee, and maintaining an open policy for membership at the national level. But nothing up to this point had so effectively opened the door for participation in the Association as did the recognition of the black dual affiliates. With representation at the RA, their voices would now be factored into the decision-making process of the governing body. By 1953, Walter Byers of the North Carolina Teachers Association had become the first black to serve on the NEA Board of Directors, and in 1954, N. R. Burger of the Mississippi Teachers Association represented MTA on the NEA Resolutions Committee.[90] Soon the doors would be open even wider for such positions.

On May 17, 1954, NAACP's legal strategy for abolishing segregation won a major victory when the U.S. Supreme Court ruled in the case of *Brown v. Board of Education* that "racial segregation in public schools is unconstitutional." Chief Justice Earl Warren wrote in the majority opinion, "In the field of education, the doctrine of separate but equal has no place. Separate educational facilities are inherently unequal." ATA and black America reacted with jubilation for this emancipation proclamation of public education. It appeared that the ultimate goal had been realized. Strangely, though, NEA was relatively silent on the decision. Although the Joint Committee reported to the 1954 convention that it was seeking "to prepare members of the profession for the proper reception" to what it termed the "May 17 decision," the Association failed to acknowledge the significance of the decision other than by printing it without commentary in the *NEA Journal*.[91] At the 1954 Representative Assembly in New York City, less than two months after the *Brown* decision, Nobel Peace Prize recipient Ralph Bunche was the keynote speaker. Bunche, a United Nations diplomat known for being outspoken on race issues, had been the first black to win the award. Anticipation ran high for what remarks he might make on integration. He steered clear of the controversial decision, however, and did not venture from his prepared text on international peace.[92] Black delegates and others were crushed with disappointment by his failure to utter a single word about the *Brown* decision. NEA's seemingly purposeful ignoring of the *Brown* case marked the beginning of a retreat by the Association on a number of earlier commitments, including those on black education issues. Under executive secretary William Carr during the 1950s, NEA was clearly becoming a more conservative organization than it had been at any previous time in its nearly 100-year history. In 1956, the RA approved a resolution recommending a study on the implications of an Equal Status for Women Amendment to the U.S. Constitution. One year later, the executive secretary reported to the RA that the Executive Committee had considered the matter and decided to withhold support because the amendment was "not a matter which is of direct concern to the teachers as such." Almost inexplicable was the conservatism which clouded NEA's 1957 Centennial Celebration at its RA in Philadelphia. For that event, it published a book, *NEA: The First Hundred Years*, which grossly underreported the Association's legacy with black educators, and limited its coverage of the *Brown v. Board of Education* decision to a single sentence. In no way did it convey the potency of school desegregation, other than to say that the Joint Committee "would work for the integration of the races in the schools."[93] During the convention, there were no sessions devoted to *Brown's* implications for educators and public schools. It was as if the Association were deliberately minimizing the magnitude of the decision. Since *Brown*—three years earlier—compliance with the decision had been virtually non-existent, though the fall of 1957 would introduce the nation to the Little Rock Nine and the widening influence of the Civil Rights Movement, compelling NEA to respond to the challenges of both.

The strategic concerns for NEA around *Brown v. Board of Education* were about balancing the racial attitudes of its southern affiliates and their membership against the interests of blacks. The South had not been angrier since the Civil War, and NEA's white southern members were closely aligned to their region's political leaders' massive resistance to the *Brown* decision. Almost overnight, a tide of aggressive defensive groups formed to denounce the decision; these included the White Citizens Council, Virginia League, States' Rights Council of Georgia, National Citizens Protective Association, American States' Rights Association, and the Grass Roots League, among other "state sovereignty" and "racial integrity" organizations. The governors of the South issued the "Southern Manifesto," a statement of their intention not to comply with *Brown*. The decision was so politically combustible that NEA feared losing the southern affiliates unless it moved with extreme caution on this volatile and divisive decision. The line between enforcing equality in segregation and proceeding with integration had been crossed, and the consequences frightened the Association.

Southerners also found themselves under siege after *Brown* when, in the aftermath of the decision, the struggles of the Civil Rights Movement were waged on their own turf, with all of the remaining systems of segregation being assaulted under the national spotlight. The Montgomery Bus Boycott, the Little Rock and Central High School resistance, the Student Sit-Ins, the Freedom Riders, Freedom Summer, the Student Non-Violent Coordinating Committee, the Southern Christian Leadership Conference with its marches led by Martin Luther King, Jr., the Mississippi Freedom Democratic Party, the integration of the Universities of Georgia, Alabama, and Mississippi, and the March on Washington of 1963, all solidified discontent over the inequities of segregation and discrimination. ATA and its members identified with the movement, while many of NEA's southern affiliates found themselves identifying more with southern politicians who stood in opposition to integration.

*****

Certainly one indicator of NEA's avoidance of integration could be found in its numerous publications. From 1955 to 1959, it did not authorize a single publication on integration. In 1955 alone, the Association and its array of committees, commissions, departments, and divisions published 20 monthly magazines, 181 bulletins, 36 yearbooks, and 1,070 other publications, none of which contained an iota of information about integration. The tilt of the Association toward conservatism in the 1950s was not exclusively about race. NEA under Carr not only soft-pedaled *Brown v. Board of Education*, or underestimated burgeoning urban education issues, but it also disdained the unionism associated with teacher rights and collective bargaining. Within the Association, the leadership was dominated by administrators who viewed strikes and collective bargaining as unprofessional activities. Teacher members in increasing numbers began to realize that the occupational interests of teachers were not the same as those of school administrators, and no organization was making that argument better than the American Federation of Teachers (AFT). Though a smaller organization than NEA, in the larger cities it was becoming competitive through its agenda addressed to the interests of urban teachers, a group largely ignored by the Association. It was the series of teacher strikes in New York City, beginning in the late 1950s and continuing into the 1960s, that required NEA to reexamine itself and its policies. This self-examination gave rise to a militant unionism in NEA which blasted the Association for failing to respond to the circumstances and conditions causing teacher unrest, and that blamed the administrator leaders and NEA's national and state associations' organizational focus for failure to position NEA proactively as a leader on urban issues. In New York, the nationally publicized strike was a brand-identity coup for AFT whose New York local had no administrator members, a fact that helped AFT handily defeat NEA in the New York City representation election. Though not competitive with NEA at the state level, AFT carved itself a niche, building strong locals in large urban areas. Concentrating primarily on the interests of urban educators, AFT's position became an attractive alternative to the conservative anti-union posture of NEA, so that a heated rivalry for membership began between the two organizations. To illustrate this point, between 1960 and 1970, AFT's membership increased from 50,000 to 205,000 teachers; while NEA during the same period increased only from 714,000 to 1.1 million members. AFT's huge growth was urban, and large numbers of black teachers in cities like New York, Boston, Philadelphia, and Cleveland—areas without an ATA legacy—found the urban agenda compelling and were to be counted in that growth.[94]

AFT did make overtures to ATA for collaboration on specific projects, with the prospect of a merger as a consideration The discussions took an inadvertent turn for the worse over an incident which occurred in New York in the early '60s when R. G. Martin, executive secretary of ATA, met with AFT officials to explore a merger proposal. The conversation was encouraging, but when the meeting adjourned, the AFT officials went to a group dinner without inviting Martin to join them. Instead, one of the black AFT officials was asked to escort him to dinner. Martin fumed over the slight, and became so incensed over the gesture of what amounted to a "segregation dinner," until he vowed that ATA would never again participate in merger discussions with AFT. The merger discussions collapsed under the weight of what was considered professional disrespect. Martin often recited the incident to ATA officials and close friends, who agreed that the dinner snub or oversight was offensive, and the incident became legendary in ATA history and culture. It also signaled that on matters of politeness and civility, ATA leaders and members demanded fair treatment in all situations. Whether or not Martin's account of the events is the sole reason for the breakdown in the merger negotiations of the ATA and AFT is open to speculation. Still, its widespread circulation through the years underscores the reality of the ATA leaders' sensitivity about being accepted as equals. Considering all that was at stake, it was this relatively small incident that prohibited any possibility of a merger of ATA and AFT. By default, NEA remained the organization, besides their own, with which ATA members most closely identified.[95]

Civil and Human Rights validated: the merger — the 1960s

By the early 1960s, NEA found itself returning to its progressive and liberal tradition, the momentum being driven largely by AFT's rise as a legitimate competitor. A group of NEA teacher activists with an urban education agenda, many of them from cities in which AFT was challenging NEA, began to take their places in NEA's highest elected offices, most notably the Executive Committee, a body that was elected by the RA. These urban educators embraced NEA's human and civil rights tradition, and NEA's black members collaborated with them to advance their agenda of claiming NEA for teachers, and focusing more of the Association's attention and resources on urban education issues. Eventually, these members formed their own NEA sub-group, the National Council of Urban Education Associations (NCUEA). From its beginning, NCUEA led by a progressive-minded group, including Frank Heinisch of Omaha, Helen Bain of Nashville, Arthur Simonds of Maryland, Forrest Walverton of St. Louis, and Curtis McClane, a black attorney and executive secretary of the Yonkers, New

York urban local, developed a strategy for promoting "urban positions" in large locals and for making NEA more accountable for urban issues. They examined NEA's structures, goals, and services within the context of urban educational environments of heated controversy and pressure for change. As calls for curriculum reform, changes in school philosophy, and direct pressures on classroom teachers mounted, urban association leaders could not avoid the pressures from their members. The mood which emanated from this incubator of change became known as "teacher militancy." NCUEA embodied the new urban spirit, and it championed human and civil rights issues, better relationships with minority educators, a closer connection with the Civil Rights Movement, and a stronger position for NEA on school desegregation.[96]

The urban movement appealed to minority and progressive educators, and among those who rode its wave into NEA leadership was Wade Wilson, president of Cheney State College in Pennsylvania, and the first black member of NEA's Executive Committee.

By 1966, an aging Carr had exhausted the good will of the members, and the changes in the Association's attitude on teacher strikes, collective bargaining, integration, and the movement toward teacher control left him vulnerable to change. Although his service of distinction since 1945 had been commendable and his contributions were many, his shortcomings in failing to promote an inclusive and socially conscious Association begged for new leadership. Wade Wilson asked Carr in the early 1960s how many black employees were on NEA's staff. The stunned executive secretary was offended by the tone of Wilson's voice, and saw no problem in replying without apology that there were none, and that he was unwilling to make a commitment to hire any. Shortly afterwards, however, the message and the changing American climate got to Carr, and he proceeded to consult with Wilson when he began hiring NEA's first minority staff members.[97]

Carol Karpinski, a scholar on NEA and the Civil Rights Movement, summarized her observations of Carr, saying that he struggled with issues related to integration, failing to grasp the meaning of the changing world around him, and was insensitive to the voices of individuals and groups calling for a more democratic education, grounded in democratic ideas. Integration by its essence pointed to a world foreign to his experiences or comprehension, and he was loath to accept a role for education in building a new social order. Later in life he conceded to Braulio Anonso that he regretted his failure to grasp the full meaning of integration for public schools and for the Association.[98]

The *Brown* decision focused on students and not on teachers, and the Civil Rights Movement exposed teachers who participated in it. Black teachers suffered under both scenarios. By the mid-1960s, black teacher dismissals resulting from desegregated schools and teacher involvement in the Civil Rights Movement reached epidemic proportions. Biased school administrators, local school boards, and politicians conspired to terminate over 30,000 black teachers, mostly in the southern and border states. NEA responded to those indignities through its Professional Rights and Responsibilities Commission, which defended teacher rights.[99] One case defended by NEA all the way to the U.S. Supreme Court involved Willa Johnson, a black North Carolina teacher who was arbitrarily fired because of her leadership in voter registration drives. NEA moved promptly to her defense with funds for her sustenance during the litigation, and bore all of her legal expenses. When the Court ultimately ruled that her rights had been violated with the termination, she was awarded reinstatement to her teaching post and received financial compensation for damages. Numerous other such cases were litigated by NEA as well as ATA and its affiliates. In North Carolina, attorney Julius Chambers and E. B. Palmer of the black teachers' association litigated more teacher dismissal cases than anyone else in the nation, and pioneered the legal approach of making many of those cases class actions.[100]

Another '60s high mark for NEA came at the request of ATA and others, after Prince Edward County, Virginia closed its schools in 1959 rather than integrate. NEA staff raised $75,000 and, in 1963, assisted in recruiting teachers for the newly created Prince Edward Free School Association, which provided integrated education for blacks who had been denied admission to local public schools.[101]

By 1965, NEA had moved closer to the front lines of the Civil Rights Movement when its staff and leaders assisted Selma, Alabama teachers in winning a black-educator voter registration campaign under a slogan that became a classic, "Fit to Teach, Fit to Vote."[102] This innovative campaign grabbed national headlines and became a model for later voter registration drives by Martin Luther King, Jr. Without a doubt, AFT had laid claim to the allegiance of many black teachers through its militant unionism and urban education agenda, but NEA landed several effective civil rights counter-punches, maintaining its core base of black southern teachers.

Nothing, however, secured the Association's relationship with black teachers more firmly than the chain of events that began in 1963, when RA delegates formally requested the Joint Committee to explore the conditions under which it would be "desirable and feasible to merge the two Associations, and report its recommendations in one year or less."[103] That single, isolated request made by NEA's most reliable and dependable interracial committee, would prove to be the one most responsible for the development of the modern NEA, not necessarily for what the committee was charged to do, but because of all the agreements that would have to be reached to make a merger acceptable to both NEA and ATA and their respective affiliates.

Never before had the Joint Committee engaged in any work that clearly foreshadowed the future direction of the organization. Forty years of creditable work on the problems of black and white teachers had developed a faith and confidence in the committee. It understood the needs and dynamics of both organizations, and, urged on by the social climate, determined that a merger of NEA and ATA would benefit both organizations and should be consummated.

In 1964, the convention acted on the Joint Committee's recommendation, passing Resolution 12, which called for the integration of all NEA affiliates. It was a courageous, bold, and optimistic Representative Assembly. Once again, NEA's progressive reputation soared, and black teachers took note that the Association had squared itself with the goals of the Civil Rights Movement.[104] For certain there was caution, because there were no templates from the past to guide the process forward. But there was also a sense of pride and even exuberance that NEA was attempting something that no organization of its size had ever done: the unification of its segregated components. Nonetheless, the lingering question that delegates took with them from the RA was whether the spirit of Resolution 12 had any meaning or support at the southern local and state levels, where members lived in communities deeply divided on race.

In the South, it was not uncommon for black and white teachers to have spent their entire careers in the same cities and towns without achieving any knowledge of or personal relationships with each other. It had been 100 years since Reconstruction had offered a fleeting experience of democracy in those places, which meant that there was no personal memory of anything but segregation and the immediate trying and painful struggles to integrate in the post-*Brown* climate. The list of concerns needing resolution before any merger could take place included membership status, state and local staff, property and other assets, ongoing priorities, traditions to be maintained, and organizational brand identity, but the most intractable one had to do with leadership. Simply put, would there be allowances for blacks to serve as elected officers at the local and state levels, where their membership numbers constituted a minority? Having long enjoyed leadership positions as black presidents, vice-presidents, and board members, and having become accustomed to being decision-makers, blacks were loath to relinquish or forfeit those traditions for a merger of any nature. Long before Resolution 12, mergers of ATA and NEA affiliates in Maryland, Delaware, West Virginia, New Jersey, Kentucky, Pennsylvania, Missouri, and Oklahoma had taken place, yet no black officers had ever been elected, nor were black education issues a priority in any of those "merged" states. ATA leaders E. B. Palmer of North Carolina, Horace Tate and Lithangia Robinson of Georgia, Joe Westbrook of Tennessee, Walker Solomon and Ellen Watson of South Carolina, and Joe Reed of Alabama, among others, were not enamored of those "absorptions." Determined that the history of such experiences would not be repeated, NEA and ATA worked together to ensure that, in every instance of a state merger, provisions for the election of black leaders would be guaranteed, and would be explicit and non-negotiable in every merger agreement. As Joe Reed said, "There would be no good faith agreements that could not be reduced to writing."[105] In all candor, it must be acknowledged that the merger resulted in major drops in white membership in some southern states, as NEA's progressive agenda pulled its politics out of alignment with the politics of the region. This situation was aggravated in late 1969 and early 1970, when NEA, under the guidance of President George Fischer, opposed the nomination of two southerners for the U. S. Supreme Court: first Clement Haynesworth, and second, Harrold Carswell were stated by NEA to be "unfit to hold this high position," because of their records on civil rights. Only a few months earlier, through action of the RA, NEA had endeared itself to blacks and progressives—though further alienating many white southerners—when it became the first national organization to suggest a national holiday to commemorate the birthday of Martin Luther King, Jr. As Allan West, however, has shown in his book, *The National Education Association: The Powerbase of Education*, by 1979 the merged organizations had increased NEA's membership by close to 200,000 over the combined membership of the two separate organizations at the time of their merger.[106]

Over a relatively short span of time, the merger agreements resulted in scores upon scores of black NEA members being elected to office in state affiliates and blacks and other minorities winning elections for all national governance positions in the Association: Board of Directors, Executive Committee, Secretary-Treasurer, Vice President and President. All of that began in 1966 at the Miami convention when both the American Teachers Association and the National Education Association voted approval of the merger. The ratification was unanimous and, in a show of solidarity for this momentous historical event, all state associations demanded the privilege of seconding the motion for merger. At that time, several separate black and white associations had not yet overcome obstacles preventing merger, but by 1977, affiliates in all states had merged. And it was only two years after the Miami convention that the membership confirmed that race and ethnicity would not handicap or exclude ethnic minorities from the Association's highest office by electing Braulio Alonso, the first Hispanic to be president of NEA. It had taken over 100 years to integrate the Association completely, and after that, less than two years to elect an ethnic minority to its highest office. The belief in inclusion that began with Robert Campbell had now found expression in a way unimaginable to any of the founding fathers or mothers. Still, their legacy of an organization representing "all the people" had been a guiding principle, and the extension of that idea into the office of the NEA president continued the remarkably progressive and much-heralded journey of the Association in the pursuit of social justice. The experiences learned from the merger of ATA and NEA provided NEA with the capacity both to notice race and ethnicity and to ignore race and ethnicity in the selection of its leaders. The organization was forever changed, and its progressive agenda and inclusive orientation would become a beacon light for minorities desiring to participate at the highest levels of the nation's largest professional union.

James P. Wickersham, NEA president, addressed the 1866 convention about the urgency of supporting the efforts of Reconstruction in providing education to the former slaves.

Thomas W. Bicknell, NEA president, threatened to move the 1884 convention from Madison, Wisconsin if black members were not provided equal hotel accommodations.

Alexander Crummell, the first black invited to speak at an NEA convention in 1865.

Booker T. Washington, the most powerful black American of his era, spoke at several NEA annual conventions.

Richard R. Wright of Georgia spoke against the concept of separate but equal education at the NEA convention in 1900 in Charleston, South Carolina.

J.R.E. Lee of Tuskegee Institute, founder of the National Association of Colored Teachers, which later became the American Teachers Association (ATA).

John Hope, ATA president in 1916 and president of Morehouse College, was a strong critic of Booker T. Washington's educational and social outlook.

Robert Russa Moton, president of Tuskegee Institute, spoke at the NEA Convention in 1929.

Credit: © 1927, The Associated, Publishers, Inc.

Ella Flagg Young–NEA's first female president.

Joseph Charles Price, founder of Livingstone
College, spoke to the NEA convention in 1890.

Credit: John E. Hood Photos, Nashville 3, TN

H. Councill Trenholm in 1926 when he first became involved with the American Teachers Association.

Martin Jenkins, Walter Ridley, and H. Councill Trenholm at the 1944 ATA convention.

American Teachers Association annual convention, Louisville, Kentucky, 1948.

Mary McLeod Bethune, first female president of the American Teachers Association, 1924.

Officers of the American Teachers Association at the 1943 annual convention, Richmond, Virginia.

Mary Williams of Charleston, West Virginia, the most active ATA black female leader and member of the Joint Committee.

Oldest member of the adult education class, Booker T. Washington High School, Pensacola, Florida, 1935.

ATA teachers had many children to try to teach from such Depression families as the one pictured.

This cooking class at Baton Heights School, Henrico County, Virginia, in the early1900s was the industrial model of education advocated by Booker T. Washington.

A "colored school" in Halifax County, Virginia in the 1930s

Dunbar High School, Lynchburg, Virginia, 1924, which later would be attended by Mary Hatwood Futrell.

ATA Teachers taught adults in the evening as well as children during the day. *Photo circa 1920s.*

John W. Davis in 1951 became the first black to chair an NEA commission.

J. Rupert Picott, an ATA official from Virginia, vigorously argued at the NEA Representative Assemblies in the 1950s for NEA to treat minorities fairly and equitably.

Mother and daughter on the steps of the U.S. Supreme Court holding a newspaper proclaiming the end of school segregation after the *Brown v. Board* ruling.

(L-R) Thurgood Marshall, Donald Murray, and Charles Houston prepare for *Murray v. Maryland*, 1935. A decision by the Maryland Court of Appeals assured Murray's admission to the University of Maryland Law School.

Nobel Peace Prize winner Ralph Bunche was a keynote speaker at the Representative Assembly in 1954. Curiously, he never mentioned the *Brown* decision of less then two months earlier.

Mary McLeod Bethune with Eleanor Roosevelt, who intervened in the infamous "Kissing Case" in Monroe, North Carolina in 1958.

NEA writer, Howard Carroll, interviewed a woman marching in support of civil rights in Selma, Alabama in the early 1960s.

Credit: Photograph by Carl Purcell, National Education Association

NEA/ATA Joint Committee which in 1961 recommended the merger of the two organizations. Seated (L-R) Louese Phillips; Webster Groves, MO; Mary L. Williams, chairman, Charleston, WV; and Madge P. Harper, Orangeburg, SC. Standing (L-R) H. Councill Trenholm, Montgomery, AL; Walter N. Ridley, secretary, Elizabeth City, NC; Ivan A. Booker, director, NEA Membership Division; Edward W. Brice, from the U.S. Office of Education (substituting for committee member Ambrose Caliver, assistant to the Commissioner); Rufus B. Atwood, Frankfort, KY; and C. Godfrey Paska, assistant director, NEA Records Division.

Mary Williams, (R), at a 1961 appreciation ceremony for H. Councill Trenholm (L).

Walker Solomon, executive secretary of the Palmetto Education Association and key figure in its merger with the South Carolina Education Association.

Joe Reed of the Alabama Education Association was a significant figure in the mergers of state affiliates.

Signing of the NEA/ATA merger agreement in Miami in 1966. Seated, R.J. Martin and William Carr. Standing, Richard Batchelder and Hudson Barksdale.

Braulio Alonso

1967-1968

Braulio Alonso
1967-1968

The Teacher Revolution,
the Urban Movement, and the Merger

As much as we would like to believe to the contrary, most history we read and write is filtered retrospectively through the lens of current definitions and social and cultural norms. While definitions and norms invariably change over time—often between one generation and another—we use those lenses when they are found to be most convenient and applicable for our needs. Braulio Alonso, who became NEA's president in 1967, is a perfect example of the ambiguous nature and changing dynamics of race and ethnic identification in our society and in the Association. Only after his term ended did the U.S. Census Bureau in 1970 provide a definition for "Hispanic" that would be inclusive of his white Spanish heritage. Hispanic then came to describe "a person of Cuban, Mexican, Puerto Rican, South or Central American, or other Spanish culture or origin regardless of race." Since the term is race-neutral, a person of Hispanic ethnicity could be of any race—white, Asian, black, Native American, or Pacific Islander.[1]

Alonso's election as president of NEA in 1967 came one year after the NEA/ATA merger, the Representative Assembly having voted him president-elect during the year of the merger. Prior to the changing of NEA's constitution in 1971, NEA presidents served one-year terms. The media did not report any historical significance in his election because he was not an ethnic minority, and at the time, the government's Hispanic designation only applied to those of Latin American origin. "I didn't qualify," he recalled, "because my father was born in Spain."[2] Thus, the Association's first minority president was not widely accepted as such until the U.S. Government provided an all-encompassing ethnic label. The shift of public perception of Alonso from white to Hispanic would occur later, and until that transformation, he was viewed as white.

Social constructs on race and ethnicity altogether too often deny the complexity of the human experience. Braulio Alonso's childhood experiences were far from typical: growing up in Ybor City—a neighborhood in Tampa, Florida—one of America's most unique and historically diverse communities. Where in most cities the different ethnic groups formed their own geographically defined and semi-isolated enclaves, Ybor City was a mixture of different immigrant groups, including Spaniards, Cubans, Italians, and Jews living side-by-side. It was one of the few places where members of at least four ethnic groups lived next door to each other. "When I was growing up we had southern blacks, Cuban blacks and whites living more or less in the same neighborhoods," Alonso said.

> "…We did not classify ourselves as Latinos or Hispanics or anything else. We grew up in a community where we considered ourselves as the children of immigrants. We considered ourselves Spanish Americans. The Italians considered themselves as Italian Americans. It was not until later, way back in the '70s, that the term 'Hispanic' had become so overwhelming that it took in different ethnic groups that really had little relationship to each other, enabling all under one label simply because they came from the language of Spanish."[3]

Alonso was born into this community on December 16, 1916, to Spanish immigrants Braulio G. and Luisa Alonso who worked in the cigar factories, where young Braulio went to work at the age of 10 to help support his two sisters. Ybor City became home to the nation's largest cigar industry, with over 50 factories in a manufacturing district that offered employment to workers producing cigars from Cuban tobacco. Neither of his parents had much formal education, but both valued learning and had come to America for education and the job opportunities that had opened up as a result of the U. S. industrial revolution. The cigar workers were unionized, and Samuel

Gompers was a lionized figure in the community, facts which contributed to his parents' respect for organized labor and the value of fighting for those things most needed to ensure a comfortable life. Alonso's fierce and deep-rooted passions for education, cultural pride and respect, mastering more than one language, unionism, equality of opportunity, political activism, and contributing to the less fortunate, were all ingrained at an early age, and they reflected his experiences in Ybor City. All were essential to the mosaic of that immigrant working-class community, molding values that would serve him well throughout a remarkable life and an illustrious career in public education.[4]

In the Ybor City of his youth, the immigrants worked side-by-side rolling cigars in the factories, and their racial and cultural differences were minimized within the community. Outside of Ybor City, however, all of the rules of Florida and the segregated South were enforced. Even within the community, the Catholic schools, which enrolled black Cubans, had to cease such educational practices when the state ruled that white nuns could not teach black students. And the theaters, restaurants, and public facilities in Ybor City also were forced to abide by some measures of the discriminatory practices. The Catholic churches, in which interracial religious services were not uncommon, were notable exceptions to the common practice.[5]

In the early twentieth century, the Ybor City of Braulio Alonso's youth—unlike most U.S. immigrant enclaves of the era—was no slum. It had the highest living standard of any working-class neighborhood in Tampa, and it provided everything the residents needed: employment, shops, recreational facilities, businesses, schools, churches, mutual aid societies, and a population of immigrants who shared the customs, languages, and traditions of the old country. Life centered around the mutual aid societies, popularly known as social clubs, which operated on dues collected from members and were generally limited to those of a specific ethnic background. The Italians, Spaniards, black Cubans, white Cubans, and subdivisions of those groups built impressive edifices for their clubs. In exchange for dues, usually five percent of a member's salary, the families of that member received library services, educational programs, and free medical treatment; could join sports teams; enjoyed special service in restaurants; and attended social functions. Beyond those benefits, the clubs were gathering places for the sharing of ideas and the development of extended families among those of common heritage. The black and white Cuban clubs are worthy of note, because Florida's racial laws limited interaction between dark-skinned and light-skinned Cubans, often requiring members of the *same* family to join different clubs.[6]

Alonso's world revolved around family, work, school, church, and the social club, Centro Asturiano de Tampa, founded by immigrants from Asturias, the region in Spain from which his family had come. Early on, he pursued education relentlessly, learning from his parents its potential value to his future and the improvement of his life. Even in the cigar factories, learning opportunities were cherished. His parents continued to learn as they worked, and they were enamored of *el lector* (the reader), the man who was hired to read newspapers, magazines, novels, and writings on current events to the workers as they rolled the cigars. Perched on elevated platforms above rows of workers below, the readers relieved the monotony of the work, stimulating the minds of those to whom they read. Long before radios became common, the highly educated and well respected readers introduced workers to the flow of current ideas and information. Spanish was the language of the factories, and some readers had sufficient multilingual skills to read from books written in English or Italian, translating them instantly into Spanish. Working in those factories from dawn to dusk, Alonso's parents admired the educated *lectores* and wanted their children to do well in school and to acquire those same learned traits.[7]

The readers were like teachers, holding power and influence from their ability to articulate values and ideas and to share information, which resonated among the workers, many of whom were illiterate and would not have found daily access anywhere else to the ideas of the world's most renowned thinkers. The power of the reader, also like that of a teacher, was not to be found in vast sums of money, property, or patronage; it was in the influence leveraged in shaping ideas. Protracted periods of labor strife characterized Ybor City's cigar-making industry, and the readers often chose or were requested to read materials that solidified workers' attention around the strength of labor and unions. More than an industrial luxury, *el lector* was a mechanism for maintaining worker and union solidarity, and an educating instrument for those whose leisure time and activities did not allow for sustained reading or familiarity with the ideas and writings of intellectuals.

Cigar makers from one generation to the next migrated to Ybor City, anticipating that *el lector* would guide them through the events, issues, and ideas central to being productive and effective workers in an industrial economy. Factory owners soon came to understand the connection between *el lector* and labor unrest, and, in 1931, their banishment of the readers resulted in a strike. "When," asked one Ybor City resident, "is the last time you ever heard of workers striking for culture?" But it was culture, and more, that bonded the readers to the workers, because the readers enabled the workers to be active and informed participants in the dialogue of the larger society and to understand better the issues of discussion between management and labor. In the world of young Braulio Alonso, this industrial "blue-collar adult education" was a source of pride and an inspiration to the poorly educated cigar makers, enabling them to define their place and significance in society.[8]

Throughout Alonso's education, both in Ybor City and Tampa, his academic prowess always ranked him at the top of his class, positioning him for a level of success never enjoyed by his parents. His first language was Spanish, but "learning English," he remembered, "especially for the children, was a priority with my family, as it was with most of the families." Eventually he would master the skills necessary to speak and write fluently in several languages. His early friendships reflected the diversity of his surroundings and the source of his appreciation for languages.

> "I remember the ethnic mixing in my neighborhood….We had Spaniards and Cubans, Italians and Sicilians in the same block and for several beyond. The names indicate it. We had Alonso, Corces, Caras, Gutierrez, Sanchez, LoCicero, Traina, Valenti, Muley, and Scaglione. And at the end of the block we had a German family."[9]

Years later he remained annoyed and vexed over the harsh discrimination experienced by his darker-skinned friends when they ventured outside Ybor City; situations he could avoid because, in his own words, "I was white." He harbored no prejudices toward blacks, equal in his eyes to all others, though circumscribed because of visual identification. "The worst the black has," he stated sorrowfully, "is the color."[10] He never forgot those painful reminders etched into his memory of the past, and as he became an adult, he vowed to revisit those Jim Crow injustices at some point in his future.

Graduating from Tampa's Hillsborough High School as class valedictorian in 1935, Alonso was accepted at the University of Tampa, which made him the first in his family to graduate from high school and attend college. While a college student, he worked at a popular newsstand in Ybor City, where the backroom card games attracted local politicians and gamblers directly opposed to the ideas espoused in the ivory towers of academe, giving him a close-up and personal glimpse into Tampa's corrupt underbelly. It was the real world and one that provided him with an education not taught in the classroom but, nonetheless, much needed. In 1934, the year before Alonso's graduation from Hillsborough High, Claude Pepper, the unabashed liberal politician and champion of the poor, ran for the U.S. Senate. As a member of the Florida State House, he had refused to support a resolution condemning the wife of President Herbert Hoover for inviting a black man to the White House for tea. Alonso's close family (totaling eight votes) was attracted to Pepper's message, and all eight voted for him. Early returns indicated that the election was close, and, curiously, the vote count in Tampa was delayed. When the votes were finally tabulated and the results announced, Alonso recalled, "The precinct where my family had voted recorded zero votes for Pepper," who lost the close election.[11] On politics, Alonso's age of innocence was lost forever.

In 1939, he completed college, and, as he had been in high school, he was again valedictorian of his class. Staying close to home, he accepted a position as chemistry and physics teacher at a local high school. Although he had been accepted to medical school at Tulane University, he had to decline owing to finances: the tuition was $1,200 a year, and, in the midst of the Great

Depression, that amount was so large that he could not have raised it even if, in his own words, he "had sold everything," he had, "and everything" his parents had.[12] Although their economic condition was fragile, Braulio G. and Luisa Alonso were active members of their community, often giving more than they could really afford to those less fortunate and surviving on whatever of their meager earnings was left over. Through the example of his parents, Alonso had seen throughout his childhood and early youth the benefits and intrinsic rewards of helping others. During the Spanish Civil War, his mother joined others to collect and send supplies to those in need, and he remembered "how good it made her feel to do this" and how it made him feel "that someday" he wanted to be like his parents, helping others whenever he could.[13]

In August of 1941, Alonso married Adelfa (Bebe) Diaz whose parents had also migrated from Spain. A few months later he entered the U. S. Army as a private, but his academic background and learned demeanor were so impressive that he was quickly enrolled in Officers Candidate School. He served with the 85th Infantry Division in North Africa and throughout the Italian Campaign as battery commander in the 328th Artillery.[14] It was during his military service that he observed the disrespectful and demeaning treatment of black soldiers, which bothered him because he expected more from the military. He saw it as shameful and no different from the racism experienced by blacks in segregated Tampa. In Italy, he witnessed the black 92nd Infantry Division, after performing brilliantly in emergency combat maneuvers, forced to perform manual labor chores from which white soldiers were exempt.[15] The hypocrisy of the treatment of Jim Crowed black soldiers defending democracy in a war against fascism contradicted and compromised all of the reasons for America's involvement. It made no sense to Alonso; it bothered him, and he was powerless to change it; but those images were seared into his mind, and he would not forget them.

Before the war was over, Alonso had risen to the rank of Major and his combat gallantry earned him the Bronze Star with Cluster, and the Purple Heart with Cluster. "It's one of those things. I was in the wrong place at the wrong time," said Alonso with characteristic modesty when replying to a comment about the honor and distinction those medals represented. "I thank the Lord that He decided that it wasn't my time to go and I was wounded instead of killed. I had so much more to do with my life."[16] Some of those serving under Alonso's leadership were not so fortunate. In his first combat encounter, 12 of his men were killed, and that remained forever his most painful memory of the war. June 6, 1944 is forever etched in America's military history and the nation's memory as D-Day, and for Alonso on that date, he and his troops would celebrate the liberation of Rome. After the festivities, he was fortunate enough to have a personal experience that he remained proud of throughout his life: he persuaded a Swiss guard at the Vatican to allow him a private audience with Pope Pius XII.[17] On that day he was fortunate to have had good luck on his side, though the courage of his request and the audacity of believing it possible, framed an outlook on life that would become his trademark over the years. He would return home after the war with that power of persuasion and optimism still intact.

After four years of service, he received his honorable discharge from the army and returned to Tampa, accepting another job in public education, but this time as a director of Adult Education and On the Job Training for Veterans. The experience of war had advanced Alonso's maturity beyond his actual age and had strengthened his resolve to make post-war Tampa a better place for all of its citizens. With determination, but without success, he tried to integrate his training program so that black veterans could re-enter civilian life on an equal footing with whites. In 1949, he was elected president of the predominantly white Hillsborough County Teachers Association and broke with racial etiquette by having meetings open to black teachers as well as white. The dangers and risks existing in segregated Florida after the war cannot be underestimated or over-stated. Black and white inter-racial groupings were strongly forbidden, and there were few organizations that went against the rules. Yet, the colorblind Alonso proceeded with his mission, impervious to the consequences of a potential backlash. Whether by instinct or pure luck, he tapped into a reservoir of good will among Hillsborough teachers desiring change through the common sense of unity. By the early 1950s, through his moral rectitude and by tireless persuasion, his leadership resulted in the integration of the Hillsborough and Pinellas County Teachers Associations, an extraordinary achievement for that period.[18] Some of the tensions created by change and black agitation for civil rights precipitated violence. Alonso was stunned to disbelief, and he grieved deeply when Florida's best-known black teacher activist, Harry T. Moore, and his wife were assassinated on Christmas Eve of 1951 by the racist-inspired bombing of their home.[19] Protesting against segregation was a dangerous enterprise, and no sane Floridian—black or otherwise—could be oblivious to the potential consequences of organizing for integration. Protesting and organizing were risks that Alonso was willing to take in advocating for integrated teacher associations, and he was relieved when black and white teachers agreed to unite for one cause. Once again, his growing optimism for the rule of justice, and his ability in persuading others to set aside differences for a common goal were becoming fundamental to the shaping of his view on unionism.

Alonso's next assignments were as principal of three local schools in succession, West Tampa Junior High (1952-1958); Jefferson High (1958-1962); and C. Leon King High (1962-1968). Always the student and always the learner, he was never found idle during the summer, and he used his vacations to earn a Master's and Ph.D. from the University of Florida. As a school administrator, his hands-on style, personal approach to relationships, and compassion for the disadvantaged earned him the respect of faculty, students, parents, and colleagues. He changed the lives of many who came under his influence. The confluence of his overarching talent, his towering presence, and his practice of leading by example, contributed to students' academic achievement in all three schools, ranking them among the best in Tampa. As a principal he was completely engaged, never missing a school dance, sports event, pep rally, assembly, or academic activity. He could be counted on to participate in everything, and he *wanted* to participate in everything. He was the first to arrive each morning and the last to leave each evening. "His presence was really felt throughout the school, and he was aware of the whole school," remembered one student. "He gave you the desire to perform, and you did not want to let him down," recalled another. The diminutive Alonso was an innovative thinker and motivator who maintained an open-door policy, making himself accessible to students and faculty alike. "The man was class, and he still is," said a former student who was inspired to become a principal in Alonso's beloved Ybor City.[20] The excitement he brought to learning stimulated the minds of students, many of whom were Hispanic and went on to become not only the first college graduates in their families, but also educators, surgeons, bankers, and judges, all tracing the origins of their success to Alonso, the role model who made all the difference for them.

Cultivating an environment in which learning flourished, Alonso became proficient in bringing out the best in students, teachers, and parents. He was especially gratified to serve students who came from backgrounds similar to this own, vicariously understanding the parents and grandparents who desperately wanted their children to succeed. Teachers applauded his style, some lobbying the school district for assignment to his schools. When asked about the secret of his popularity with staff, he responded, "If you treat a teacher with dignity, if you become a facilitator for their teaching, if you allow them to teach without interrupting them all of the time, if you become a person that a teacher would look to for help, then you can become successful."[21]

Not only was Alonso known to his faculty members and students as an exemplary educator, but from the early 1950s, he was recognized as a man of stature and influence in local education, as well as in the wider community. When he entered the education arena after World War II, his administrative acumen and professionalism quickly brought him local acclaim, and he soon became well-known throughout the state, serving on the board of directors of the Florida Education Association (FEA) from 1951 to 1956. During that period, he was a highly regarded and much-sought-after speaker. FEA members solidified his role as a leader in the education community by electing him president of the organization in 1957. On the larger stage, he continued the work of social justice that he had begun in Tampa, by developing a plan for FEA to move towards correcting the injustices of segregation. "When I became president," he said, "we had a lot of black teachers" in the FEA, "but they had a black organization in Miami." His approach was basic, "Why don't we just combine?" No one from FEA had ever publicly questioned the separate arrangements, but Alonso initiated discussions with white and black teachers, which ultimately led to one organization for all of them. To the surprise of many, he reflected, "Nobody protested and there was no problem." Earlier, Alonso had gone against the grain of southern sentiment when he traveled throughout the state speaking to civic and community groups about the importance of complying with the *Brown v. Board of Education* decision, which had also been supported by his local association while he was president.["]

Following his presidency of FEA, he went on to serve on NEA's Board of Directors (1958-1964), and Executive Committee, where his consensus-building skills, intellectual capacity, faith in public education, and organizing abilities were revealed to a national audience. The number one issue for NEA at that time was preparing the membership for the merger with the American Teachers Association. Alonso brought to NEA a background and experiences more diverse than most, and he understood the issues surrounding the merger. He shared all that he had learned about mergers and integration in Hillsborough, Pinellas, and the FEA. For those members and leaders who needed direction on this pivotal, though fragile and often precarious, issue, Alonso, the southerner, was positioned to provide assistance. "I had been involved in that area for a long time," he reflected, "and that's probably one of my greatest achievements."[23] Prominent NEA personalities Helen Bain of Tennessee, E. B. Palmer and Lois Edinger of North Carolina, Bob Chanin of NEA, and Joe Reed of Alabama, all single out Alonso for his skills of developing consensus around the merger and other sensitive race issues.[24]

In 1967, one year after the merger, Alonso became president of NEA. Given the politics of the merger and integration, a better and more qualified person for the job could not have been chosen. No NEA leader had the hands-on experience and success of integrating and democratizing the Association at all three levels: local, state, and national. But there was an exacting family and community price to be paid for taking over the reins of the NEA. The position required him to relocate to the Washington, D.C. area, causing anguish and great pain. "It was the worst time in his life, having to leave

Tampa," remembered his wife. "It was the first time I saw him cry."[25] Like
the memorable character George Bailey, made famous by Jimmy Stewart in
the movie *It's A Wonderful Life*, Alonso found that it was not easy to leave
home.

Braulio Alonso, like all of the NEA presidents who preceded him, was limited
to a one-year term by the NEA constitution, which would not change to
consecutive two-year terms—pending reelection—until NEA adopted a new
constitution in 1973. Aside from the politics of implementing the merger,
however, the overlapping issues of organizational structure, collective
bargaining, urban education, teacher strikes, political action, and competition
from the American Federation of Teachers (AFT), were inherited by Alonso,
and would prove to be the challenges of his presidency. Those issues would
also test NEA's ability to adapt to changing perspectives on teachers and
unionism.

Organizationally, the NEA structure was a bureaucratic maze of divisions,
and one of those—the Division of Classroom Teachers—which gave NEA its
brand identity, was the largest, but, arguably, not the most authoritative. The
decision-making power and authority resided with the executive secretary,
the Executive Committee, and the Board of Directors, all disproportionately
represented by administrators. The relationships between the national office
and the state affiliates were clear when NEA went about the business of
lobbying the federal and state governments for legislation supporting public
education. In that equation, however, the interests of the local affiliates
were often slighted. All of this was exacerbated when urban education
issues took on distinct identities in the early 1960s, and with the advent of
collective bargaining. Urban education leaders and their locals needed more
recognition and access to NEA, as well as autonomy from state affiliates
in defining and representing issues unique to their home areas. Collective
bargaining, a distinct function of a local affiliate, would bring these issues to
a crisis in the Association.

Since the founding of NEA, the organization had embraced teachers and
administrators as members, though the latter dominated the leadership

positions, decision-making, and operation of the Association. As one scholar noted, "The fundamental difference between NEA and AFT was that whereas the Association enrolled all educators, the union proscribed superintendents from membership and confined the ranks of its locals only to classroom teachers. Administrators other than the superintendents—that is, principals and assistant principals—could join AFT only by forming their own local organizations apart from the teachers' local."[26] With collective bargaining— which NEA had no choice but to endorse—it was fundamental and obvious that the occupational interests of teachers and school administrators were not the same. Collective bargaining divided the NEA house against itself, and the internal dynamics which would decide if the structure could stand, would not be determined until the new constitution was adopted in 1973.

The weakness and vulnerability of NEA's inclusion of administrators in its membership became more transparent when laws were passed respecting teachers' rights to collective bargaining. The movement swept the larger cities. When the teachers in New York City, led by AFT, won the right to collective bargaining, the effect rippled nationally. Teachers nationwide understood the implications, organized at the local level, and demanded the same treatment as that achieved by their colleagues in New York City. On the heels of the New York decision, AFT won collective bargaining elections in Detroit in 1964, and Philadelphia in 1965. While NEA continued to debate the issue and not provide its large city members with resources to compete, it lost ground and lagged behind AFT in large city systems. By 1967, when Alonso came to office, Chicago, Boston, Kansas City, Cleveland, Washington, D.C., Newark, Toledo, and cities elsewhere had gone to AFT.[27]

The teacher revolution found its counterparts in other American labor movements of the era, one of which was closely followed by Alonso. The National Farm Workers Association (NFWA) and the Agricultural Workers Organizing Committee (AWOC) merged in 1966 to form the United Farm Workers (UFW). Led by Cesar Chávez, UFW sought economic justice and advocated strikes, picketing, boycotts, marches, and other non-violent means to achieve the union's aim. The movement involved risks for those who joined it, and, though largely Hispanic in composition and leadership, it found support among organized workers and socially conscious Americans much as Martin Luther King, Jr.'s Civil Rights Movement and his Ghandian philosophy on civil disobedience had done earlier. A life-long learner and son of lower-income industrial union workers, Alonso had come to appreciate personally those movements, and he understood the relationship between struggle and change.

As early as 1966, when Alonso was a candidate for the office of president-elect of the Association, urban leaders had approached him about the need for structural changes in NEA in the hope of minimizing the influence of conservative administrators. Since 1962, the urban leaders, who were to become the National Council of Urban Education Associations (NCUEA) had organized and succeeded in establishing through their militant campaigning teacher-school board relationships, strikes, collective bargaining, and urban education problems as the dominant topics at NEA's annual conventions. Alonso identified with NCUEA and delivered an address to the group in which he embraced their goals, though he did not go so far as to endorse their proposal for a constitutional convention whose major function was patently clear: ousting the administrators, empowering teachers, and streamlining the organization. But he impressed the group with a demonstrated awareness of urban education problems, a vision for the future, and an honest sense of urgency. Urban leaders were pleased with Alonso's perspectives and priorities, both of which identified NEA's recalcitrant administrator leaders as restraints on the Association's relevancy to modern teacher unionism. The confidence placed in him to promote a progressive urban agenda spoke to his emerging stature as a national leader. He was not a classroom teacher, and his credentials were those of an administrator, but his instincts had no allegiance to the privileges of position, and he trusted his moral compass to direct him toward fairness. The ultimate and most severe test of his loyalty, however, would surface in his home state while he served as president of NEA.[28]

The year 1968 will be remembered as one of political assassinations, war protests, race riots, the Black Power movement, and the Kerner Commission report. In public education, the U.S. Supreme Court ruling in *Maryland v. Wirtz* energized NEA, among other public employee organizations, to continue its campaign to secure a federal collective bargaining law for public employees, and Congress passed the Bilingual Education Act, following years of lobbying by NEA. On the public education landscape, however, the teacher revolution took a gigantic leap forward and became a front page story when Florida teachers staged the nation's first statewide teachers' strike.

Deteriorating conditions and political neglect of public education in Florida made it a prime target for teacher militants. The state education misery index was alarming and indefensible, causing the rise of militant unionism over professional associationism among Florida's teachers. School deficiencies were rampant, including low teacher salaries, overcrowded classrooms, inadequate physical plants, insufficient kindergarten programs, and policies rife with racism, including a regular practice of recycling used and worn textbooks to schools populated with black students. Instigated at first by FEA's urban leaders who sought NEA's support after their pleas for increased school funding had been ignored by the governor and state legislature, the movement for a strike gained momentum, attracting statewide teacher support. But at NEA, support for a strike aroused mixed feelings with a clear break visible between administrators and teacher leaders.[29]

On the eve of the Florida teachers' strike, Alonso assumed the presidency of NEA. In his first address to the RA, he spoke about inadequate public financial support for education at all levels and singled out the 55,000 teachers in Florida as an example of teachers who were frustrated to the point that collective action was inevitable as a process for igniting a more responsive professional association. The issues raised by the Florida teachers placed the Association at the crossroads of past and future. Its anti-unionism, anti-strike elements were embodied in executive secretary William Carr and the administrator members; while the pro-union, anti-administrator proponents were personified by the militant urban leaders and growing numbers of sympathetic teacher members. The subject of teacher strikes was a sensitive one in the American Association of School Administrators (AASA), an NEA affiliate, and had been raised at every AASA convention since the early 1960s. That organization flatly opposed strikes and NEA's support of them. The Florida situation, however, was statewide, and NEA had learned from AFT in New York City the value of strikes to membership and organizing. Alonso's urban credentials were impeccable; his identification with the urban militants was creditable through his active support of NCUEA, and, since 1962, he had chaired FEA's Urban Committee.[30] He was an ideal flag-bearer for the urbans. And it was a parade he wanted to lead.

Janet Dean, president of the NCUEA, sought a new NEA Board policy to support the impending strike. In 1967, she led a lobbying effort that persuaded NEA's Directors not to abandon the strike movement, and she offered an impasse procedure for her position. Carefully worded, Dean's language fell short of promoting strikes, but in the event of a strike, it authorized NEA "to offer all of the services at its command to the affiliate concerned to help resolve the impasse." Phil Constans, executive secretary of FEA from 1967 to 1969, and Pat Tornillo, leader of the Dade County Teachers Association welcomed the much-needed support, which represented a sharp break with NEA's past position on strikes.[31] William Carr had unequivocally repudiated teacher strikes, once saying in a speech to the RA, "I think I can speak on your behalf" that the "members of the National Education Association…will keep their pledged word and they will never walk out on the students in their charge."[32] Alonso broke sharply from Carr and saw it differently, vehemently asserting that to secure better education for all students, the teachers had no alternative but to strike. This philosophical division between the NEA executive secretary and its president, highlighted the growing internal strife between teachers and administrators, placing both on an unavoidable collision course that would define the future for NEA.

In a show of strength and solidarity, 35,000 FEA members—more than half of Florida's teachers—packed Orlando's Tangerine Bowl in mid-August of 1967. It was a meeting, not a strike. An aerial photograph of the teachers crowding the football stadium appeared in newspapers throughout America and became iconic of teacher unrest. Nothing teachers had done since the 1961 strike in New York City had brought as much national attention to public education. It put Florida's Governor Claude Kirk and the state legislature on notice that the teachers were organized and could not be wished away. It also alerted NEA that the Florida teachers' movement was genuine. Governor Kirk and the legislature, however, feigned indifference and continued their adversarial politics, refusing to pass a budget satisfactory to teacher demands. Over the next several months, the impasse continued in Florida, and NEA continued to wrangle over how far the Association should go in support of the teachers.[33]

During this period fraught with back-and-forth allegations, Alonso went on a media blitz, explaining teacher discontent and seeking public understanding of teacher militancy. Appearing on NBC's Today Show, ABC's Network News with Peter Jennings, NBC Radio with Barbara Walters, and giving interviews to *Time, Newsweek, Saturday Review, Parade, McCall's, Look,* and *The New York Times,* he stayed on message in explaining the cause. Teachers were not participating in the nation's current affluence, he pointed out, and he explained what motivated their unrest and kept them going, stating that:

- Teachers wanted more voice in education.

- Teachers were reacting against the frustrations of poor teaching conditions.

- More men, as breadwinners for their families, were teaching than ever before.

- Teachers were the best educated in history.

- Teachers would never go back to the old days.[34]

By presenting variations on these main themes, Alonso was effective in making the case for teacher unrest to the American public, and thus he made himself the best-known public educator in America, though his characteristic humility compelled him to avoid celebrity status and resist the cult of personality in the Association. Alonso's strength had always resided in his ability to downplay his personal role and shift attention from himself to the causes he advocated. Since his childhood, learning had always come easy to him, though he never used it to intimidate others, or to create a marquee for himself.

On Monday, February 19, 1968, 35,000 of Florida's teachers took action again, this time going on strike. Florida had not conceded to their budget demands. A federal judge ordered Alonso to call off the strike with a 24-hour mandate. "There was no way I could do that. . . . I never considered turning my back on those teachers who stood for what I believed in for all of my life," he recalled. He defied the court order and traveled back to Washington as a warrant was being issued for his arrest. In solidarity with the striking teachers, he defiantly resigned from his principal's position in Tampa just before he was summarily fired.[35]

On March 7 the strike ended when the Florida legislature passed an education bill with funding provisions to satisfy the demands of the strikers, including an additional $2,170 for every classroom and an increase in salary for every teacher, which lifted Florida teachers from 22nd to 13th among state averages for teachers' salaries. The strike ended one day after passage of the legislation, though the chaos that followed splintered the Florida movement, when returning teachers faced different realities in their school districts. Some locals worked out agreements acceptable to the teachers, while others, facing vengeful school boards, offered the teachers only retribution ranging from demotions and harassment to termination. The press, which had never supported the teachers' job action, pointed out that the post-strike chaos proved that the strike had failed, despite the increased education funding. Quite the contrary, the strike achieved other goals for the urban militants of FEA and NEA in that it altered Association thinking to accept that professionalism could not be artificially severed from public activism for fair treatment. The publicity around the Florida strike served as a tourniquet for the potential hemorrhaging of members to the rival AFT, whose image until then had been more in tune with urban education. It signaled the arrival of unionism in Florida, setting the stage for an NEA-AFT statewide power struggle. And, it fueled the dialogue on unionism at NEA, forcing the Association to make policy decisions on strikes that would be more commensurate with teacher attitudes than with those of administrators.

NEA and the nation were jolted on April 4, 1968, when Martin Luther King, Jr., who had journeyed to Memphis, Tennessee to take part in a strike, was slain by a sniper, James Earl Ray, as he stood on the balcony of the Lorraine Motel. Alonso admired King's civil rights leadership, and his more recent involvement in organizing and supporting labor movements like that of the sanitation workers of Memphis. The assassination was followed by riots and other disturbances in over 125 American cities, despite pleas for calm by King's associates and national leaders. Braulio Alonso joined Libby Koontz, NEA president-elect, Jimmy Williams of NEA's Southeast Regional Office, J. Rupert Picott of the Virginia Education Association, and others in traveling to Atlanta to attend the funeral services. "Considering what Dr. King had done to improve this country, which contributed directly to the climate and timing of the merger," said Alonso, "NEA had to be there, and I was proud to represent our members by being there."[36]

When NEA's 1968 RA convened in July, Alonso, now at the end of his one-year term of office, chaired the assembly. By now, he was the symbol of Florida and the strike, as well as a hero to many because of his personal sacrifice in losing his principal's job rather than betray the striking teachers. Sam Lambert, who had replaced the recently-retired William Carr as executive secretary, gave an opening address to the delegates praising the gains won by teachers through collective bargaining and, thus, setting the tone for the debate on strike policy. Janet Dean of NCUEA led the fight for a resolution on strikes, which passed in a vote that must have been influenced by Alonso's presence. The resolution read in part, "Strikes have occurred and may occur in the future. In such instances the Association will offer all of the services at its command to the affiliate to help resolve the conflict."[37] That language was a stronger and more binding version of the impasse procedure adopted by the NEA Board a year earlier, and was used to sustain NEA's support for the Florida strikers. NEA had strengthened its strike policy and the activists, urbans, and others—including Alonso—who wanted NEA to become more of a union in policy and attitude had achieved their goal.

Alonso stood close with those at NEA who believed good labor policy and practice starts at home, and during his term as president that philosophy had been put to a defining test. Although the Association had come to support collective bargaining for members, it was hesitant about extending it to NEA staff. In 1966, the Executive Committee—with several seats now being held by active urbans—had initiated a survey to gauge opinions on the issue, but before the results were reported, the 1967 RA had adopted a resolution recommending that staff members of NEA and the state affiliates have the same right to negotiate as teachers. Following adoption of the resolution, Alonso appointed a committee of Executive Committee members, administrators, and staff to develop a framework for bargaining procedures. Though hand-picked, the committee represented balanced experience and views. The plan it developed in 1967 gained Alonso's approval and led to the formal recognition of the NEA Staff Organization (NEASO) as the bargaining unit for staff.[38] On the matter of collective bargaining, NEA's position was now Association-wide and complete in a way unimaginable a decade earlier. The policy that was to have been a test of organizational character was, for Alonso, an opportunity of a lifetime, and the efficiency with which it was brought into being was in large part attributable to him. Anyone vaguely familiar with his background and upbringing in Ybor City would have known where he would stand on NEASO. He wanted it to exist and was politically astute enough to assist in creating it.

During Alonso's year as president, NEA continued to position itself in ways more relevant to the modern needs of teachers, and when he spoke, he was deliberate in reminding his audiences that teachers had to express themselves politically to advance their causes. "As long as we depend upon government for funds" he concluded pragmatically, "we must be active in politics."[39] His strong support of teachers' labor activity was especially apparent when teachers went on strike in the Washington, D.C. suburbs. Long-time NEA general counsel Bob Chanin commented on his leadership, "Braulio was important to NEA as a result of his experience with the Florida strike and was helpful to NEA with the 1968 teacher strike in Montgomery County, Maryland. He knew what to say to the teachers and leaders in Maryland because of his experience with the statewide teachers' strike [in Florida], and as president of NEA, his stature helped that cause. At that place and time, when teacher strikes were relatively new, he was quite a valuable NEA resource."[40]

Braulio's regular meetings with President Lyndon Baines Johnson at the White House were not only a sign of his status as a force in national education, but they also sharpened his understanding of the relationship between politics and power. Though he and LBJ, a former teacher, developed a lasting friendship, he entertained no illusions that those meetings were indicators of anything more than NEA's political strength. So, rather than engage in trivial conversations during the meetings, Alonso sought to nurture a relationship built on shared personal experiences. "We talked about civil rights, education funding, the war on poverty, but every meeting with Johnson started with one question, 'Braulio, how is integration going?'" Johnson understood the enormity of the NEA/ATA merger and drew on Alonso for wisdom and direction on how it was progressing in the public schools.[41]

The Florida teachers' strike deepened membership tensions between teachers and administrators, making them more pronounced and contentious. The coexistence of both groups under one roof made attitudes combustible, difficult to manage, and impossible to reconcile. Although he was an administrator, Alonso was claimed as their own by urban militants and Association activists. Ethnic minorities encircled him because he had appointed more of their number to committees and commissions than any previous NEA president. He had also advanced their issues and helped fashion a human and civil rights agenda that brought NEA recognition as a partner in the Civil Rights Movement. Blacks held him in high esteem because of his determination that the NEA/ATA merger should succeed. At the end of his term, his imprint on the Association was unmistakable, but his accomplishments had exacted a high personal toll. To paraphrase the writer Thomas Wolfe, he could not go home again, at least not to the Tampa he had left. His public school career in Florida had been decimated; he had been fired. Florida had lost a remarkable principal and education leader, but now others sought to recruit him for his many demonstrated skills. The employment opportunities that poured in from elsewhere offered only a small measure of consolation and comfort for all that he had lost. He was still a fugitive in Florida, and it would be several more stressful months before the court order for his arrest was lifted so that he could return to Tampa and Ybor City. Fortunately, the Association recognized that he had much more to offer NEA once his term of president was over, and he accepted a position at NEA, becoming director of International Relations, in which capacity he worked closely with the World Confederation of the Organizations of the Teaching Professions (WCOTP). Becoming an ambassador of good will, he met with numerous heads of state in Latin American countries where he continued to speak on teacher unionism, civil rights, school funding, and political involvement. In the international arena, he strengthened NEA's reputation as an organization finely tuned to the issues of public education and social justice.

In 1983, Braulio Alonso retired and returned to Tampa, where he became active in many organizations, counseling young scholars and educators, studying history, and continuing as a living example of moral courage. He exemplified the changes he had initiated. His sense of humility never lessened, and when a local high school was named in this honor, he was bashful about the attention it brought him. "I don't think," he commented, "the person who has a school named after them should be alive."[42] Now over age 90, the same modesty applies whenever he sees his name listed for the sizeable financial contributions he has made to a scholarship fund that he co-founded for needy Hispanic students at the University of South Florida. He wants no special recognition for himself, preferring that the attention be given to his causes.

Before and since his retirement, he has received several honorary degrees and many other national and international honors—the United Nations Association's Human Rights Award, the Russell Medal Distinguished Service Award from the WCOTP, NEA's H. Councill Trenholm Award, as well as recognition from other groups worldwide, among them the Canadian Teachers Association; the Kenya National Teachers Association; the Israeli Teachers Association; Confederação do Profesores do Brasil; and Asociación Nacional de Educadores of Costa Rica. Life in retirement continues to be a victory lap for his achievements, and at frequent intervals on the track, he stops to remind us eloquently and passionately of the essence of public education in America—the system that caused his parents to leave Spain for America and that was valued as highly in his home as democracy itself. In fact, in the world of his parents education and democracy were inseparable, and he remains anchored in the values his parents instilled in him. Knowledge and learning are the keys to his existence, and the inquisitive mind of Alonso allows him to read two to three books a week, from science and biography to literature, language, and history.

"I am a great promoter of public education," says Alonso, reflecting on his life. "I and others like me have benefited so much from it. The greatest thing this country will ever give to Western Civilization is not the Declaration of Independence, but the idea of free public education for all. We provide education for free to every citizen of this country. Public education is the greatest form of affirmative action this country has ever had. No one is denied an education, regardless of color or ethnic background."[43]

When the torch passed from Braulio Alonso to Libby Koontz, who succeeded him as president of NEA, she spoke of his year in office with admiration. "He has been a leader with courage to lead by his example showing the way to a commitment to action," Koontz said. "Mr. Alonso, for that courage, and for that leadership, and for the conviction that it is better to be right than safe, I salute you."[44] Alonso's moral strength, intellectual aptitude, compassion for those less fortunate, burning passion for social justice, and demand for equity in the distribution of quality education, all converge to justify the title he most deserves, "the first, the best, and the brightest."

Elizabeth Duncan Koontz

1968-1969

Elizabeth (Libby) Duncan Koontz
1968-1969

Human and Civil Rights,
Decentralization, and Black Power

With the notable exception of the merger of the National Education Association and the American Teachers Association in 1966, no single event in the Association's celebrated history aroused the attention of the black community more than the 1968 election of Elizabeth (Libby) Duncan Koontz to the office of president. Every major newspaper and media outlet in America reported on the Representative Assembly's choice to lead the organization. *Time* magazine called her "a fighting lady for NEA" for the problems plaguing schools—racial tensions, bureaucracy, outmoded methods, and inadequate resources—and for the hope of the nation's teachers clamoring for change. "No one," wrote *Time*, "symbolizes that hope better than Mrs. Elizabeth Duncan Koontz...the first Negro to head the 1.1 million member organization."[1]

Not since Ella Flagg Young's election in 1910 as NEA's first female president had the significance of an election held such historical importance. Koontz' race and gender made it unique. Although she followed Braulio Alonso as president, because of ethnic minority definitions then prevailing, Koontz was the first person to be recognized as a member of an ethnic minority when elected president or while holding that office. Rarely, if ever, had the election of an education organization's president competed for front-page coverage or claimed lead-news status in major print and broadcast journalism. The media, unable to resist the connection of the election to the powerful Civil Rights Movement, drew parallels between the two. Overnight, Libby Koontz had become a top-tiered national personality, and the nation's network of black press, teachers, and other professionals proclaimed her accomplishment to the extent that she became not only a household name but a bona fide celebrity as well throughout those communities. Indeed, few in all sectors of education and public service were unfamiliar with her name. Even aside from the professionals, her name recognition was strong among less socially and economically prominent blacks, including domestic workers, doormen, seamstresses, sanitation workers, waitresses, cooks, barbers, chauffeurs, janitors, blue-collar industrial workers, Red Caps, and other less formally educated citizens of the multi-layered black community.

The changes occurring in America in the decade leading up to her election had been nothing short of meteoric. A plausible case could be made that more progress was made in race relations and the entry of blacks into the mainstream during that relatively brief time-span than in the entire century preceding it. The Supreme Court ruled favorably on, or upheld, every civil rights case, and though *de facto* often presented a different reality, *de jure* meant those decisions were enforceable by law. NEA was not isolated from the Civil Rights Movement or LBJ's vision of a Great Society; and Koontz' rise to influence in the Association was a by-product of both.

A summary of black *firsts* during the 1960s helps illustrate the national climate that made Koontz' election possible. In municipal politics, Carl Stokes in Cleveland and Richard Hatcher in Gary were elected mayors of major cities; and Tom Bradley was elected to the Los Angeles City Council. Robert Weaver became a member of the U.S. Cabinet when Lyndon Johnson appointed him Secretary of Housing and Urban Development, while Andrew F. Brimmer was appointed to the Board of Governors of the Federal Reserve. Edward Brooke was elected Attorney General of Massachusetts before becoming a U.S. Senator, the *first* black to attain that position since Reconstruction. Thurgood Marshall was appointed to the U.S. Supreme Court. And Martin Luther King, Jr., won the Nobel Peace Prize.

Black women were also gaining legislative and judicial power, as well as diplomatic prominence. Yvonne Braithwaite Burke of California and Barbara

Jordan of Texas won elections, making them the *first* of their race to serve in their state legislatures, and many other women and men were elected to serve in southern state legislatures for the first time since Reconstruction. Patricia Harris became the *first* black female appointed to an ambassadorship. Constance Baker Motley was appointed a federal judge, and Shirley Chisholm of New York won an election in 1968, making her the *first* black female U.S. Representative. With two first-time black male Representatives, she joined six black male incumbents in Congress.

By the beginning of Libby Koontz' term as NEA president, the universities of Georgia, Alabama, and Mississippi had all reversed school and state segregation policies and admitted black students. Most previously segregated institutions of higher education followed by enrolling their *first* black students.

After the 1966 merger of NEA and ATA, photos and articles on black educators appeared in every issue of the monthly *NEA Reporter*. Several of the southern affiliates, however, had been unable to reach state merger agreements despite pressure from NEA, including the threat of sanctions. In 1967, the RA decided it wanted to send a stronger statement on integration to its members, to the nation, and to the unmerged state associations, and it made that statement by electing Libby Koontz from North Carolina to the position of president-elect of the Association. Coming in the wake of the merger, her election had symbolic importance to those who questioned the commitment of NEA's leadership to the Association's verbal support of integration, as well as to those who may have been uncertain of NEA's commitment to a merged Association.[2] The urban activists, now positioned to leverage influence at all levels of NEA, aligning themselves and the organization with the Civil Rights Movement and the social changes that were producing black *firsts*, waved Koontz' banner in the urban battlegrounds where AFT was competing with NEA for members. A year and a half later, the politics that inspired the appointment of black *firsts*, coupled with Koontz' increasing celebrity beyond the Association and her courtship by the media, would place her at a major crossroads in her career and would return to disturb NEA in ways no one could have predicted at the time she became president-elect.

Elizabeth Duncan Koontz, affectionately known as Libby throughout her life, was born on June 3, 1919, to Samuel Edward and Lena Bell Duncan in Salisbury, North Carolina. Both parents were college-educated teachers, and despite rigid segregation, they saw that Libby and her brothers and sisters were well educated. Until 1923, with the establishment of the J. C. Price High School, Salisbury did not provide a public high school for black youth. Private schools, both secular and parochial, operated by blacks were the only alternatives for those who wanted to secure an education, and though the tuitions were low, the incomes of many uneducated and unskilled black parents would not allow for formal schooling for their children. Salisbury, however, had a small population of highly educated blacks who worked at Livingstone College, an HBCU founded by Joseph C. Price in 1882 and operated by the African Methodist Episcopal Zion Church. Price had been one of America's most respected black leaders in the late 19th Century, and in 1890, he had spoken to the NEA's convention, an honor extended to only a handful of his race.[3] Most Livingstone graduates went on to teach in black southern schools, as had Libby's parents.

In her early years at home, Libby decided that "teaching was for me" when she helped check the lessons and examinations of illiterate adults whom her mother was teaching to read. That experience touched her in deeply personal ways, providing her at an early and impressionable age with an appreciation for the value of teaching and learning at the most basic and practical level. And though her family enjoyed black middle-class status, she observed and later modeled their sense of obligation and responsibility to those less fortunate.[4]

Libby's world was one of massive prejudice, discrimination, and injustice, as was that of all other black southerners growing up under the doctrine of "separate but equal." Everything in Salisbury was segregated—schools, parks, churches, public transportation, libraries, hospitals, movie theaters, restaurants, cemeteries, swimming pools, and neighborhoods—and restrictions were imposed on basic rights such as voting. Blacks in Salisbury formed their own organizations and institutions, including Livingstone College, and proceeded to build a community somewhat remote from white Salisbury.[5] On a personal and organizational basis, genuine friendships between the races did develop and were tolerated as long as they did not openly challenge racial laws and etiquette. In North Carolina, such relationships had proved beneficial to local businesses and commercial interests, in large part because twelve other HBCUs existed in the state, all substantial contributors to their respective local economies.[6] Still, Koontz' parents—like others of their generation—raised their children in close-knit families and communities where the conventional wisdom passed on from one generation to the next required the children of blacks to be twice as able as those of whites to compete in a world subject to racial restrictions. The admonition to be the best possible was drilled relentlessly into black children by their elders for two purposes: to place a premium on academic excellence, and to cushion black youth against the inequities of a society that discriminated based on race. Whether Libby or anyone else ever reached the lofty and highly improbable standard set by her parents remains a matter of speculation, though the observations and testimony of those who knew her, black and white, demonstrate convincingly that she stood head and shoulders above the crowd intellectually and academically.[7]

Libby was the youngest of seven children, all raised with an abiding faith in the protestant ethic and taught by lesson and example to share their advantages with others less fortunate. Learning at school was reinforced by learning at home, and academic success for each child was the product of that blend. The expectation that the Duncan children would attend college was never questioned, and the drive to excel, rather than be merely average students, was a challenge each accepted without reservation. All of the children worked while attending college, relieving their parents of some of the financial burdens associated with college expenses, and those who had already graduated contributed to the education of their siblings who were still in college. This staggered system of financial assistance worked well for the Duncans, allowing each to pursue a career in education or other public service. Samuel Duncan, the eldest of Libby's five brothers, became president of Livingstone College, served as North Carolina's State Supervisor of Negro Schools, was president of the North Carolina Teachers Association during the merger period, and was a member of the U.S. Commission on Civil Rights, as well as the North Carolina State Board of Higher Education. A sister became Livingstone's registrar; two brothers went on to become high school principals; and another became an education administrator in the District of Columbia. Lois Edinger, a fellow North Carolinian and former NEA president, fondly remembered the Duncans as the state's "first family in education."[8]

A black person of status and position such as Libby's father, who was a school principal, was able to escape many of the indignities often unavoidable for those of lesser influence and means, and occasionally developed stable, trustworthy, and trusting relationships with well-disposed whites. Samuel Sr., patriarch of the Duncan family, worked under the authority of the white school board and superintendent, and on some social issues and on all education matters he was the official link between white and black Salisbury and Rowan County, frequently interacting, sharing information, and engaging in dialogue across the color line. Contacts of that variety in southern communities sometimes led to mutual respect and lasting friendships, but segregation and its code of conduct governed by law and tradition, with its ability to monitor and regulate interracial personal relationships of a non-sexual nature, was a complex proposition. Craig Phillips, son of Guy Phillips, the Salisbury school superintendent, spoke about the relationship of his family to the Duncans. "We did not live far apart," he recalled, "and everyone in our city knew the Duncans. They were smart and they were kind." The Phillips and Duncan families were close, and Phillips remembered his father saying that Libby "was the smartest child—black or white—in all of Salisbury." He and Libby were childhood friends, but—as was common in the South—as they grew older, segregation pushed them apart. The bond they developed in childhood, however, was lasting. "We were friends all of our lives," said Phillips.[9]

Inside the Duncan home family values were cultivated and passed on to the children. The family dinners, Libby recalled, were her first "classrooms," where teaching on all subjects took place around the table. Those soul-food lessons included the ingraining of the central family value: the sharing of resources and responsibility. Each child had specific responsibilities from cleaning the bathroom to washing and ironing the laundry. Sometimes the sharing extended into the community, as when her father brought groceries through the front door, while her mother parceled out some of them to the children who would exit through the back door to deliver the food to needier families.[10] Those experiences with family shaped Libby's worldview, but nothing external to the family caught her attention more than a court case in Durham that made her and others acutely aware that the legal foundation for administering segregation policies held obligations for equity that had yet to be challenged in the courts.

The segregated educational world of the South, as defined and legalized in 1896 by *Plessy v. Ferguson,* had an intriguing loophole that made it vulnerable in higher education. Separate but equal theoretically meant that what a state provided for whites must also be provided for blacks. During Libby's senior year in high school, the National Association for the Advancement of Colored People (NAACP) made plans for Thomas Hocutt, a graduate of the North Carolina College for Negroes (NCC), to apply for admission to the School of Pharmacy at the University of North Carolina (UNC). NCC did not have a pharmacy program, and NAACP attorneys Charles Hamilton Houston and William Hastie argued that refusal to admit Hocutt was a violation of the equal protection clause of the Fourteenth Amendment. The alternative would be for the state of North Carolina to open a School of Pharmacy at one of the black state colleges for a single student, Hocutt. Banking on the assumption that North Carolina would view that alternative as cost prohibitive, NAACP sponsored Hocutt's application. UNC, of course, informed Hocutt that his application would not be considered because of race. Hastie, then, with the assistance of black Durham attorneys Conrad Person and Cecil McCoy, proceeded to file a lawsuit.[11]

Libby and all of North Carolina intensely followed this unprecedented school integration case, fully cognizant of what it might portend for the future. Hastie's performance, in this *first* NAACP separate-but-equal education case, was reported widely as breathtaking and brilliant. And while he was winning by large margins on all legal points in the courtroom, the state attorney general argued the case in un-coded words far removed from legalese. "I think there is a deep motive behind this suit," he stated to the judge, "and that motive is that this 'Nigra' wants to associate with white people."[12] Despite the strength of NAACP's case, however, it was undermined outside of the courtroom, when NCC President James Shepard, succumbing to pressure from state political operatives, declined to release Hocutt's undergraduate transcript to UNC, effectively throwing the lawsuit out of court.[13] While Libby was a student at Livingstone, NAACP won college integration cases in Maryland and Missouri, but for her it was the Hocutt case that broadened her horizons and opened a window to the possibilities of the future.

Libby was an attractive, smart, social, and popular student on the Livingstone campus. Her grades kept her on the dean's list, and her many extracurricular activities included joining the Zeta Phi Beta Sorority. After graduating in 1938 with a Bachelor's Degree in English and Elementary Education, she followed the paths of her parents and siblings, accepting a teaching position in Dunn, North Carolina. It was in that small lumber town the Libby came up against a practice she fought to change: the assignment of the most inexperienced teachers to the most demanding jobs. "They gave me all those children they were absolutely certain couldn't learn anything—when, naturally, beginning teachers need the most help." Despite her inexperience and misgivings, Libby did well with her students in the twelve-grade, all-black school. Her toughness and tenacity emerged when she organized a teacher revolt following her discovery that the principal was overcharging the teachers for board in a school-owned boarding house, after which he refused her demand that the costs be reduced. Her employment was hastily terminated, and she was forced to leave, but the leadership skills she displayed in Dunn would travel with her.[14]

In the early 1940s, she taught in the small town of Landis and in Winston-Salem before returning to Salisbury in 1945, where she worked at Monroe School and Price Junior and Senior High Schools up through 1968. On November 26, 1947 she married Harry L. Koontz, a teacher and athletic director at Dunbar High School in Spencer, North Carolina. They had no children, and although their careers meant that they were often apart, their 40-year marriage centered on their home in Salisbury.[15]

While teaching in Salisbury, Koontz attained her Master's Degree from Atlanta University and then went on to undertake further study at Columbia and Indiana Universities, with additional work at North Carolina Central University in a field closest to her heart—special education for intellectually challenged students. After ten years of teaching "the supposedly mentally retarded," she became critical of that label and the low expectations that accompanied it. Too many of those students, she concluded, "are not mentally retarded" and those who are have "all the basic needs and urgings of other kids, but lack the perception and skills of others because they have been neglected." Most could achieve much more than too many educators believed possible. With "understanding and patience," said Koontz, they, too, could grow academically.[16] She expressed these beliefs in the 1940s, long before Ron Edmonds of Harvard launched the Effective Schools Movement in the 1970s with the powerful credo, "All children can learn." In the classroom, Koontz' task was to use her pedagogical skills to help special education students achieve academically, develop healthy self concepts, and learn the survival strategies required to live in a segregated world.

In the mid-20th century, southern black teachers and parents feared for the safety of their children if they came into conflict with white codes of racial conduct. No age was exempt from reprisal in such situations, and lessons on avoiding such conflicts had to be learned by black children as early as elementary school. In 1958, after Koontz had been teaching for more than a decade in Salisbury, fears turned into nightmares in the town of Monroe a few miles away, when two black children, ages seven and nine, were arrested for participating in a "kissing game" with a white girl during which the girl playfully kissed one of them on the cheek. Subsequently, the girl told her

parents, who promptly had the sheriff arrest the young boys on the charge
of attempted rape. After they had been detained in jail for a week, a judge
meted out a harsh penalty when he summarily sentenced them to reform
school until they reached age 21. It was outrageous, and despite protests
of teachers and community leaders, no judge would overturn the decision.
Former first lady Eleanor Roosevelt intervened, however, and, with the help
of President Dwight D. Eisenhower, pressured the governor to release the
boys after three months' detention.[17] The infamous "kissing case" troubled
Koontz deeply, and it made her realize that the efforts of individual teachers
and individual parents would not be enough to ensure that justice triumphed
in such cases.[18] Injustices required organized responses, and black teachers
alone could only accomplish so much change in the classroom. Effective
action against injustice would require organizational strength.

Koontz' concern led her to become active in the state and local black teachers'
organizations. As early as the 1940s, while teaching in Winston-Salem, she
had joined the North Carolina Teacher's Association (NCTA), which had
served black educators since 1880. Livingstone's founder, Joseph C. Price,
had been among NCTA's first vice presidents, and from its beginning, most of
the state's HBCU presidents, black principals, and a large number of teachers
enjoyed membership in the prestigious association. Her parents had been
long-time members, and her brothers were actively engaged in its work, so
it was logical that she would join. The group was attractive to her because it
gave black teachers an organized identity, facilitated the interchange of ideas
among professionals, and, through its affiliation with the American Teachers
Association (ATA), offered access to a national network of black educators.
At the time that she joined NCTA, the organization assisted in introducing
her to colleagues in the school system and professors at Winston-Salem
Teachers College, local black leaders, and the black social fabric of the city.
Thus, over and above her professional needs, it served an important social
function for her, along with other teachers new to the community.[19]

NCTA's agenda called for more and better schools, equitable funding, and
equalization of teachers' salaries. As early as 1934, it had made its position
known by presenting the governor with a list of problems in black schools,

requesting that a committee be appointed "to study the state's program for Negro education" and present its findings to him. Governor John Ehringhaus agreed and appointed a diverse interracial committee to carry out the task. The committee assembled, met several times, and divided into sub-committees to work on specific problems. A report of its findings was submitted to the governor, and one of its recommendations called for a reduction in the differential in white and black teacher salaries and the establishment of a single salary schedule. Although the committee went about doing its work diligently, it had no political clout and its report was flatly rejected. No actions were taken on any of its recommendations. The problem with the committee and its report was that it had taken its work too seriously, believing that the governor valued its work and welcomed fair and reasonable change. On both counts the committee members were wrong. When Koontz had begun teaching in 1938, the average annual salary of a black teacher in North Carolina was $647.00, compared with $915.00 for a white. The all-white North Carolina legislature did not see such a difference as a problem. The worth of black teachers was not to be measured against the white salary schedule, and the governor offered no explanations for his cursory dismissal of the report.[20]

Koontz increased her involvement with NCTA when she returned to Salisbury, so that by 1959, the organization had nearly 20 years of close exposure to her intellect, energy, speaking ability, courage, leadership skills, and sheer force of personality. Her commitment was rewarded by her election as president of NCTA's division of classroom teachers (NCACT). Ten years earlier, in 1949, NCTA had added this new division to meet the needs of its growing teacher membership. With a structure similar to NEA's, by the late 1950s, NCTA, while including many high-profile principals, college faculty, and administrators, was essentially supported by its large number of teacher members.[21]

When Koontz began her term of office, NCACT appointed a full-time executive secretary who was instrumental in expanding the number of locals from 20 to over 100 within a year. It was clear that the organization's involvement in the Civil Rights Movement was accountable for this phenomenal pace of growth. In her first year in office, Koontz began to participate in the Southeastern Regional meetings of NEA's Department of Classroom Teachers (NEA-DCT). While the meeting arrangements were somewhat awkward because of NEA's pre-merger recognition of dual affiliates in North Carolina, Koontz's participation was so impressive that Margaret Stevenson, executive secretary of NEA-DCT, recommended that she be made a member of its advisory council. Her attendance at council meetings resulted in a growing respect for her intellect, language skills, passion for the issues, and engaging personality, and she soon became a regular at NEA national meetings, as well as one of the best speakers on the current issues of public education, particularly those directly related to the frustrations of classroom teachers.[22] NEA could not ignore this budding talent, and in the early 1960s she became a member of the NEA Commission on the Education of Disadvantaged Youth, the first NCTA member appointed to a commission on the concerns of classroom teachers. When she became assertive in helping the Florida Teachers Association pass a resolution against segregated accommodations at NEA-DCT's Southeastern Regional meetings, it was a clear signal that her participation in NEA-DCT would not be that of a token or a silent observer.[23]

During her presidency, from 1959 to 1963, NCACT published *Guidelines for Local Associations of Classroom Teachers*, which was essential to the operation, growth, and capacity-building of newly established and inexperienced locals. In addition to *Guidelines*, Koontz' term produced hands-on publications for all six districts; statewide workshops on the Conditions of Work Project; a revised newsletter; and a publication on African contributions to world culture. Largely due to her leadership in improving communication with members through *Guidelines* and the newsletters—a far more effective program than any initiated by the administrators who had served as NCTA presidents between 1959 and 1963—the membership of NCACT surged from 9,700 to 11,500.[24] Even her brother, Samuel Duncan, who served as NCTA president from 1964 to 1966, came nowhere close to equaling her leadership or her record in membership growth. NCTA exploited the public relations value of Koontz' acceptance of appointments at NEA, issuing press releases about them to the black press. Nothing, however, matched the publicity she received in 1960, when she was elected secretary of NEA's Department of Classroom Teachers, a position she held for the following two years. That story even earned coverage by the white press of North Carolina.[25]

Although one black member, Wade Wilson of Pennsylvania, had previously been elected to the Executive Committee, NEA had not had a black in a prominent national position. Increasingly viewed as friendly, capable, and sophisticated, with her attractive and well-groomed physical appearance, Koontz was well-liked, and excelled in the previously white executive world of NEA. With a style that combined grace, dignity, and humility with great intellectual capacity, she was ready to be chosen as NEA's first-ever black national leader. NEA's choice was a great experiment that served several purposes: it better positioned NEA organizers to recruit and retain black members in the urban battlegrounds; it helped erase the memory of NEA's innocuous position on *Brown v. Board of Education*, and it represented a fundamental change in the organization from its conservative stance in the 1950s. One of the most reliable indicators of that conservative mood can be found in NEA's mid-century publications, which disclose the main focuses of the organization's attention. Beginning in 1955 and up to the eve of Koontz' election as NEA-DCT secretary in 1960, NEA did not authorize a single publication on integration, a fact best understood in comparison to the volume of NEA's annual publications totalling over 1,200, completely ignoring the most compelling issue in public education and in America's domestic policy. [26] From Koontz' election in 1960, and for the remainder of the decade, NEA's publications would reflect integration, black teacher dismissals owing to either civil rights participation or desegregation, teacher strikes, urban unrest, and disadvantaged student populations. In fact, for the 1960s, the monthly *NEA Reporter* is an index to the Civil Rights Movement. The nation was changing, NEA was changing, and, in terms of NEA's elected personalities, Libby Koontz was the most visible symbol of that change.

For two years, Koontz served as NEA-DCT secretary, continuing to receive national exposure and impressing members with her abilities, passion, and drive for teacher issues. On matters dealing with race she was forthright, but her broad knowledge of race-neutral issues was such that her brand identity leaped far beyond race. Her style appealed to large numbers of members, including those who were pessimistic about effective collaborations between whites and blacks, but were relieved to learn that her agenda was not exclusively black, and that she represented the issues of all members of the Department of Classroom Teachers. At the same time that she was building her national persona at NEA, she was serving as president of NCACT, where she developed friendships and solid working relationships with the white North Carolina Association of Educators (NCAE) during the continuing period of dual affiliates. "On anything political such as test scores, and teacher salaries," recalled Lois Edinger, former president of both NCAE and NEA, "we worked closely with Libby and the black teachers."[27] Libby and Lois—a southerner who was active in the desegregation causes of NEA, and those of her state and church—developed a personal friendship. Each helped the other gain respect and credibility with the members of their respective organizations. This relationship of mutual support also reaped dividends at the national level.

Following her term as NEA-DCT secretary, Koontz was elected its vice-president in 1962, and one year later she became heir apparent to its highest office when she became president-elect. Among her biggest boosters in that 1964 campaign were NCAE and Lois Edinger, who, in her own bid for the NEA presidency that year, had received the backing not only of Koontz and her brother, NCTA president Samuel Duncan, but also of the membership of NCTA.[28] NCTA and NCAE decided to share one campaign booth at the 1964 RA, a pioneering collaboration for dual affiliates, which garnered much attention. Under an overhead banner that featured the photos of Libby and Lois to indicate their co-endorsements, the booth was staffed by members of both organizations. Both women won by sizable margins, and years later Edinger remembered that for the entire duration of the campaign she "never heard anyone utter a single word about race."[29]

Of major importance to Koontz in 1960, when she entered the political world of NEA, was that her organizational identify not be solely defined by race. Based on the election results and the later reflections of her contemporaries, both white and black, that professional image had been perfected and validated in the successful 1964 campaign for president-elect of NEA-DCT. A year later she assumed the DCT presidency, representing 825,000 teachers, close to 90 percent of NEA's total membership. "We figured once Libby got inside the system," said E. B. Palmer, former NCTA president and NCAE associate director, "she would chart a course and there would be no limits. Her smarts and people skills could not be ignored, and she knew how to connect with NEA members. Her ability to remember [facts] and recall names was truly amazing," Palmer recalled.[30] It should be noted that Koontz' election to president of NEA-DCT took place before NEA's constitutional changes of 1971-1973, at a time when the Association was an organization of many divisions, with the power residing with the executive secretary and the administrator-members. Teachers had yet to take control of the organization, and there were no minority guarantees. Changes that were but a few years in the future were already brewing.

Koontz' rise to the top of NEA was given a major boost in 1967 when she became president-elect of the entire organization. During that year of involvement and preparation, she gained firsthand and front-row experience of the issues managed by President Braulio Alonso, who was thrilled to have her next in line. Collective bargaining, teacher strikes, urban education and unrest, the internal friction between teachers and administrators over organizational control, and monitoring the process of merging the unmerged affiliates in six states—Alabama, Arkansas, Georgia, Louisiana, Mississippi, and North Carolina—dominated Alonso's year in office, and when the torch was passed, those unresolved issues would be inherited by Koontz.[31]

There is virtually no in-depth documentation on Libby Koontz, though scholars of NEA history, Wayne Urban, Michael John Schultz, and Alan West, contend that her election as its first black president boosted the morale of minority members, while serving as indisputable evidence of NEA's position on the principle of racial equality; and that its symbolic importance was transparent to all participants in NEA affairs, particularly those in the unmerged state associations. In urban school districts in which AFT engaged NEA in fierce competition for members, her election gave NEA organizers bragging rights for minority teachers.[32] And, coming only three months after the assassination of Martin Luther King, Jr., her leadership represented to liberal and progressive elements of NEA the personification of his famous dream.

The president-elect system of NEA had given Koontz a full year to prepare for the demands of the position, and it had also given the media and Association pundits the same amount of time to contemplate the meaning of it all. Having been president of the local, district, state, and national Departments of Classroom Teachers, she was no stranger to either the politics or personalities of NEA. As far back as the early 1960s, when she first entered the national scene, she had observed the momentum of a feeling that NEA's governance structure was inadequate for a teacher movement that championed militancy in the profession and teacher control of the Association. The movement also insisted that NEA presidents play a stronger leadership role. In that connection, the one-year term was questioned because it did not allow enough time for a president to develop and implement an initiative or to represent organizational identity in a way that was sufficiently clear. As one observer cogently described it, "NEA presidents at that time served single one-year terms. The delegates to the annual Representative Assembly chose a president-elect who was in the wings to become president the following year. Every NEA president was, in effect, a lame duck."[33] Still, while waiting in the wings and representing the Association at important political and public relations events, she absorbed all of the internal dynamics of NEA and honed her media skills.

As NEA president-elect, Koontz traveled the nation, introducing NEA's Teacher-in-Politics weekend, an initiative introduced by Braulio Alonso that was designed to motivate teachers to become more involved politically and to make them aware of the crucial relationship of politics to public education. Equally important, NEA used the program in seeking opportunities to explain "teacher militancy" and teachers' strikes to the American public. Appearing on NBC TV's *Today Show*, she explained to viewers throughout the nation that teachers were taking part in politics because the NEA Citizenship Committee found that teachers had to enter the political arena to end public apathy about schools and poor school conditions. She told moderator Hugh Downs that she thought it was "an atrocity any time a person expects a teacher simply to be dedicated, and not worry about salaries" or working conditions. She hastened to emphasize that teacher militancy was based on more than compensation. "First of all," she said, "the local property tax" needed a larger contribution from the state to ensure quality schools. In explaining why the Teacher-in-Politics events were being held in every state, she said, "A community should be proud if it has teachers that are concerned about the buildings, the conditions under which they work, the number of children in the classroom, and the curriculum."[34] Her media appearances as president-elect, linked to the offices she had held consecutively in her state, and at the national level, made Koontz a well-known quantity in NEA circles, allaying any doubts from would-be critics about her qualifications for the position of president.

In an era of black *firsts*, Koontz received more media coverage than most, and because she was a teacher from a segregated southern school for students viewed as "mentally retarded," blacks identified with her achievement and made her a larger-than-life icon of black success. In 1968, there were few educated blacks who did not know the name Elizabeth Duncan Koontz, president of the 1.1 million member National Education Association.

At the NEA Representative Assembly in Dallas, Texas on July 2, 1968, Libby Koontz became the Association's 110th president. Selecting "A Time for Educational Statesmanship" as her theme, she outlined a nine-point program that called for a unified, secure, respected, informed, and socially aware profession; one that was undivided by artificial differences, that guaranteed decent retirement income, that valued teacher leaders, and that defended against unfair criticisms. She urged the more than 7,000 delegates not to withdraw from the societal issues raised by the urban unrest of the previous year when cities throughout the nation experienced more than forty race riots, and close to a hundred disturbances of the peace. The most serious occurred in Newark, where 26 people died, and in Detroit, where at least 40 were killed. Other outbreaks of violence took place in New York City, Atlanta, Baltimore, Washington, Chicago, Ocean City, as well as in medium-sized and smaller cities. The Kerner Commission, which was appointed by Lyndon Johnson to study the disturbances and issue recommendations, gave the nation a chilling and sobering report stating that "the nation is moving toward two societies: one black, one white—separate and unequal," and concluded that "white racism" was the principle cause of the upheavals.[35]

"Every state and community in the nation has been touched by riots, by tragic deaths of leaders, and by growing division among the races," Koontz told the RA, making the connection between urban unrest and dysfunctional schools, neglect of which resulted in underserved students and parents. "The school community is acutely concerned, as desegregation and integration take place, with factions insisting upon or opposing decentralization, neighborhood schools, centralized control, busing, compensatory education, closing of Negro schools, elimination or demotion of the Negro principals and teachers, and the absence of nonwhite personnel in administrative positions."[36] She went on to talk about the unrest on college campuses, "student takeovers, lock-ins, lock-outs, and lock-ups," indications all pointing to the more serious problems of the exclusion of nonwhites in textbooks and curriculum relevancy—an obvious reference to the Black and Chicano Studies movements. She then proposed what would become the most publicized event of her administration, the NEA Critical Issues Conference, which would assemble informed individuals with influence, representing diverse points of view to "come to grips with selected major issues." She promised that no issues, regardless of how potentially explosive they might be, would be avoided.[37]

That same RA responded to the racial unrest in the nation by endorsing the establishment of an NEA Center for Human Relations (CHR) recommended by a special task force on human rights. The CHR assumed the work of the Professional Rights and Responsibilities subcommittee on Civil and Human Rights of Educators. Sam Ethridge, who in 1964 had become NEA's first black professional staffer, was made assistant executive secretary for the Center, which was given cabinet-level status in the Association. Thus, he became NEA's first black insider at the staff decision-making level. Promoting the establishment of Human Relations Councils in NEA's 50 state and 10,000 local affiliates, the Center changed the culture of the organization by infusing human relations throughout NEA. Over time, the Center would evolve into the Association's Human and Civil Rights Department. Although the ceremonial ribbon-cutting for the Center was done by Koontz, the origins of the task force that recommended its establishment, could be traced to NEA executive secretary Sam M. Lambert, who also appointed a Task Force on Urban Education, headed by George W. Jones of Alabama, to explore the problems of urban education.[38]

In the fall of 1968, both Koontz' Critical Issues Conference and the Task Force on Urban Education were confronted by the Black Power movement and the politically sensitive issues of decentralized and community-controlled schools. The phrase "Black Power" was first enunciated in 1966 by Stokely Carmichael of the Student Non-Violent Coordinating Committee (SNCC). Within a year, chanting of the slogan, "Black Power," could be heard at almost every protest, and the concept the phrase embodied resonated so well that within a year the term "black" had replaced "Negro" as the preferred designation for people of African descent. It was a cultural movement with varying manifestations of black pride, and it was a political movement to those who felt hopelessness, neglect, and outrage over the effects of racism. The phrase meant different things to different people, but to most it signaled black pride, self-determination, recognition of heritage, and a rejection of institutions and ideas that marginalized blacks. It was by far the greatest resurrection of black pride since the Harlem Renaissance of the 1920s.

The issue of decentralization and community-controlled schools crystallized in the Ocean Hill-Brownsville controversy in New York, in the spring and fall of 1968, culminating in the longest and largest teachers' strike in the nation's history. The struggle pitted black community activists, parents, and militant teachers against the AFT in protests over the *mis*education of black and other minority—especially Hispanic—students in schools with largely white staffs. The union was brought into the fray when white teachers were arbitrarily terminated from those schools without due process. Black community leaders embraced Black Power, demanding community-controlled schools and black teachers to replace the fired white teachers. The firings took place without apology, sympathy, or explanation, the only reason cited being the huge and unacceptable achievement gaps between black and white students, and placement of the entire blame for those gaps on white teachers, with the claim that they had no real affinity for the educational needs of black students, or the pedagogical frame of reference required for a relevant curriculum.[39]

The bureaucracy that oversaw New York City schools agonized and frustrated parents of minority students lost in the system, and proposals for community-controlled schools and decentralized oversight appealed to these desperate citizens. After several weeks, the concept of community control was politically sanctioned when John Lindsay, the liberal Republican Mayor of New York, and McGeorge Bundy of the prestigious Ford Foundation issued a commission report entitled *Connection for Learning*, which called for city-wide community-controlled schools to be governed by boards composed of elected parents and mayoral appointees. Authority to hire school personnel and set educational policy—normally the responsibility of district administrators and school boards—would reside with the community boards. The implications of the report were troubling for unions, but there was some measure of relief and justice when the fired teachers were finally reinstated. Rhoda McCoy, the black district superintendent, and members of the community were vigorous in opposition to the reinstatements, however, and threatened retribution if the teachers were returned to the schools from which they had been fired. McCoy even went so far as to pledge all-black teaching staffs, maintaining that they would serve the best educational interests of black students. Black Power activists sided with McCoy and the community, opposing any plans of the union that would have encouraged white students to integrate those schools. Moreover, they resisted provisions proposed by the AFT that would have made it easier for teachers—largely white—to remove "disruptive" students—largely black and Hispanic—from the schools. On that point, they cited alarming statistics on minority student school suspension in the districts.[40]

Ocean Hill-Brownsville epitomized the worst in urban school districts, and conditions such as those prevailing in the area were prime factors causing riots and ongoing crises in urban communities throughout the nation. A graphic description of Ocean Hill-Brownsville by one journalist could have applied to any number of urban school districts nationwide that were populated by poor blacks and other minorities. Fewer than a third of the adults had finished high school and two-thirds were receiving public assistance. The student population was 70 percent black and 25 percent Puerto Rican. Over 80 percent of the teachers were white, and dropouts were excessive. The area resembled "Berlin after the war: block after block of burned-out shells of houses, streets littered with decaying automobile hulks."[41] It was a situation tailor-made for Black Power advocates and demagogues who placed little faith in integration and even less in whites teaching black students. Carmichael called for black parents to take control of schools, the hiring and firing of teachers, and the selection of curriculum. Integration, as he saw it, had shortcomings in that it forced blacks to devalue "black culture" for "white culture," ultimately making black students feel inferior because it promoted "the maintenance of white supremacy."[42] Within a few months after the Dallas convention, decentralization and Black Power would converge on Koontz, becoming a stern test of her leadership and the "statesmanship" she had talked about in her RA address.

When in November Koontz followed through on her promise to the RA delegates to hold a Critical Issues in Education Conference, the Ocean Hill-Brownsville situation was at its height. The agenda of the conference, which was held in Washington, was comprehensive, covering a broad spectrum of issues. Workshops, panel discussions, and speeches were given by a diverse range of presenters. No education issue that fall season, however, was larger than the teacher strike in New York City and the community-control, Black Power, and urban school concerns in which it was ensnarled. What was transpiring there was looming larger for other cities, and the implications for the Association could not be ignored. Indeed, they were causing urban militants within NEA to organize rapidly. At stake was the core value of the teachers' place in a labor movement: workers having the right to organize and protect themselves from capricious and arbitrary dismissal. This fundamental tenet of liberalism was the bedrock of collective bargaining, whose explosive effect on teachers nationally had caused Association membership to skyrocket earlier in the 1960s. In a period of dramatic decline for the trade union movement, teachers' union membership soared, and teachers clamored for the power it bestowed on the profession, hoping to leverage it for better compensation and improved conditions of practice.[43]

In less than a decade collective bargaining had made teacher unions the most influential force in American education. Though NEA leadership had initially been hesitant to accept it, by Koontz' term of office it had become essential for Association survival. The merging of professionalism and unionism—concepts once considered mutually exclusive—became the challenge and the goal of most members. The resistance was stiff, but not enough to sway the tide of changing attitudes. "If NEA hadn't changed its stripes," on collective bargaining, opined Don Cameron, former NEA executive director, "it would have been surpassed by the AFT."[44]

Black urban communities, justifiably discontented with education practices and policies that underserved black students, provided a base of support for Black Power advocates. Some level of community control seemed reasonable, but community control that usurped collective bargaining agreements, violated due process, and condoned arbitrary race-based teacher reassignments and dismissals, was more than the Association could endorse. This direction of community-controlled schools split civil rights leaders Martin Luther King, Jr., Bayard Rustin, and A. Phillip Randolph from the younger black militants who, surprisingly, had won influential white liberal support for community control such as that recommended by Lindsay and Bundy. Richard Kahlenberg, a scholar specializing in the '60s battles over schools, unions, and race, summed the seemingly contradictory liberal assault on the foundations of organized labor. "The old liberal idea that unions should protect individuals from arbitrary dismissal," he said, "and the idea that race should play no part in who is hired and fired were abandoned by many who considered themselves liberal."[45] This was, in part, the beginning of a wedge between blacks who believed that some past injustices required race-based remedies, and those who saw race-based solutions favoring blacks as reverse discrimination.

The Critical Issues in Education Conference found itself in the middle
of that split and opened NEA's doors to issues its leadership had not
anticipated. In the general session, black dissidents confronted Koontz with
two organizational challenges: the involvement of disadvantaged people
in Association policy-making, and enforcement of community control
over schools. One conference participant, Frank Wilderson of Minnesota,
introduced himself as a member of NEA's Black Caucus—the first time that
term was ever used to identify an NEA constituency group—and advocated
for "black youth, parents, and leaders" to be a part of NEA's decision
making. Calling for a restructuring of the Association that would "allow
for black participation from a source of strength rather than frustration," he
asked that NEA consult with black groups before making decisions affecting
those communities. Out of respect for the new president, whose position was
considered by some to be token, Wilderson's Black Caucus applauded Koontz
for convening the conference, while blasting NEA's "hypocritical hierarchy."
Pointing to the few blacks on NEA's 96-member Board of Directors,
Wilderson charged that NEA maintained "a lily white leadership," while
hosting the conference on issues "most of which relate to black people."[46]
This ingenious ploy was calculated to challenge Koontz on two levels: her
personal blackness and her professional position. She remained poised,
gracious, and polite while the Black Caucus made its claims, which posed a
baffling dilemma for NEA's many members who touted community control
as a corrective mechanism for dysfuntional schools. Those same members,
on the other hand, firmly believed in the protection of teacher rights, which
would be endangered by unacceptable propositions for teacher hiring and
firing. Whitney Young, Director of the National Urban League, spoke at the
conference but chose not to take sides in the contentious discussion, though
he urged NEA to become involved with more than teacher welfare issues.
Young encouraged NEA to place failing students in poor and urban school
districts among its priorities.[47]

The conference and the dialogue were important because despite the NEA/
ATA merger, they publicly exposed NEA's leadership as overwhelmingly
white; brought Black Power expression to NEA; forced NEA to define

decentralization and community control in a way that would protect its union interests; and cautioned NEA that "window dressing" the Association with Koontz as president carried with it expectations for policies and actions for black and disadvantaged students. Each of those considerations would either begin or continue conversations within NEA that would ultimately contribute to it being a more diverse and inclusive organization.

Shortly after the conference, and following careful thought about the issues raised, Koontz outlined her response to decentralization, community-controlled schools, and Black Power advocacy at a news conference at the NEA Center in Washington. Holding firm on union turf, she decried the decentralization attempts in New York City as "little short of bedlam and complete disorder" and "a mad scramble for power and influence." The school, according to her, belonged to the public and not the parents or teachers. "It is established not only to serve the children in it, but to serve as the indispensable source of national unity, common purpose, and equality of opportunity." This cautiously constructed argument implied schools had no obligation to maintain either a Eurocentric or an Afrocentric perspective, and that their responsibility was to build a national consensus and identity. Any attempts "by organized groups to interfere with or stifle" programs developed by teachers and parents served "not the pupils, not the public, not even the teaching profession."[48] Koontz, however, empathized with students literally trapped in failing urban schools plagued by overcrowding, deteriorating facilities, bureaucratic neglect, insensitive and poorly prepared teachers, and other problems identified anecdotally by Jonathan Kozol in the then shocking book, *Death at an Early Age*. She had not forgotten the separate and unequal schooling she had received under segregation, and a generation later she found herself loath to accept the separate and unequal education still being dispensed in daily dosages under integration. Yet, if Ocean Hill-Brownsville had done anything, it had disclosed the stark reality of the urban education experience to which ethnic-minority students were subjected. It also pushed her to articulate a vision for a decentralized and community-controlled school system, which she printed and distributed at the news conference. Specifically, then, within each school, the following was to occur:

- The principal and a personnel committee selected by the faculty organization should be responsible for recruiting, screening, and selecting new staff members. They should seek the advice of the community in so doing.

- Joint committees of faculty and citizens should have substantial authority to plan school programs.

- Financial support of individual schools should be based on an equalization arrangement whereby the schools with the toughest problems get more money per pupil.

- Except for functions such as the observance of system-wide minimum salary schedules, licensing requirements, and appropriate business procedures, schools should be allowed wide discretion in allocating their financial resources.

- Staff employed should work under a system-wide negotiated contract designating such matters as salary, personnel standards, and grievance procedure with binding arbitration. This contract should also contain provision for negotiating building level contracts on all matters not covered by the master agreement such as extra class activities, program innovations, and instructional materials.[49]

The plan demonstrated the brilliance and political shrewdness of Koontz in that it did not compromise the integrity of collective bargaining; it advocated shared decision-making with defined community stakeholders; and, equally important, it sustained her blackness and beliefs that too many urban schools short-changed students, teachers, and parents. Still, the plan was not advertised as the final word on decentralization. It was to set a framework for ongoing inquiry. She sought more information and recommendations on the subject from George Jones and Father Joseph Devlin of NEA's Urban Task Force, and from Sam Ethridge, of the newly-established Human Relations Center. In a time of crisis, Koontz' style of leadership, tact, and diplomacy prevailed, and she was lauded for her protection of sacred union ground for the Association's liberals, urban militants, and collective bargaining proponents. On race-neutral issues common to all teachers, she was also proficient. Capable of speaking in the reserved tones of a diplomat, when required she could comfortably shift into the role of a furious and deeply passionate teacher advocate. Skilled at the craft of language, Koontz often employed metaphors for dramatic effect in speeches and interviews. In an interview with *Time* magazine shortly after becoming president, she spoke plainly of the pressures and stresses on overworked, under-appreciated, and under-supported teachers. "It's like hiring a surgeon to perform delicate surgery, then expecting him to do it with a can opener, by candlelight, with everyone standing around telling him where to cut."[50]

Allan West's *The National Education Association: The Power Base for Education*, credits Libby Koontz for the understated role she played in the affiliates' reaching merger agreements following the 1966 Representative Assembly. "Through the force of her personality, and the prestige of her position," he writes, "she was able to intervene effectively at critical points in the merger negotiations, her influence, often subtle and low-key, was a major factor both in keeping merger talks moving in a constructive way and in achieving equitable results."[51]   None of the remaining six unmerged states, including her own, reached merger agreements during her presidency, though all were making progress around difficult issues, including disposition of assets; racially balanced staffs; guarantees for black elected officials; black representation on boards, committees, and commissions; and the selection of names of the "new Associations."

NEA and AFT remained the dominant organizations competing for unionized teachers, NEA being the larger, with its strong state affiliates positioned to influence budgets at the state government level, where state constitutions designated the legal responsibility for public education. AFT, the smaller, with a structure built on the local level, where members lived and worked, leveraged its influence on decisions made by local school boards. The militant urban teacher movement within NEA in the early 1960s now led to more emphasis on larger locals, in addition to the formation of NCUEA. Given the relative strengths of the two organizations, it was not surprising that proposals would frequently surface for the merger of the two. During

Koontz' presidency, AFT president Charles Cogen approached NEA with a merger proposal. After consultation with the Executive Committee and Board, Koontz responded with their authority to reject the proposal flatly. David Selden, then president of AFT, recalled the difficulty of discussing a merger with Koontz.

> "When I became president of the AFT, Elizabeth Koontz was the NEA president. I tried repeatedly to arrange a luncheon conference with her, but she proved extremely elusive. Koontz did not return my phone calls, and when I ran into her at Washington social functions, she was polite but aloof. Finally, I managed to meet Koontz for breakfast. . . . I soon realized, however, that the NEA president had only come for breakfast and not for discussing merger. My efforts to talk about teacher unity evoked no response. In forty-five minutes I was out on the sidewalk. . . ."[52]

The two obstacles were membership affiliation—NEA included *all* "professional" school personnel, and AFT almost exclusively teachers—and the AFL-CIO affiliation of AFT, which carried with it obligations and priorities beyond public education. In the future such proposals would arise periodically, and for a range of reasons the AFL-CIO issue always proved insurmountable.

Just as Koontz was entering her comfort zone as president, the unexpected happened. In January 1969, President Richard M. Nixon offered her an appointment to head the Women's Bureau of the U. S. Department of Labor.[53] Exactly six months into her term of office, and with only six months remaining, she initially kept the offer under wraps, only confiding it to her closest friends and family, whose opinions she solicited in helping her make a decision. Her brothers Samuel and Joe, along with E. B. Palmer and Edna Richards of NCTA were among those she consulted in North Carolina. They all listened with patience as she weighed the pros and cons of the offer. Palmer saw the position as a promotion, and Sam leaned towards her acceptance of the offer when he reminded his sister that "you get only one invitation in a lifetime from a President of the United States." She did not make up her mind that day, but within a few days she told the Executive Committee by telephone of the offer.[54] From the call, it was clear that they would be supportive if she decided to accept the position, though there was reluctance about losing her to the Nixon Administration. Braulio Alonso and other insiders thought the offer would provide her more national recognition, and felt that she should accept the federal post.

Though reluctant to leave NEA, she felt that the timing of the offer favored her acceptance of the appointment. On the one hand, she was at the halfway point of her presidency, with only six months left to influence organizational policy on public education. For the past eight years she had held a progressive series of elective positions, and after her term as president, she would have exhausted all NEA positions. On the other hand, the Nixon offer to head of the Women's Bureau would provide at least four years to influence women's labor issues at the national level and would offer a platform from which she might address specifically the neglected topic of black women's issues in the workforce. There was, however, one major difference in the two positions. At NEA, she never represented herself as a "black" president and had always downplayed race whenever the subject arose. At the Department of Labor, she would have to keep in mind the politics of the appointment and consider herself a token, though one who might have an impact on policy. She told her close friend Lois Edinger, "President Nixon needs a southerner, a democrat, a woman, and a black—he got them all in me."[55]

Understandably, all of the feedback Koontz received was not pleasant. Some members felt betrayed that she would accept another position prior to the end of her presidential term at NEA. The criticisms of her becoming president were now matched by boxes of mail chastising her for leaving the Association. In some things in life, said wise sage Joe Reed, "you lose either way, so you accept it and move on." When she spoke with George Fischer, the NEA president-elect about her decision, she also confided to him that she had received stacks of hate mail when she became president of NEA, something she had chosen never to make public. In referring to the negative reaction she received on accepting the federal appointment, E. B. Palmer said, "she was wounded by the harsh word-of-mouth criticisms from those who were horrified that this first black president would show her gratitude to the Association by leaving for another job."[56]

After her acceptance of the position as head of the Women's Bureau, Libby Koontz wrote an article, "An Agonizing Decision," for the *NEA Reporter*, in which she sought to explain her reasons for leaving NEA. In it she said that she hoped for compassion and understanding.

> "To accept the new post and leave the NEA presidency was, for me, an agonizing decision. I felt a responsibility to complete the term of office for which the NEA members had elected me. I did not want to leave the membership in the awkward position of having no president-elect to serve with George Fischer this year. Further—despite the fact that I was not elected because I am black—there were blacks, and other nonwhites as well, to whom I was a symbol, and I didn't want to disappoint them as they looked forward to seeing a Negro perform in the capacity of NEA president.
>
> "One of the main factors that encouraged me to accept the job as Director of the Women's Bureau was the knowledge that I would be undertaking a task in which my effectiveness could be as great as it would have been as NEA president. I felt it would permit me to be effective in influencing opportunities for those to whom I was a symbol as well as women and girls in general.
>
> "First of all, I am a teacher, an educator; I could see that a heavy accent on education is important in the whole field of employment in which I'd be working in the Department of Labor.
>
> "Every member of the NEA Executive Committee agreed that this was a tremendous opportunity for me to serve in a role that is, in a way, an extension of the work I was doing. It too would be concerned with education and employment. . . .

"I have many regrets about leaving my position as NEA
president, but I leave with the faith that the Association can
fulfill the promises it has made to society and to our nation."[57]

Following her resignation, the *NEA Reporter* carried photos of her in the
next several issues. For all practical purposes, Libby Koontz was gone from
NEA, and, other than ceremonial appearances at the annual Human and
Civil Rights Awards Dinner, she was never again actively involved in NEA.
Shortly after assuming her new position at the Women's Bureau, she was
also named U.S. Delegate to the United Nations Commission on the Status of
Women. In that capacity she helped the Bureau share research and expertise
with women around the world, especially in developing countries, and she
took great pride in her role in those international efforts.

When Koontz arrived at the Bureau, the momentum for the passage of the
proposed Equal Rights Amendment (ERA) to the U.S. Constitution had
gained substantial strength owing, in large part, to the impetus of the Civil
Rights Movement. Where for years the Bureau had stood in opposition to
the ERA, by 1969 its stance had changed. Utilizing a sophisticated public
relations campaign to position the Bureau as a more aggressive advocate for
working women's concerns, Koontz brought specific attention to the unique
issues of black and other minority women. Labor policy for white women
needed much attention and action, but when compared with the injustices
still suffered by minority women, racism could not be excluded from the
discussion.[58]

To the chagrin of the Nixon Administration, Koontz was the first to admit
that her appointment represented "tokenism," although in an unprecedented
era of black *firsts*, she was far from alone in that capacity. Under Nixon,
however, only three other blacks were appointed to major posts—James
Farmer, Assistant Secretary for HEW; Arthur Fletcher, Assistant Secretary
for Labor; and William Brown II, Chairperson of the EEOC. Determined
to broaden the focus of the Bureau, Koontz initiated an awareness of the
differences between black working women and white working women. She
made public that black women worked in higher percentages than whites, in
the worst conditions and poorest paying jobs, many as domestic workers in

the homes of white women who most often were not a part of the workforce. She led the Bureau in an extensive outreach effort to inform historically disadvantaged women of their newly confirmed rights, encouraging them to report violations to federal and state enforcement agencies. "Women hold the lowest paying jobs. Black women are at the very bottom," she said when creating an awareness program that sponsored minority consultation workshops. For many minority women who attended those workshops, it was the first time they learned that the ERA and the Bureau had any applicability to their unique labor concerns.[59]

Koontz, without a doubt, put a face on the black and minority women whose labor issues had been relegated to the level of a mere footnote or "statistical" component of the Bureau's studies and standards policies. But she never lost sight of the shared problems of all working women, regardless of economic standing, educational background, or social status. "Our society has set aside rules for women—the pedestal approach. However, the fact is that many women can't stay home even if they want to. . . . Women are learning that 'til death do us part doesn't mean her death but her husband's death," she said.[60] Lois Edinger recalled a discussion at a conference on the problem of prostitution in Washington, D.C., and the need for stronger criminal sanctions. Libby Koontz waited until all had spoken, then told the conferees that she "would be glad to punish the prostitutes, if we agree to punish the buyers. . . Remember, there would be no prostitutes and no crimes to [punish] if there were no buyers." Edinger remembered that incident as an expression of both Koontz' analysis of a problem when only viewed from a male perspective, and as a classic example "of her great sense of humor."[61]

Under her directorship, major strides were made for women's rights, particularly the Department of Labor's regulations requiring federal government contractors to take action to eliminate discrimination against women and minorities. Libby was a team player for Nixon in the sense that she did her job and she did it well, but she could not be controlled and would not go along with any script that omitted black and other minority women from labor issues. "Libby was not jumping rope the way Nixon wanted," said Edinger, "and he decided not to reappoint her for his second term."[62]

It was politics, pure and simple, and Koontz understood the game and left quietly, without fuss or fanfare. Class and dignity had been her trademark when entering the national scene, and they would remain with her when she exited.

After leaving national politics, Koontz continued to receive recognition wherever she went. In 1975, she was among five women honored by the American Newspaper Women's Club with an award for distinguished service in international affairs, which was presented by President Gerald Ford. A year later she was the recipient of the College Board Medal for Distinguished Service to Education. During that year, too, long after her departure from NEA, she spoke at a symposium on "What's Right in American Education" and pointed especially to the split of national opinion between a higher tax structure and high quality schools. "Until all institutions which bear responsibility for the education of our people accept professional responsibility for the entire spectrum of education that transcends structural lines and attainment levels, there will be gaps and chasms that prohibit or impede programs. . . . The public must provide funds to furnish modern equipment and materials for schools. The educator must readjust his or her approach to teaching and learning. Is it reasonable—is it in the interest of society—to expect students to learn when outmoded equipment and methods of teaching are used in the schools?"[63]

Returning to North Carolina from her stint at the Labor Department, she accepted a position coordinating nutrition programs for the State Department of Human Resources. In 1975 she was offered a post as Assistant State Superintendent for Teacher Education. The offer came from Craig Phillips, once her white neighbor in Salisbury and her lifelong friend. Phillips, then State Superintendent for Public Instruction, said nothing delighted him more than having Libby Koontz join his team. Both Craig and his father Guy, who became Dean of the School of Education at the University of North Carolina after being a superintendent in several state school districts, had followed her career and thought it fitting that she should return home and share her abilities and experiences at the state level.[64] It was Guy who years earlier, while superintendent of Salisbury schools, had commented that Libby was the brightest of all the children in the city. The prodigal daughter was now returning home. The appointment was prestigious, making her the highest ranking black employee in North Carolina state government. She excelled in the position until her retirement in 1982, when she was able to return to Salisbury for good. She continued to travel widely, both nationally and internationally, and was a popular speaker on the lecture circuit, receiving various awards for her activities on behalf of women, honorary degrees from over three dozen colleges and universities, and citations of recognition. In her hometown of Salisbury, she was honored with the naming of the Elizabeth Duncan Koontz Elementary School.

On January 6, 1989, three years after the death of her husband Harry, Libby Koontz suffered a massive heart attack in her home in Salisbury and died. A few weeks later, during her confirmation hearing as Secretary of Labor, Elizabeth Dole, a fellow Salisbury, North Carolinian, adopted a solemn tone as she eulogized Libby, and remembered her as a personal friend and a pioneer whose life and contributions had inspired her own career.[65] Secretary Dole was not alone. Libby Koontz touched many lives in her own incredible life of service.

James Alexander Harris

1974-1975

James Alexander Harris
1974-1975

Project Urban Neglect and
the Constitutional Convention Transition

James Harris of Des Moines, Iowa became president of NEA on July 2, 1974 in Chicago, following a year in the position of president-elect. He was the first black man to hold the position, though in terms of public relations value and newsworthiness, the distance between the first and second black presidents was more than one notch. Elizabeth Duncan Koontz had become NEA's first black president in 1968, during an unusual period of historical firsts for blacks. By 1975, however, the news of a second NEA black president failed to attract major media attention, and, within NEA, race had been so muted when Harris had run for president-elect a year earlier, that to most delegates his election was seen as business as usual. The relative silence or lack of commentary on the historical significance of his election speaks volumes about the progress of race relations in NEA after its merger with the American Teachers Association (ATA), as well as in society in general.

Between Koontz and Harris, NEA elected five presidents and all continued the trend of defining NEA as an organization to be controlled by classroom teachers, who comprised the majority of its membership. The most vociferous and charismatic in advancing that cause was George Fischer, who replaced Koontz before serving a term on his own. Fischer thought Koontz did not do more towards limiting the role of administrators because "she had too much baggage from her role with the merger."[1] In his first interview as president, he sent shockwaves through NEA calculated to send a message to the NEA membership. "I don't give a damn," he said, "about administrators and superintendents. If they really were leaders in education, we wouldn't need the NEA. All I care about is teachers." In fact, that interview was so laced with expletives and offended administrators to such a degree that it prompted an effort to remove him from office, a first for an NEA president.[2] Fischer and the presidents who followed over the next five years—Helen Bain, Don Morrison, Catherine Barrett, and Helen Wise—all identified with a stronger role for the president and greater involvement in the ongoing programs of the Association. This agitation eventually led to a constitutional convention in 1971, which began the restructuring of the Association to allow for greater representation of classroom teachers and to provide minority member guarantees. By 1975, the new constitution extended a presidential term to two years with an opportunity for reelection for an additional two.

When Harris assumed the NEA presidency, the Association was beginning the process of making a transition from the old to the new. His route to NEA's highest elected position had no template and defied all odds. Every step along the way, beginning with his poor rural origins, he consistently became an exception to the rules of probability. But the class, dignity, sense of purpose, and reserved manner in which he conducted himself throughout his NEA career, could all be traced to his experiences and the lessons he had learned early in life from his parents and teachers. "He was smooth and he was polished, and there was nothing in his style which offended whites," said Lauri Wynn of Wisconsin. "We saw him as a gentleman and no one could question his intelligence," she reflected, "because it was so obvious that he was exceptional."[3]

Harris' parents, Alonzo and Gertrude, were not unlike black teachers in small towns like Boonesville, Missouri where he was born on August 26, 1926. Though neither had college training, both were from the breed of well-read and self-taught educators. Hired as poorly paid instructors to teach in segregated black schools, they were held in high esteem by the parents and communities in which they taught. In Boonesville, education for blacks was not taken seriously by school officials, and was secondary to the need for child labor during the farming season when the school term for black students was shortened. This policy irritated Harris' father, who objected and adamantly protested the practice, though he found himself unable to change it. The lowering of standards for black education was routine and across the board, enabling both Alonzo and his wife to obtain teaching posts without either having ever attended college. The looseness and corruption of the system for black education was further evidenced when Alonzo paid the white teacher-credentialing examiner 50 cents to give him a passing score on a teacher examination he never took.[4] In small towns and rural villages throughout America in the first half of the twentieth century, such transgressions were ordinary, overlooked, and exceedingly detrimental to the educational prospects of black students, whose parents expected excellence from school districts that had no intention of placing them on an even par with those of whites.

Harris was the second of six children, and at an early age his parents, seeking to improve their lives, moved to Des Moines, Iowa where his mother found employment as a cafeteria manager, and his father secured stable work in a defense plant until suffering a heart attack, which forced him to find less physically strenuous work. To support his family during the Depression, he started a small real estate firm in which the principle business strategy consisted of his selling his own home every few years at a modest profit. One remarkable episode from that period remained vivid in his son's memory. His father wanted to buy a building, but the owner would not sell to a black. To complete the transaction with an unwilling seller, Alonzo devised a scheme whereby he had a white realtor purchase the property while accompanying him to the inspection under the guise of being a painter. With his nod of approval the realtor made the purchase of the property, but when Alonzo's identity was finally disclosed, the incensed seller, although he could not reverse the transaction, out of vindictiveness refused to convey the building furniture to Alonzo as he had agreed to do with the white realtor. Alonzo objected, but the seller pointed out that the furniture deal was word-of-mouth and not a part of the contract, making the agreement non-binding by law. Alonzo was furious, but conceded his mistake, chalking it up to experience, and proceeded to negotiate a separate contract for the furniture, which both parties signed. The lesson Harris learned from this experience passed on to him by his father was that black men must always secure legal documents to protect their interests in business arrangements, the inference being that a legal document might prevail, whereas decisions based purely on a black man's word against that of a white man would not likely be favorable.[5]

The schools in the Des Moines of Harris' youth did not hire teachers without college training, and no black teachers were hired in the entire system. Throughout all of his schooling, Harris never had a black teacher. The public schools in Iowa were not segregated by race, though the practice of students being assigned to neighborhood schools virtually assured that black students would attend schools heavily populated by one race, particularly in the elementary and middle grades. In Des Moines, where less than three percent of the population was black, over 50 percent of the students in Harris' early schooling were of his own race. Later, because of his good grades, academic prowess, and intellectual curiosity, he was assigned to East High School, the best in the district, where only one percent were black.[6]

Harris remembers that his teachers were kind, took an interest in his academic growth, and encouraged him to take college preparatory courses at a time when only eleven of several hundred blacks who began elementary school with him were enrolled in college. Only academically exceptional black students in Des Moines public schools were motivated by the all-white teaching staffs to continue education beyond high school, and Harris was fortunate to be among the chosen few. "Because there were so few of us in Iowa, racism was generally not overt, and in growing up, my life was somewhat sheltered from the experiences of those raised in more segregated environments," said Harris.[7]

On one occasion in high school Harris was involved in a fight with a white student, and both were called into the teacher's office where she scolded them. After the reprimand, she discreetly called Harris aside to "express how disappointed" she was in him "lowering himself" to the level of a student around whom he "ran circles academically." Harris never forgot that stern lecture, and was surprised that anyone, especially a teacher, cared about him or respected his ability so much that she would demonstrate to him so openly that, in her view, he was best in comparison with a white student.[8] The flattery was consoling, but in that predominantly white school setting the effect of the experience on his self-esteem and confidence was beyond measure. Teachers regularly open up doors to the future for students, forever changing the direction of their lives. Often the door-opening experiences go unnoticed. On that day, however, a teacher changed young Harris' life, and over a half century later, he recalled the incident as vividly as if it were yesterday.

Boxer Rocky Graziano titled his autobiography, *Somebody Up There Likes Me*, because of the many dangerous pitfalls and precarious situations he managed to escape as an adolescent. In Harris' young life he, too, often found himself on the brink of failure, financially destitute, or simply needing encouragement to lift his sagging morale, and each time someone or something—almost providential—would intervene and direct him on a course leading towards success. Later in life when, with tears in his eyes, he recalled those incidents, attributing his good fortunes to "Somebody up there, and down here, too" guiding his life along the way.[9] The spirituality of those experiences augmented his faith, and would remain with him over the years. A deeply religious person, he was committed to combining the secular and the sacred all of his life.

At East High School, Harris took an art course as an elective, and one of his teachers, Harriet Meins, saw enough promise in his skills that she set up a special room for him to develop his craft. He enjoyed having the space, the prestige of it being his own, and proceeded to produce several paintings. Impressed with his work, she proceeded to enter several of them in three separate categories in a scholastic art exhibit and competition in California. When it was announced that he had won first place in one of the categories, he and his teacher were thrilled. The award was publicized in Des Moines, bringing honor to Harris and to his school. Moreover, it established his reputation as one of the school's most talented students. Another student in his class was George Fischer, a good friend who would also become a president of NEA, giving East High the distinction of being the only high school to produce two NEA presidents. Fischer remembered Harris as a student whose abilities were recognized by the entire student body.[10]

As graduation drew near without Harris having any plans or financial resources for college, Harriet Meins became personally involved in planning for his future. She took his prize-winning artwork to Drake University, also in Des Moines, and showed it to the faculty of the art department, asking that the talented student be considered for a scholarship. She was relentless in her efforts and determined that Harris' artistic talents and academic ability be nurtured in a college setting. It became her personal crusade. Drake officials were initially hesitant, but eventually relented to Meins' pleas and agreed to award Harris a partial scholarship, dependent on his ability to maintain a B average. Meins was relieved, knowing that the academic requirement would never be a problem for her prize student.[11] Years later, Harris would fondly remember Harriet Meins, his favorite teacher, and often invited her to his home for holiday dinners with his family. He wanted to show appreciation for her kindness during a vulnerable period in his young life, and wanted his children to know her personally.

At Drake, Harris supplemented the scholarship with a full-time evening job as a maintenance worker, while staying at home with his parents, since the university did not provide on-campus housing for its two percent black student population. For the first year, his daily regimen of school, work, and home not only isolated him from his black friends who did not attend college, but it fostered a discipline that resulted in both maturity and top grades. He never forgot that, after his first semester at Drake, he went to a board where student grades were posted and heard a white female student marvel at his high grades. She told him how she wished her grades were that good. "At that precise moment, my confidence soared because it first struck me that I could compete, and that all white college students did not receive solid grades," recalled Harris of that amusing incident.[12] Never again did he doubt his academic ability.

The freshman year matured Harris, and his academic work impressed several professors who took an interest in his intellectual growth, but like many others of his generation, he sought adventure. Putting his patriotism ahead of his personal academic ambitions, he enlisted in the military, joining the Air Force. By 1944, when Harris left home for military training, the nation was fully engaged in World War II. Up to that point in his life, excluding his brief early childhood in rural Missouri, all of his experiences had taken place in Des Moines. Educationally he had benefited from integrated schools and caring teachers, though his black family, neighborhood, church, friends, and social gatherings all played roles in developing a sense of racial solidarity and pride. None of that, however, prepared him for Tuskegee, Alabama where he was stationed after passing the rigorous set of examinations that qualified him for the Tuskegee Airmen's program– -the 99th Fighter Squadron—the most prestigious for a black man in the military. The Tuskegee Airmen became America's first black military aviators during a time when much conventional wisdom held that black men lacked the intelligence, skills, courage, discipline, and even patriotism for such high-level military training and preparation.[13]

It was a badge of honor to have been selected for this elite squadron, and Harris accepted the challenge and the meaning of fighting two wars, as hailed by the "Double V" campaign in black communities; one for victory over America's enemies overseas, and the other for victory over racism and discrimination at home. The principles worth shedding blood for in one place were no less basic in the other. The spirit of the Double V captured all the hopes for change in a post-war America. NEA's Joint Committee also used black participation in the war effort to justify a fairer distribution of public funds for black education. It created a new sub-committee on National Defense, which called for "fair and adequate" treatment of blacks "in all phases of service in war and peace." The movement was contagious and caught on in black America. Los Angeles attorney Loren Miller noted, "The Negroes used it in a way which I thought was effective and ingenious. They had what they called the Double V sign, you know, victory over the fascists in Europe and victory over discrimination here. So when another person would go around giving the V sign for victory, the Negroes were giving the Double V sign." Publications of the American Teachers Association and those of its state affiliates often referenced the symbol. Harris, too, thought his personal fortunes and those of his race stood to benefit from exemplary black military service. Of the thousands who applied for entry into the Tuskegee program, an elite group of 994 pilots was trained and graduated. The selection of Harris for the distinguished group, secured for him recognition as one of the best and brightest of his race, providing an early sign that his post-war prospects for success might be promising. The black airmen posted a record of outstanding accomplishment, and their bravery and behavior, projected throughout World War II were catalysts for the post-war movements for social equality and wider economic opportunity.[14]

More than the home of the Tuskegee Army Air Field, Tuskegee, Alabama was also important to black Iowans because it was the location of Tuskegee Institute, where Iowa's most celebrated black college graduate, George Washington Carver, had been a renowned scientist and legendary member of the faculty. "When I saw the all-black professional world of Tuskegee Institute and the military base, it was an eye opening experience, like seeing another world," Harris remembered. "It was so different than Des Moines" and all that he had ever known. Almost all of the professors, doctors, lawyers, and business people in the institutions of Tuskegee were black, well-educated, independent, and confident. Harris' only disappointment was that Carver had recently died, which denied him the opportunity of meeting the great scientist in person, something his mother had hoped he would be able to do. But he did get to know one soon-to-be famous person, Colonel Benjamin O. Davis, commander of the Tuskegee Airmen. Harris told the story, perhaps apocryphal, of a game of blackjack in which Colonel Davis was dealing to a lower-ranked officer who "asked for a hit." Davis slowly raised his head from the table coming face-to-face with the officer, and with a stern look and clenched jaw queried, "I beg your pardon." The officer reconsidered and promptly replied, "Oh, I am sorry, I really meant to ask would you please give me a hit, Sir."[15]

After his honorable discharge from military service, Harris returned to Drake to complete his degree. Generally, living in Des Moines relieved him from many of the indignities blacks faced in the South on a consistent basis. Segregated public facilities, voting restrictions, physical intimidation, and other more overt and aggressive forms of discrimination were not institutionalized components of Iowa's race relations. No one could deny that there were racial transgressions in Iowa, though, comparatively, they were more subtle and less confrontational. Some professors at Drake, who were as sensitive to his race and financial disadvantages as had been some of his teachers at East High, often intervened offering assistance and support where necessary and appropriate. Even as a member of the college track team, his coach purchased track shoes for him when he observed Harris running faster in basketball sneakers than his teammates with proper equipment. Other examples occurred during track team trips to out-of-town events, when, to avoid possible embarrassment as the only black member of the team, the coach arranged separate travel and housing accommodations for himself and Harris.[16] Wrapped in a support system of caring and compassionate white mentors, Harris, for the most part, was able to steer clear of the unpleasant racial experiences those less fortunate might have been unable to avoid.

Yet, Drake University could not always assure a black student that racial incidents would not occur. The infamous Johnny Bright football incident of 1951, Harris' senior year, jolted intercollegiate athletics and was a coming-of-age experience for Harris. Because there was no on-campus housing for blacks, arrangements were made for Bright, a black football player being recruited by Drake, to stay with Harris' family on his visit to the campus. Harris, a war veteran, was older, and, after Bright's acceptance of a football scholarship, the two became friends. By the fall of 1951, Bright, though the only black on the team, had become the school's star player and a pre-season Heisman Trophy candidate who during the preceding season had led the nation in rushing. That season, the team traveled to Stillwater, Oklahoma to play Oklahoma A and M, a rival in the Missouri Valley Conference. During the first seven minutes of the game, the unimaginable happened to the only black player on the field, when he was knocked unconscious three times by deliberate and malicious blows from an opponent. Well after another play ended, an Oklahoma player targeted Bright and landed an elbow in his face, shattering his jaw and forcing him to leave the game. Even the packed all-white stadium crowd was aghast at the incident. A reporter from the *Des Moines Register* covering the game, discovered that the egregious injury had been planned the week before the game, and that the Oklahoma coach had implored his players to "get that nigger." After the game, the incident made national headlines when a cameraman for the *Des Moines Register* published what would become a Pulitzer-Prize-winning six photograph sequence of the injury, clearly showing that the blow was intentional. Black leaders and organizations demanded an official investigation of the incident. No such action was taken, however.[17]

To Drake University's credit, it withdrew from the conference for several years over the incident, because the conference refused to take any disciplinary action against the player who had caused Bright's injury. Nor did Oklahoma A and M take any corrective action. The incident deeply moved Harris, and what he learned from that unforgettable athletic lynching was that being one of the few blacks or the only one in a white environment was not risk-free and did not imply acceptance as an equal. None of his privileges made him think for a moment that any amount of education he acquired could exempt him from racism, or serve as an insurance policy for the race-based unexpected, to which all blacks might be subjected at any time. Over a half century later, Oklahoma A and M—now Oklahoma State University—sought redemption by issuing a full apology to Drake, which named its football field for its all-time greatest player, Johnny Bright.[18]

Harris graduated from Drake in 1952 and married his campus romance Jacqueline Meesen, also a Drake graduate, on his graduation day. The best job offer he received after graduation was from an elementary school in Kansas City, Kansas. From 1948 until 1952, he taught in Kansas, returning home in the summers to complete his master's degree at Drake. During his last year teaching in Kansas, he became upset when he learned that, despite the many tributes he received for teaching, his actual salary was below the salary schedule for the district. He became infuriated and protested to the superintendent, who then decided to correct the situation by awarding him the proper salary. The sense of betrayal and the flagrant violation of his teaching contract so overwhelmed him that he resigned, angrily vowing never to return to the district that had finally agreed to pay him appropriately—though not retroactively. Again, it was a learning experience and he vowed never again to enter into a working arrangement without understanding all the provisions of the contract, and holding the district accountable for fulfilling them. Ironically, the superintendent who allowed the violation to occur was none other than Frank Schlagle, a former NEA president.[19]

Harris' next job was in a school on the campus of Langston University in Oklahoma, where he taught for a year before returning to Des Moines and accepting a teaching position. In his hometown he became active in the local teachers' association. So great and effective was his involvement that he earned the respect of his colleagues—almost all white—who came to see him as a leader. He was smart, well spoken, dependable, and an advocate for teacher rights and better conditions of practice. He was also an excellent teacher and friendly colleague in Des Moines schools, whether predominantly black or white. By the late 1950s, several local association members approached Harris, encouraging him to run for local president and committing to work on his campaign. He was well aware of his status as one of a handful of black teachers in Des Moines, but that had always been typical of his experiences in Iowa. With a young man's optimism, he had grown accustomed to it. Race, he figured, would not be a crucial variable in his chances for election, mainly because well-connected white union leaders had persuaded him to run for office, and he had not detected any racial overtones when his name was being floated.[20]

Then, as the campaign was underway, rumors began to circulate that were patently untrue. One was that he was a conscientious objector during World War II, which was easy to disprove, and the other was that the NAACP was sponsoring his election campaign. The latter was interesting in that it sought to exploit what must have been anti-NAACP sentiments in Des Moines. While Iowa was not in violation of the NAACP-engineered *Brown* decision, it maintained neighborhood schools largely attended by one single race. Most likely, however, it was the fear of the period that the NAACP represented change, and even though its Civil Rights Movement strategies were less threatening to the status quo than those of SNCC, SCLC, and CORE, the brand identity of the NAACP defined its marginal association with Martin Luther King, Jr., and the civil rights and Viet Nam war protest movements. Whatever the reasons, in the Des Moines local where there were only five black members, the rumors were effective, and Harris lost his bid for local presidency.[21]

Though defeated in the election by virtue of the negative campaign against him, Harris did not quit, and he remained active with a core of loyal supporters. Many of them appreciated the value he brought to the organization, not only because he was gifted, but also because his physical presence represented a symbol of progressive thought. Soon afterward, he ran for the NEA Board of Directors, and won the first of three consecutive three-year terms. It was during those years on the Board that Harris gained notoriety and started to emerge as a legitimate, informed, and respected NEA leader. It also helped that George Fischer, his high school friend, was president of NEA for a year and a half during the time that Harris was on the Board. That personal friendship gave him access to Fischer's inner circle and network of relationships—all important prerequisites for his advancement in the Association. Harris was moving forward in the Association, but, unlike Libby Koontz, he was doing it without a black support base. His blackness remained intact through it all though his independence from race was creating distance between him and southern blacks, who admired him but were uneasy with the dynamics of his rise to influence.[22]

In his Board position, Harris' identity became prominent within the Association when he took the lead in advocating for poor children, particularly around the school lunch program, insisting that free meals be provided for students who could not afford the cost. At the 1967 Representative Assembly, he presented an action item seeking funding for school lunches to be administered by the Department of Education, rather than the Department of Agriculture. NEA President Braulio Alonso felt so strongly about the item that he allowed Harris to make his presentation from the RA podium rather than the floor "to showcase it" and give it the attention it merited.[23] The RA unanimously accepted the item, and years later Harris would view that opportunity as one that promoted his name recognition throughout the Association. Harris praised Alonso for that RA action, which brought him attention he might otherwise never have gotten. According to Joe Reed of the Alabama Education Association and E.B. Palmer of the North Carolina Association of Educators, Harris and other minority members benefited greatly from the generosity of Alonso, NEA's first ethnic minority president.[24]

In late 1972 and early 1973, a group of teachers, some of whom were Board members, approached Harris about running for NEA president. Because he had never been either a local or state president, there was some hesitation about whether his NEA Board experience was sufficient and, of course, he had to factor in his race as a consideration. But when the influential former NEA President George Fischer and the white Mississippi state president endorsed the idea and committed to support his campaign, he decided to run for the office. When Joe Reed told him that he felt confident he could win and could count on active support from the black delegates of the merged affiliates, Harris officially announced his campaign. Some southern black members, however, had hoped that a black candidate would have come forward from one of the merged affiliates. Horace Tate of Georgia, George Butler of Alabama, Walker Solomon of South Carolina, and E.B. Palmer of North Carolina, among other blacks, were lukewarm to Harris' candidacy for those reasons, but were excited about his base of support among whites, which legitimized his efforts, increasing his chances of winning.[25]

Actually, to Harris the reluctance of some blacks to endorse him fully was the result of a discussion in which he found himself "uncomfortably in the middle." In a number of the states, merger agreements had been reached or were being hammered out on black and white rotating terms as president. Even at the national level there were discussions about whether rotating terms would be necessary to assure full black participation at all levels of the Association. George Fischer wanted black participation in all NEA elective positions, though "he did not feel rotating terms" were required for that to happen. "He went as far as to say I could be elected on my own, without a guaranteed rotation, and that did not sit well with many blacks," remembered Harris.[26]

A lot had changed at NEA between the 1966 NEA/ATA merger and 1973. Two members of ethnic minorities, Alonso and Koontz, had served widely popular terms as NEA president. Of all the merged state affiliates, only Mississippi and Louisiana had yet to reach merger agreements. Minority groups had formed caucuses to advocate positions and policy before the Representative Assembly, Board of Directors, and Executive Committee, as well as to endorse candidates for office. Formerly segregated state affiliates had rebounded from some membership loss following the merger, and the inclusion of blacks at the local and state levels had replaced the racial isolation, which had bred fears and mistrust while promoting stereotypes. As early as 1968, NEA's Association of Classroom Teachers had met in Portland, Oregon to explore ways to ensure minority group involvement and participation in ACT. Later, minority involvement programs had been instituted by Don Morrison, who became NEA president in 1971, to encourage more minorities to become active and seek election as delegates to the NEA annual convention. Blacks had met with Morrison during his campaign to express concerns about their low representation at the RA and the need to systemically train minorities for Association leadership. What captured Morrison's attention was a press conference called by Lauri Wynn of Wisconsin at the San Francisco convention in 1970 and reported in the *San Francisco Chronicle*. It was a time when black discontent attracted the news media, and by calling the news conference, Wynn hoped to bring attention to the problem of black members not being properly trained to participate as active delegates to the RA. She figured that the chances of NEA responding favorably would be enhanced by publicity. Actually, NEA did not officially respond to the story in the *Chronicle*, but Morrison, then a candidate for NEA president, decided to meet with Wynn and the Black Caucus. After listening to their concerns, he made a campaign pledge that, if elected president, he would establish a minority involvement program. Since his childhood in Oregon where he had attended school and made friendships with Japanese Americans, he had become incensed over the internment camps of World War

II, the Marine Corps' racist propaganda training films, and the discrimination against blacks in the military, including an incident in which he had observed a white officer "put a gun to the head of a black soldier" for merely asking a question about an unplanned military maneuver. Those experiences were unsettling to Morrison, and they remained with him through the years, making him especially sensitive to Association issues regarding minorities.[27]

At that time Lauri Wynn, Pat Browne of Indiana, Ester Wilfong of Washington, Vivian Bowser of Texas, Joe Duncan of North Carolina, Wade Wilson of Pennsylvania, Lithangia Robinson of Georgia, John Lucas of North Carolina, and Walker Solomon, E. B. Palmer, Joe Reed, George Butler, and Horace Tate, among others, had become the leading voices of black members and of the NEA Black Caucus, which in 1971 was recognized as the Association's first ethnic minority caucus.[28] It was those leaders who brokered deals for black members, and it was the Black Caucus that endorsed Morrison and held him accountable, though his predisposition to honor his promise was such that little monitoring of his pledge was required. He felt the logic was persuasive, the timing good, and that it was simply the right thing to do. Upon his election he immediately secured funds to establish a minority involvement program, which went on to become the NEA's Minority Leadership Training Program.

The power base for black leaders in NEA in the 1960s and early '70s was the National Council of Officers of State Teachers Associations (NCOSTA), whose membership consisted of those who had served as executive directors of the state affiliates of the American Teachers Association. NCOSTA advised NEA on the state mergers and insisted that fair standards be set to establish acceptable merger arrangements. It pushed for black staff positions at the local, state, and national levels, and claimed credit for the first wave of black staff hirings at NEA. Its composition was mostly southern members, though in a glaring oversight, it failed to ensure that there were active classroom teachers in its membership. As mergers were consummated, its members began joining the former white state affiliates, causing a dilution of the membership of NCOSTA and diminishing its relevance and influence.[29]

At the 1969 RA in Philadelphia, E.B. Palmer and Lauri Wynn had gathered with others to develop the concept for a Black Caucus. Wynn and Palmer started daily morning meetings with black delegates, usually inviting participants by word of mouth, and within a year the ritual had built a critical mass of 30 to 40 members who were interested in collaborating to advance black issues and concerns in the Association. Initially, another group of black members had called themselves the Black Caucus, but it had been largely inactive since the presidency of Libby Koontz, and aside from their presence at the Critical Issues Conference at NEA in 1968, its members do not appear to have continued as an identifiable and structured black group. Hence, the new group initially adopted the name "The Official Black Caucus" to distinguish itself from the earlier short-lived black constituency group. NCOSTA had been run by southern blacks, and others, like Lauri Wynn and Pat Browne, wanted a more geographically diverse organization and one whose membership included teachers. Lauri's rise in the Association had been nothing short of remarkable. Politically savvy, a spellbinding speaker, and alert to the full range of national education and union issues, the native New Yorker had begun teaching in Milwaukee in 1965, and by 1973, had become the Wisconsin state president, and a member of NEA's Executive Committee. "I joined NEA primarily because a fellow teacher told me it had been good to blacks in the South," recalled Wynn. She was determined to make it good to black members from all regions. Most contemporaries who remember Wynn believed she was on course to become NEA's second black female president. She had a sense for the dramatic and made national headlines when she brought a lawsuit against the Milwaukee School District for maintaining segregated schools. Jackie Gilmore of South Carolina, Eleanor Coleman of Arkansas, and Lillie Carswell of Texas, all remembered the anticipation that something important and profound was to be heard when Laurie Wynn's name was announced as a speaker from either the floor of the RA or at an NEA Board meeting. Helen Bain, a former NEA president, witnessed Lauri outshine Al Shanker during a panel discussion at a conference. "I had not ever seen anyone more dynamic in advocating for teacher interests. Lauri had to be seen in action to be believed," said Bain. As to Lauri's style, she is remembered as strident; and as to abilities, she is remembered as exceptional. Her oratorical skills were powerful, and her huge personality and equally large afro hairstyle commanded attention. She was an extraordinary person, and a symbol around whom many rallied and identified. Lauri Wynn was a force that even Al Shanker of AFT courted to secure Black Caucus support for a prospective NEA and AFT merger. According to David Selden of AFT, in 1972, "Shanker met with Lauri Wynn, the leader of the NEA Black Caucus. Wynn held liberal views on most social issues, but she was adamantly opposed to AFT-NEA merger, mainly because of Shanker's record in the Ocean Hill-Brownsville conflict. The NEA Black Caucus remained an important stumbling block in the way of organizational merger.[30]

Both Wynn and Harris were based in the Midwest and became close friends. Harris saw promise in Lauri and encouraged her to attend NCUEA meetings, and the 1971 NEA Constitutional Convention (known as "con-con") in Fort Collins, Colorado. He mentored and cautioned her on appropriate style, language, and Association image. E. B. Palmer, on the other hand, had been groomed by Koontz, and their North Carolina backgrounds also contributed to a mutual affinity, but one quite different from that of Harris and Wynn in terms of the base of their support systems and their priorities. E.B. was focused on equity in the merger affiliates and the desegregation issues of southern teachers, while Lauri brought attention to northern desegregation issues and sought to extend the active black membership base beyond the South.

At the Detroit RA in 1971, Wynn became the first elected president of the Black Caucus, defeating Horace Tate, a longtime influential member of NCOSTA and executive secretary of the Georgia Education Association. E.B. thought a black southerner was best for the position and considered Lauri's victory to have been a by-product of the Detroit location, where large black attendance from the region gave decided advantages to a candidate from the area. Despite their differences of opinion, both Palmer and Wynn contributed to making the Black Caucus a force in Association culture. After Lauri had served several terms, Palmer became president, and both continued to build the membership and credibility of the caucus. On most issues, they were the same. But on Harris, they did not share the same opinion, though both thought he was highly competent. To Wynn, he was "a gentleman, statesmen-like, subtle when expressing anger, and receptive to varying viewpoints." To Palmer he was all of that, too, "and more." "We thought he had class and his parliamentarian skills were excellent, but he came from outside of NCOSTA and was not familiar to black southern members, the largest segment of NEA's black membership," said Palmer.[31]

Harris had not been active in black NEA groups, and some believed that to be a prerequisite for a black NEA president. While on the NEA Board he had become one of its most outspoken advocates for poor and disadvantaged students, and he never retreated from his belief that urban school districts were in decay and should be NEA's top priority. Southern blacks would have preferred one of their own, but when Harris ran for election they showered him with support. "He was a good president and he presented and conducted himself well," said Palmer, though at the outset there were expectations "that his agenda might be someone else's and not ours." Wynn took pride in nominating him for NEA president, and when he was president-elect in 1973-1974, aside from his service on the NEA Board, she was familiar with his work on NEA committees, including, the Committee to Study Critical Issues Facing Schools; the Planning and Organizational Development Committee; the Committee to Study Organizational Structure; and the NEA Bicentennial Committee; as well as the work he had done when he represented NEA as a consultant to the National Association of Art Educators. "I knew James, and I knew he was ready," said Wynn. President Helen Wise also liked Harris, wanted him to succeed, and helped immensely to make the transition successful.[32]

During his year as president-elect, the NEA adopted a new constitution that called for a fundamental shift in organizational power from administrators to teachers; provided for three salaried full-time executive officers: a president, vice-president, and secretary treasurer. Membership categories were redefined pending individual state discretion to include education support professionals. The role of chief policy spokesman became that of the president rather than executive secretary, and the presidential term was extended from one to two years, with eligibility for reelection for an additional two-year term, effective 1975. Those changes highlighted the new constitution, but almost nothing was as controversial, bold, or revolutionary as the minority guarantees. Under the new constitution, minority representation on the Board of Directors, Executive Committee, and Association committees was set at 20 percent. Representation at the RA was set at the proportion of the ethnic minority population in each state, and state and local affiliates were trusted to elect minority delegates equal to the proportion of the ethnic minority population of the state.[33] No organization of NEA's stature and size, before or since, has ever gone that far to ensure an ethnically diverse governing body.

NEA officials celebrated the new constitution, and minority members took pride in the progressive direction of the organization, while NEA organizers were delighted over the implications of the minority guarantees for recruiting and maintaining minority members. Al Shanker of AFT strongly opposed what he termed NEA's insistence on racial quotas. "The NEA has gone from one form of racism to another," he argued in trying to make a flawed and failed case that NEA was discriminating in favor of minorities.[34] What Shanker could not deny, but would never bring himself to admit was that NEA was on the verge of electing three minority presidents in less than a decade, compared to none for AFT; and that scores of others were in the training pipeline. He also must have come to grips with the realization that AFT would perhaps never again seriously challenge NEA for the loyalty of its minority members. NEA's minority goals, judged by a scholar of Shanker and the AFT, "were arguably more extensively used than in any other major U.S. organization."[35] The minority guarantees came only three years after a new term, "reverse discrimination," had been introduced into American politics, making them open to criticism from those not inclined to support either affirmative action or quotas. Though the legal status of the minority guarantees would be challenged over time, reducing them to goals, by definition they were nonetheless a constitutional expression of organizational intent and commitment to sharing power with ethnic minorities. NEA had already been moving in the direction of right-sizing the staff to reflect the diversity of its members. Since Sam Ethridge had been hired in 1967, becoming NEA's first minority professional staff member, the doors for others had been opening progressively wider.

By 1975, the number of ethnic minorities on NEA's national staff had grown to over 40, including many who went on to establish niches in NEA culture through stellar careers and reputations for their contributions. Among the first wave were Eugene Dryer, Sal Varela, Evelyn Temple, Pat Perez, Malinda Miles, Marian Clayton, Mary Sosa, F.J. Johnson, Howard Belton, Charles Bolden, George Jones, Columbus Rich, Maria Viegas, Ray McFarlane, LaMar Haynes, Dale Robinson, Eloise Sykes, Felicia Haynes, Larry Billups, Jessie Muse, Fredrika Blackmon, Janice Jackson, and Barbara Floyd. All of the early NEA hires were important not only because of the inclusive image the Association wanted to project to its diverse members throughout the nation, but also because their performances assisted in dismissing any internal notions that affirmative action reduced the quality of the workforce. The first wave was important because of the proof it provided that excellence was not compromised by diversity in hiring at NEA.[36] Later, when succeeding waves of minorities were hired, NEA would find itself well positioned to boast— based on experience—of the benefits of a racially diverse staff whose origins could be traced to the NEA climate created by the minority guarantees of the 1971 Constitutional Convention and the 1973 Representative Assembly. Not enough can be said about the impact of the minority guarantees on the changing of NEA's culture.

As president-elect, James Harris traveled widely, meeting members and speaking to affiliates about the programs of President Helen Wise; and about the Association's policies and issues for which he had a special passion: disadvantaged students and opposition to a merger with the American Federation of Teachers. On the AFT subject, Harris plowed fertile soil, galvanizing a large NEA following who agreed with his explanation that there was one fundamental issue working against a merger and prohibiting the establishment of "one independent, autonomous united teaching profession." That major concern "is affiliation with the AFL-CIO," Harris told the delegates at the Portland, Oregon RA in 1973. "I want you to make sure that there is no question where I stand on this issue," he said, in emphasizing that he could not endorse "affiliations with the AFL-CIO at either the local, state, or national levels." Closer working relationships, however, "with other teacher groups" allowing NEA to form coalitions without sacrificing independence, was the strategy he argued for advancing teachers and education interests. "And that is the critical issue," said Harris, "unity with independence." Harris maintained that his base of core support in NEA was derived from members who trusted him to oppose any merger with AFT. More than purely professional, there was a troubling personal experience with an AFT official that he never forgot. Reminiscent of R. J. Martin of the American Teachers Association, who in the early '60s terminated merger discussions between ATA and AFT over what he determined was a racial slight, David Selden of AFT made the mistake of assuming Harris was a chauffeur when they first met. Only years later did he discover that "the driver" would go on to become NEA president. To his credit, Selden had the courage to write about the embarrassing incident in his semi-autobiographical book, *The Teacher Rebellion*. After attending NEA's Constitutional Convention at Colorado State University in Fort Collins, where his mission was to encourage merger considerations, he sought a ride to the airport. In his own words:

> "I am taken back to Denver by my friend George Fischer, the former president of NEA. A friend of Fischer's drives, but Fischer and I do most of the talking during the hour long journey. Several years later the driver introduces himself to me—again, for of course we were introduced at the time. I am much embarrassed. The "driver" was James Harris. . . ."[37]

When he became president in 1974 in Chicago, he continued to build on the work of his immediate predecessors, Catherine Barrett and Helen Wise, in strengthening NEA's Political Action Committee (PAC) and lobbying efforts. But like all of those who preceded him, Harris had only one year to make his mark and to initiate programs that emphasized his own special interests. As a result of con-con, he also knew that he would be the last NEA president limited to a one-year term, and the first to have prospects of running for a second.

Soft spoken, eloquent, erudite, and low-keyed, Harris was a skillful speaker whose every word could be measured for meaning and efficiency. "Declaring war on ignorance and neglect" was the theme of his RA address, and it became the focus of his term in office. In that speech, he reminded the delegates that every politician understood the term "teacher power" because organized educators were expressing their views and priorities at the ballot box. It was the political reality of unionism, and teachers were admonished to become more politically involved. "We must bring about substantial changes in the political scene. We must raise more money, make more phone calls, and ring more doorbells," he implored in support of NEA-PAC activities. Shifting to urban schools, he spoke of an educational crisis facing the nation, calling it "a national disaster" despite "courageous efforts by thousands of administrators and hundreds of thousands of teachers." To solve these problems, teachers needed to be appreciated for not being "superhuman" and would "not be scapegoats." Instead they should be better utilized as primary resources for providing a fairer share of both input and solutions. NEA's role was to raise the nation's awareness of and commitment to the resources required for improved education through the election of politicians who shared its views. The children of the economically disadvantaged deserved more from public education, and NEA, he insisted, must play a role in raising that awareness. Beginning with Lyndon Johnson and his war on poverty and continuing through Richard Nixon, who by 1974 had not backtracked from that goal, the nation's consciousness of poverty had been raised. But, as Harris noted in his closing, no one had "declared war on ignorance" or "war on neglect," and NEA was challenged to assume the responsibility of enlisting teachers to fight those wars.[38]

In deference to each president, NEA had a tradition of providing a budget for programs and initiatives promoting their special priorities, and for Harris that included funds for his brainchild, Project Urban Education Neglect. It debuted with a major urban educational conference in Washington as a component of the initiative. Included among the distinguished political and civic leaders who gave presentations were Congressman Norman Y. Mineta of California, Congresswoman Barbara Jordan of Texas, Jesse Jackson of Operation Push, Senator Walter Mondale of Minnesota, Carmen Delgado of the National Urban Coalition, and many others. Coordinated by Sam Ethridge, then Director of NEA Teacher Rights, the conference drew major media coverage, and a special edition of the *NEA Reporter* was produced on it so that NEA members would have access to the highlights of the various presentations and conference proceedings. The conferees pushed forward a set of proposals, many of them calling for NEA's immediate action. In retrospect, many of those proposals—of over a third of a century ago—remain current and illustrate the length of time often required to solve difficult and seemingly intractable education problems. Among the proposals for NEA action were the following: develop a program to inform parents of students' due process rights in suspensions, expulsions, and court referrals; encourage school districts to actively recruit bilingual, multicultural teachers, guidance counselors, and other ancillary personnel at all grade levels; develop formats for teacher training programs that would deal with problems of crime, violence, and major disruptions at schools; work for the goal of no suspensions of students; and continue to address the educational neglect of youths in detention.[39] The proposals from the conference would remain relevant and follow NEA and public education into the 21st Century.

Harris keynoted the conference with his own list of action steps to combat educational neglect, and they served as poignant reminders of issues as yet unresolved, which are important because they provide a glimpse of Harris' views at that moment in time. All the items on the list suggest what some have called "the changing same" because of their continuing relevancy. They included:

- Reduce class size to 10.

- Provide free higher education for neglected students.

- Provide better health services for neglected families.

- End standardized testing for ability grouping and labeling students.

- Provide job assistance for neglected families.

- Employ specialists such as psychologists, reading teachers, and nutritionists.

- Eradicate discrimination based on sex, race, language, religion, and national origin in policies, practices, and curriculums.[40]

When Gerald Ford replaced Richard Nixon, he called a White House meeting on inflation, and extended an invitation to Harris. At the meeting Harris spoke at length to the participants on the devastating blow dealt to teacher salaries as a direct result of inflation. He reminded them that teacher salaries prior to the crisis had lagged behind those of other professionals requiring college degrees, and that it would be unfair to request that teachers suffer any further reductions in compensation. Responding to economists at the meeting who outlined budget reduction policies to fight inflation, he warned, "Unlike economic spokesmen, I can give you an iron-clad guarantee that cutting back education will bring reduced national income and lost government revenue at every level—funds that might have helped lessen deficits. Underfunding also guarantees increased crime, with all its varied attendant expenses; increased welfare rolls; and increased unemployment— with all these costs to be borne by a proportionately smaller segment of the population." Harris went on to tell the esteemed group that schools could ill afford any "anti-inflation gimmicks that chip away" at the foundation of America's productivity—public education. Referring to NEA Project Urban Education Neglect, he told President Ford of NEA's work "in the urban areas where large numbers of students were shunted aside into poverty and crime because of poorly financed schools lacking the staff, materials, and facilities to educate them effectively." He closed by reminding the White House conferees that redirection of local budgets had forced teacher layoffs and unemployment in the vast majority of states where teachers were not eligible for unemployment benefits, and he urged development of federal policy in that respect. He also took exception to those who claimed the existence of a teacher surplus, when he indicated that if class size were factored into the calculations, "an additional 670,000 teachers" would be needed.[41] His performance was an auspicious White House debut, and he accurately expressed the sentiments of the Association's more than 1 million members. It would be one of the finest moments of his presidency. President Ford was so impressed by Harris that he accepted his invitation to speak at the NEA Board Meeting. There Ford spoke optimistically of "bright clouds" which would soon be due to the teaching profession.[42]

When traveling throughout the nation promoting Project Urban Education Neglect, Harris was careful that there would be no perception that only black students were victims of poor schools. He understood that his message must alert NEA and the nation that blacks did not have a monopoly on poverty. "Pockets of neglect surround us," he told an audience of Baltimore members, and "are on the verge of consuming us. Urban inner cities where one-third of our students live, Indian reservations, barrios of the Southwest, Appalachia with its disadvantaged whites, youth detention and correctional centers. . ."[43] Harris was one of the first NEA presidents to speak often on bilingual education. As early as 1973, when he was president-elect, he spoke on that topic at a conference of the National Bilingual and Bicultural Institute in Albuquerque, New Mexico. "Over seven million kids sit in class," said Harris, "mostly Hispanic and Asian, with special language needs" that were being ignored. He cited the Mexican American Education Study of the U.S. Civil Rights Commission, and hailed it for addressing Mexican American educational concerns and for "pointing out for teachers that the same institutionally racist patterns that had been destroying blacks and Native Americans for over a century had been operating against Mexican Americans." Schools desperately needed bilingual teachers who were culturally sensitive and possessed skills to also "teach the history and culture associated with the children's language, and the personal qualities of being able to conduct sessions with parents and interact individually with the children." Harris repeated variations of that theme in many of his speeches on bilingual and multicultural education, usually closing with the words of the great Indian poet, Rabindranath Tagore, who warned of the long term effects of educational neglect when he wrote, "The flower lies dying in the dust. It tried to be a butterfly."[44] It was important to Harris that he be seen as a president who represented the interests of all of the members, and the issues of all of the students, all of the time.

Another Harris initiative, Educators Deployed to Underdeveloped Countries Affecting Total Education (EDUCATE), was a concept that hoped for an international curriculum in which American teachers would take assignments in underdeveloped nations and incorporate the principles of democracy and international understanding and cooperation into lesson plans. The project was ambitious for a one-year term of office and did not gain enough Association traction to survive for any length of time beyond his presidency. "That project was about globalization, world peace, democracy, and the extension of quality education throughout underdeveloped countries," said Harris in retrospect, "and it was something in which I deeply believed!"[45]

During his term in office, Harris launched a bid to become NEA's first two-term president, and though he was unsuccessful, that election in 1975 certainly demonstrated the interracial progress made by NEA since the NEA/ATA merger of 1966. He was opposed by three white candidates, and to the credit of NEA members and the delegates, race never emerged as an issue. Throughout the campaign, the candidates stayed on the issues, and their supporters did the same, whites and blacks favoring the candidates equally. On the first day of voting, though none achieved a majority, Harris and John Ryor of Michigan took the lead. In the run-off election, Harris was defeated by Ryor.

Keith Geiger, who followed Mary Hatwood Futrell as president, later commented on that election, "Harris never demonstrated class more than he did when he lost the presidency to John Ryor in 1975. After the run-off election, he had to run the RA, and he showed no bitterness or animosity. He was majestic and above the politics of it all. It was, ironically, one of his finest moments."[46] One delegate, Billie Cherry of Texas, voiced an opinion on the election that summarized the interracial growth and maturity of NEA's RA delegates. "In the run-off election, I voted for Jim Harris," she told the *NEA Reporter*. "However, before I left home I had read the platform of Ryor and I was very much impressed by it and the things he proposed to do. So I felt that we could not lose with either man."[47]

After leaving NEA, Harris became a principal in Washington, D.C., before retiring to found the Faith Baptist Community Church which thrives today in Silver Spring, Maryland, where he serves as pastor. When asked what he most wanted to be remembered for, Harris did not blink or hesitate, and he gave a response which reflects on his personal background, expectations, and beliefs. He said, "One person can be the key to the future; teachers can make a difference; school personnel change lives daily; communities must be closely connected to children and their educational well-being; and adults can learn from kids, because kids are resilient. For those reasons and views, I want to be remembered."[48] James Harris will be remembered for all of that and much more. He was NEA's first black male president, and he was the quintessential politician, education advocate, and, above all, a gentleman and a scholar who helped NEA to appreciate the need for providing improved opportunities for neglected students, the children of migrant workers, the poor, the incarcerated, the handicapped, and those who suffered from racial discrimination. He will also be remembered as the transition between NEA controlled by administrators, and NEA controlled by teachers.

Sam Ethridge, NEA's first black professional staff person.

Credit: Photograph by Fabian Bachrach

Braulio Alonso frequently lunched with President Lyndon Baines Johnson, a former Texas teacher.

Credit: Photograph by Carl Purcell, National Education Association

Braulio Alonso addresses the 1967 Representative Assembly.

The July 1967 rally of 35,000 teachers in the Citrus Bowl, Orlando, Florida, which preceded the statewide teachers' strike.

(L-R) J. Rupert Picott, Floyd McKissick, Braulio Alonso, Libby Koontz, and James Williams attend the funeral of Martin Luther King, Jr., 1968.

On becoming NEA President in 1968, Libby Koontz attracted more media attention than any other person who had held the position.

Opening of the NEA Center for Human Relations. (L-R) Sam Lambert, Libby Koontz, Sam Ethridge, and Wade Wilson, October 1968.

Credit: *NEA Reporter*

Credit: *NEA Reporter*

NEA president, Libby Koontz, tells viewers of NBC's "Today Show" how important it is for teachers to be active, involved citizens.

Lois Edinger, NEA president in 1964-65 , was from North Carolina and a close friend of Libby Koontz. She was important in Libby's rise to influence in NEA.

Vivian Bowser, president of the Texas State Teachers Association, was the longest serving member of the NEA Executive Committee. Bowser was active in the 1960s and 1970s.

Credit: Joe Di Dio, National Education Association

Helen Bain, NEA president, 1970 and Don Morrison NEA president 1971. Bain was a leader in NCUEA, and Morrison promoted the minority involvement program.

George Jones of Alabama, a prominent NEA staff person after the merger and director of NEA's Mid-Atlantic Region.

Credit: Joe Di Dio, National Education Association

Eugene Dryer, an early minority staff member, worked closely in the field with the merger agreements in the South. He also became an NEA regional director.

Credit: Cliff Moore

Tuskegee Airmen of World War II. James Harris, the first black male president of NEA, was a member of this famed group.

James Harris was NEA's first president to run for reelection as a result of the NEA Constitutional Convention.

Lauri Wynn, president of the Wisconsin Education Association and member of the NEA Executive Committee, was one of NEA's most dynamic leaders in the early 1970s.

E. B. Palmer of North Carolina, one of the founders of the NEA Black Caucus.

NEA teachers plan for minority involvement at a 1968 meeting in Portland, Oregon. (L-R) Ruth Trigg of Barrington, Illinois, Lithangia Robinson of Atlanta, Georgia, and Ouida Ott of Charleston Heights, South Carolina.

Credit: *NEA Reporter*

Herman Coleman of the Michigan Education Association was the first black to serve as an NEA state executive director, 1973-1981.

Mary Hatwood Futrell with Andrew Young, U.S. Ambassador to United Nations.

Reg Weaver, NEA's fifth minority president, speaking at the NEA Representative Assembly in July 2008.

Credit: NEA Reporter

Governor Bill Clinton defends Arkansas' new teacher testing law as NEA Executive Committee member Odetta Fujimori listens skeptically.

Representative Assembly, July 2008 at which Barrack Obama's candidacy for U.S. President was endorsed by NEA.

Mary Hatwood Futrell

1983-1989

Mary Hatwood Futrell
1983-1989

The Education Reform Movement and
the Rise of Presidential Identity

The rise of Mary Hatwood Futrell to the ranks of power and influence in the National Education Association caught no alert observer by surprise. Just as a trusted almanac often predicts a storm well before it crosses the meteorologist's radar screen, NEA insiders and political pundits had detected her future eminence long before she burst upon the national stage. They recognized that a uniquely gifted future leader with extraordinary talent was on her way to the top tier of the Association. In a progressively upward spiral, every single position she held at the local, state, and national levels had been a textbook example of exemplary leadership, gathering for her a broad and inspired following all along the way. Members connected with her both professionally and personally, maintaining a vicarious relationship with her passions, issues, and classroom experiences. Her personality blended the most contradictory characteristics into a balanced whole: she could be simultaneously courteous and outspoken, firm and flexible, practical and visionary, humorous and no-nonsense, candid and confidential, a cautious yet bold risk-taker.

Considerably before the concept of identity politics came into vogue, and likely before Futrell grasped its full meaning, her inimitable style, engaging personality, and command of message resonated with members from diverse backgrounds, including those who categorized their primary Association identities by race, ethnicity, gender, sexual orientation, regional background, distinct issue advocacy, or membership designation. Whether they saw their roles in education as professional or unionist, they connected with her and she with them in a way that was natural, genuine, and authentic. She was a phenomenon, and like those who personify the intangibles of class and dignity, she was a challenge to describe. To all of NEA's members, however, she was easily recognizable. A mesmerizing speaker on stage, she was even more captivating in individual and small group conversations. "One by one, and group by group, the members wrapped themselves around Mary," recalled longtime NEA staffer Chuck Williams, "and one by one and group by group, she wrapped herself around them."[1]

In sharing common ground with more Association constituent groups than perhaps any president before her, Futrell became a consensus builder for all factions of the organization, fostering dialogue and collaboration among what might otherwise have been competing NEA entities. On July 3, 1983, at the Representative Assembly in Minneapolis, that broad-based coalition expressed its confidence by electing her NEA's fourth ethnic minority president in the short span of 16 years—a record simply remarkable for an organization that had elected no members of minorities to any office in its first 100 years. As evidence of how much the Association and the nation had been transformed since the NEA/ATA merger of 1966 and the Civil Rights Movement, Futrell's election, unlike that of Libby Koontz in 1968, was not a major news story outside of education and union circles.

Within NEA the culture and organizational structure that had been so greatly changed by the merger and the Constitutional Convention (con-con) of 1971 coincided with the transition of the old NEA governance and staff guard to the new. At the national level, the minority guarantees had been translated into organizational goals, and the commitment to compliance had filtered to the state and local levels. Conversations on the need to hire minority staff—begun in the early 1960s when black Executive Committee member Wade Wilson had chastised NEA executive secretary William Carr for not hiring black staff—had resulted in an affirmative action program that placed minority staff in every NEA department. Minorities continued to serve on the Executive Committee, and nearly 20 percent of the members of the Board of Directors were minorities. All of the appointed committees and NEA meetings had minority participation, and the Representative Assembly had record numbers of minorities from almost every state.

The energy of minority involvement could be seen in the minority caucuses, members of which were courted for endorsements by most NEA political candidates. Further, NEA had a Minority Affairs Committee and a Minority Leadership Training Program. Moreover, the most prestigious and anticipated event of the Representative Assembly had come to be the Human and Civil Rights Awards Dinner, a proud legacy of the American Teachers Association. Another gauge of NEA's progress was that all of the presidents in the intervening years—George Fischer, Helen Bain, Don Morrison, Catherine Barrett, Helen Wise, James Harris, John Ryor, and Willard McGuire—had come of age during the Civil Rights Movement, the teacher revolution of the1960s, and the merger, each continuing to build on the organization's agenda of diversity and inclusion.

Few organizations in all of America had made so much progress in minority inclusion as had NEA, and no other school personnel organization could compete with the Association's commitment and results. Making the argument that NEA "was better for minorities than its competitors became much easier for our organizers," claimed regional director Eugene Dryer.[2]

At the state and local levels where members most closely interacted, the transformation of the organization had been nothing short of sensational. Where members of different races in formerly dual affiliate states did not know each other, all now collaborated to share ideas, advance issues, forge friendships, and elect officers. By 1983, most southern states had elected at least two black presidents, Futrell being one of them in the Virginia Education Association. Even in states like Illinois, the trend toward minority guarantees in the mid-1970s was making the leadership of the state affiliate much more representative of the membership and state population, recalled Ann Davis of the Illinois Education Association. "We had blacks and Hispanics," she continued, "on all state committees and attending all state meetings."[3]

The formerly segregated affiliates effected mergers between 1966 and 1977, and the dynamics of those power-sharing negotiations and the lessons

learned from them initiated a ripple of change that spread from the local
to the state associations, and onto the national level, creating a "bottom up
effect," which E. B. Palmer and Joe Reed—former ATA executives—contend
drove the minority guarantees of the Constitutional Convention.[4] All in
all, minorities performed as well as whites, the membership continued to
increase, and the fears and suspicions fueled by isolation were giving way
to the trust and confidence bred by familiarity. On race-related matters,
this was the NEA inherited by Futrell, far different from the Association
led by her minority predecessors, Braulio Alonso, Elizabeth Koontz, and
James Harris, all pre con-con presidents. Organizationally, those presidents
had served an Association in which administrators dominated and their
privileges were disproportionately larger than those allowed to the largely
teacher membership. Coming a full decade after con-con, Futrell assumed
leadership when school personnel—then primarily teachers—controlled the
policymaking apparatus of NEA. As George Fischer noted, "It was simple
as making a decision whether you wanted staff," referring to the executive
secretary, "or whether you wanted your aspirations reflected through the
elected leadership."[5] Thus, con-con made the president the chief policy
spokesperson, and Futrell became the first member of a minority to exercise
that authority for the Association. Con-con had changed the title of executive
secretary to executive director, and the redefined duties of that position
included employment and supervision of the national staff and administering
the budgets authorized by the governing bodies, but being spokesperson on
matters of established policy only at the discretion of the president.[6] This
meant that Futrell's relationship with executive director Don Cameron as
spokesperson would be decidedly different from that of Alonso and Koontz
with pre con-con executive secretaries Sam Lambert and Terry Herndon,
the latter of whom continued in the position of executive director after the
new constitution was adopted. The teacher revolution of the 1960s had not
only established the profession as a force in American politics, but it had
also established teachers as their own agents, fully in charge of charting the
destiny of the Association.

What had occurred within NEA along the lines of human and civil rights and minority inclusion since the merger and con-con was trend-setting, and it mirrored the historical progress taking place in America, which gained momentum with the presidency of Lyndon Baines Johnson. In just the eight years between James Harris and Mary Hatwood Futrell, barriers continued to be broken with the flexing of black political muscle and the prevalence of black influence. The number of blacks holding public office doubled, with mayors being elected in Atlanta, Philadelphia, Chicago, and Charlotte to complement those serving in over 20 other cities with populations of 100,000 or more. Tom Bradley of California, former mayor of Los Angeles, narrowly lost in his bid to become the nation's first black governor. William Coleman, Pat Harris, and Sam Pierce held Cabinet level positions under Gerald Ford, Jimmy Carter, and Ronald Reagan.

Among federal appointments, there was optimism with Clarence Thomas heading the Equal Employment Opportunity Commission; Clarence Pendleton and Mary Francis Berry leading the U.S. Civil Rights Commission; and Andrew Young representing the U.S. as Ambassador to the United Nations. Ruth Love became superintendent of Chicago schools; Jewell Cobb, president of California State University at Fullerton; Faye Wattleton, president of Planned Parenthood; and Franklin Thomas president of the Ford Foundation. Those appointments attracted major media coverage, though nothing came close to rivaling President Jimmy Carter's increase of the number of black federal appellate judges from two to 56.[7]

Yet, while those accomplishments generated pride and were indications of progress, the intractable vestiges of segregation remained formidable. Despite the U.S. Supreme Court rulings that separate educational facilities were "inherently unequal," almost 30 years later—on the day Mary Hatwood Futrell would become President of NEA—almost 46 percent of minority students were still educated in segregated schools. Herself no stranger to segregated schools, with all of her public school and undergraduate study taking place in institutions that had not been integrated, Futrell could look forward to the possibilities of continued progress, and she could also reflect on her most personal experiences as a black woman growing up poor in the

Jim Crowed and rigidly segregated Virginia of the 1940s and '50s. Maybe it was her habit of revisiting her past as a yardstick for progress, a source of introspection and inspiration, that kept her always searching and probing for the lessons in life worth remembering and never forgotten. Over the years, Futrell would resort to her autobiography as a reminder of the roles that caring families, communities, and teachers played in preparing students for productive lives. None of her NEA ethnic-minority predecessors shared the experiences of her upbringing. Braulio Alonso had come from a working-poor background in the segregated South, but he had been considered white. Libby Koontz had come from the segregated South, but her family was of the black educated middle class. James Harris' family had been of modest means, but he had benefited from and excelled in Iowa's well-funded integrated public schools. The disadvantages of Futrell's early life were anchored in poverty, discrimination, and policies of "separate but unequal."

Mary Alice Franklin Hatwood was born on May 24, 1940 in Altavista, Virginia. Her mother, Josephine Hatwood, was a domestic worker, performing the kind of common low-paying job held by an overwhelming number of uneducated black women, and her father was a construction worker. Her parents were unmarried, but during Mary's childhood her mother married a responsible man, John Ed Calloway, who was the man she considered her father. He died when she was only five years old. Mary Alice had a sister, Ann, and her mother raised three other children as a foster parent. All were treated equally, and the extended family would not allow distinctions to be made between those who were biologically related and those who were fostered.[8]

Because there was no hospital for blacks in Altavista, the family moved to Lynchburg when John Ed Calloway suffered medical problems. He was treated in Lynchburg, and Josephine remained there with her children after his death, working as a maid and cleaning woman. "My mother took me and my sisters along with her on jobs, always reminding us that there was nothing wrong with honest work," Mary remarked. It took the family eight years to pay off the hospital bills. Josephine worked 15- to 18-hour days as the sole support of the family, pledging never to consider remarrying until the daughters were grown. "She would be gone before we'd wake up for breakfast, and still not home by dark," Futrell remembered. As a measure of her generosity and compassion, even with her meager financial resources, she accepted her "non-biological" daughters after the mothers of two of them died, and the third had been virtually abandoned by her mother. Josephine herself had lost both of her parents by the age of 10, and had been raised with four siblings by her grandparents.[9]

When she was forced to seek employment at an early age, like others of her race and generation, her schooling had ended before she was a teenager. At some point, she came to understand the tragedy of that circumstance and determined that her daughters would not repeat her experience. "She ingrained in us that education was everything, insisting that nothing was more important than getting a good education," said her daughter. Only education, Mary concluded, could lift the family from poverty. Josephine was considered smart by her peers, and perhaps the frustration of being intelligent but without education credentials, motivated her special emphasis on education. Whatever the reasons might have been, her children were the beneficiaries. Despite the fact the she only had a sixth-grade education, endured financial hardships, and worked long hours, Mary's mother found the time to assist in the education of her daughters. "My mother always read to me and my sisters, had spelling contests with us, checked our report cards, and came to school any time it was necessary," Futrell recalled, "even though it might mean changing buses two or three times."[10] Years later Josephine took pride in talking about her precocious daughter Mary and remembered that "people and books were all she ever cared about." The young girl also asked questions about everything from segregation to homework assignments, and her mother remembered that she "could ask nine million questions in three minutes flat."

Mary enrolled in the segregated schools of Lynchburg, where she was taught and nurtured by teachers who observed her academic talents and pushed her to the limits of her potential. "They recognized something in me that I did not recognize in myself, and they encouraged me to excel," recalled Mary, who also took jobs on weekends to supplement the meager income brought home by her mother, who qualified for, but refused to accept, welfare. That stubborn pride transferred to Mary who shrugged at her school nickname, "See Mo," which mocked her clothes, as if there were more holes than fabric. Even as an adult, Mary would find more humor than bitterness in those memories. "I refused to let it bother me," she said, "because my mother and teachers told me it is not what you wear, it is who you are, and the boundaries do not define you, unless you let them define you."[11]

Living in poverty taught Futrell how to survive, and one humiliating situation after another forced her to maintain faith in the belief that education would ultimately allow her to triumph over adversities. One incident of her childhood is exemplary of the coexistence of poverty, love, and hope. Futrell wrote about it in the *Readers Digest*:

> "I remember when Ann and I walked barefoot to school one fine September day because our shoes had worn out and there wasn't enough money for Mama to buy us new ones. The principal looked at us and raised his eyebrows, but didn't say anything. The next day we thought he would speak, but he didn't. The third day he met us at the door.
>
> "'Why don't you have shoes on?'
>
> "We explained that Mama couldn't afford to buy us shoes.
>
> "'Well,' he said, 'you'll have to go home. We can't have you attending school barefoot. You'll have to tell your mother.'
>
> "Ann took my hand, and we turned to go back home. Being the more mischievous one, I suggested we spend the day in a nearby cornfield instead. Just about the time school was over we went home. There was Mama, waiting for us. That was most unusual, but the gossip line is faster than Western Union in a town like Lynchburg.
>
> "Mama was frowning—and standing straight as a tent pole. She asked us where we had been. I made up a story rather than upset her. Then she started crying. 'You were not in school today,' she said.

"It was clear she knew everything. She told us how important it was to get an education. She also told us never to be ashamed of being poor. 'It's not what you wear, it's who you are,' she said. '*That's* what matters.' A few days later, when she got paid, she took money she would have used to pay bills to buy us new shoes."[12]

At times when the stress of school and work weighed on her spirit, Mary remembered Mrs. Henry, her fourth grade teacher, who privately took her aside and cautioned, "You seem like you want to give up, but you cannot do that, you must keep trying." Another of Futrell's teachers punished her for talking in class by requiring that she write a thousand-word essay on education and its impact on the economy. Every draft she completed was rejected for either lack of neatness, poor punctuation, wide margins, or grammar or sentence structure. Finally, after the fourth draft of the paper was accepted, Futrell fumed over the punishment until three weeks later the teacher interrupted the class to announce, "I am happy to inform you that Mary has won third prize in the essay contest – on the impact of education on the economy."[13]

Segregated schools were consistently short on resources, but rarely were they deficient in teachers who understood, cared for, and protected the hopes of the next generation. Unfortunately, within the segregated schools and communities in cities like Lynchburg, there were class, complexion, hair texture, and other artificial divisions prevalent among blacks, and, unfortunately, some academic decisions were based more on those considerations, and less on scholastic merit.

Lynchburg had a black middle class of teachers, doctors, dentists, contractors, small merchants, funeral directors, entrepreneurs, and faculty and administrators of the HBCU, Virginia Theological Seminary. Prominent black residents included famed Harlem Renaissance poet Ann Spencer, and Dr. Robert Johnson, a physician and the nation's leading patron of black tennis players, who trained Althea Gibson and Arthur Ashe, both Wimbledon champions. Regardless of background, almost all black Lynchburg students went to Paul Laurence Dunbar High School, which had served the community since 1923, after blacks petitioned and lobbied for a new school. Initially, the faculty was white and the curriculum focused on classical scholarship, and during the 1920s, as many as 90 percent of its graduating students—one of the highest rates in the nation—went to college. By the mid-1950s, when Mary was a student there, the faculty and administrators had long been all black, and the school continued to excel academically, while simultaneously offering cultural, athletic, and educational programs for the community. General education and vocationally-oriented courses supplemented the established curriculum in the fully accredited school.[14]

Some of the students at Dunbar received preferential treatment from teachers and were encouraged to succeed. Often less was expected of others, who were tracked into vocational education programs, rather than the more demanding college preparatory curriculum. On balance, Clarence Williams Seay, the principal, championed both programs and promoted fairness, though it was not always practiced by his staff. "When I entered high school, I applied to be in the academic program and I was denied," said Mary. Unable to reconcile the rejection with her honor-roll grades, she needed consultation, but instead sought explanation from the school counselor. "Basically, what she told me was that my family was poor and that I was not going to college anyway, so I needed to be trained to get a job."[15]

With no option to contest the decision, Mary was enrolled in the vocational program for several years before she was moved to the high school academic program as a result of a high score she made on a standardized examination. She was a junior, however, before that placement correction was made.[16]

Throughout the time she was trying to enroll in courses leading to college, Mary had teachers who took a special interest in her development, imploring her to "never give up." Even when she failed in her attempt to become a cheerleader—a role ensuring popularity that guaranteed acceptance by her school peers—she continued to practice all of the routines, and when a vacancy opened, she made the squad and eventually became captain. When Mary was being considered for the National Honor Society, some teachers questioned whether she should be a member, although her grades showed clearly that she was deserving of enrollment. Another student, however, whose parents owned a business, was invited to join despite borderline grades. "That upset some of my teachers, who saw the unfairness of it all, and I joined the Honor Society after they intervened." Again, her teachers were guardian angels who built confidence while guiding her through a challenging course of high school experiences.[17]

During the year Mary entered high school, the U.S. Supreme Court handed down its ruling in *Brown v. Board of Education*, declaring unconstitutional schools segregated on the basis of race. Virginia's resistance to the decision was massive, led by Congressman Harry F. Byrd, who endorsed the Southern Manifesto signed by 101 politicians, claiming the decision was an abuse of judicial power, and promising to resist its implementation. More than a decade would pass before school integration would come to Lynchburg, and then only after blacks began filing lawsuits to expedite the desegregation process. Mary remembered the *Brown* decision, the Little Rock Nine, the kidnapping and murder of Emmett Till, the stand taken by Rosa Parks, the non-violent protests of Martin Luther King Jr., and the Montgomery Bus Boycott, all of which occurred during her high school years, but she had few recollections of conversations in her home, community, or school about these volatile events. Parents and teachers were loath to excite black youth in the wake of the early Civil Rights Movement, fearing retaliation from angry whites. "We knew what was going on," Mary reflected, "but the adults wanted to maintain our safety and manage the optimism of our youth." The black culture of Lynchburg placed limits on conversations determined to be more appropriate for adult discussion. Josephine Hatwood appreciated the Civil Rights Movement and hoped for a changed America for her daughters, but all of her dreams were invested in their educational pursuits. Since Josephine was a strong disciplinarian and no-nonsense when it came to homework and family chores, Mary thought her mother did not like her, but later she came to understand that "she was hard on me because she wanted me to stay focused, she did not want to lose me."[18]

At the Dunbar High School graduation, the address of the superintendent helped Mary appreciate that her mother had not lost her, when she heard him state that of the 400 students who had started school with that class, only 87 were graduating. The euphoria of completing high school with honors was tempered by a shortage of funds needed to attend college. At first Mary had trepidations about applying for college admission, and she only changed her mind at the insistence of several of her teachers by applying to one institution, Virginia State College, an HBCU near Petersburg. Several of her teachers collected $1,500 from local businesses, churches, and individuals to help pay her college expenses. A few months earlier, she had completed an application for a scholarship provided by her high school, but before the announcement of the scholarship winners, one teacher had experienced so much guilt that he confessed to her that the scholarship committee had denied her application, not on the basis of academic ability, but because they had concluded that her family's poverty was such that "it would be a waste to invest in someone who would likely not finish college." That information was a heavy load to bear for 18-year-old Mary Alice Hatwood, who had been an exemplary student, had followed all of the rules with model conduct her entire life, and was on the brink of becoming the first high school graduate in her family. Her innocence was shattered, through no fault of her own. But with the eternal optimism of Scarlett O'Hara in *Gone with the Wind*, she believed that tomorrow would bring a change of fortune, and she set her sights on a future to which Josephine could not have aspired, preparing for the fall of 1958 when she would be a member of the freshman class of Virginia State College.[19]

In September of 1958, Mary boarded a segregated bus in Lynchburg bound for Petersburg. Other than working in the summers as a domestic for wealthy white families in the resort town of Virginia Beach, it was her first extended trip from home. On the Virginia State campus, she soon discovered that she would be judged solely on her academic abilities and not her impoverished background. Besides, there were many other students on the campus whose families were no better off than her own. All that mattered was her will to succeed. It was a new experience, a new setting, a perfect match for her abilities, and it was ripe with new opportunities. Because the business teachers in her high school were those who had influenced her most, and because her professional role models had been teachers, she chose business education as a major. But her decision was also based in part on her ongoing insecurity about college financing. "I figured," she reasoned, "that if I didn't finish college, at least I would acquire some skills to help me get a job." It was a practical assessment of her situation, but an alternative she never had to explore. Early in her first semester, college counselors told her about financial aid programs for which she qualified. The $1,500 scholarship that her teachers had secured from the Lynchburg community was enough for a full year's tuition, room, and board. And with financial assistance available from the college, the remainder of her undergraduate years were more secure, which allowed her to concentrate on her studies and enjoy the vibrant life of the college.[20]

The students at black colleges after the *Brown v. Board* decision were eager to participate in the Civil Rights Movement, and those institutions, most of which were located in the segregated South, took the lead in desegregation campaigns in southern cities and towns, with their attendees eventually forming the Student Non-Violent Coordinating Committee (SNCC), a national group of student activists founded on the campus of Shaw University in North Carolina. Virginia State students were actively involved in civil rights activities designed to desegregate Petersburg, and Mary soon gained a reputation as one of the leaders in the campaign. On February 1 of her sophomore year, four black students at North Carolina A & T in Greensboro occupied seats designated for "whites only" at a Woolworth's lunch counter and were refused service. In less than two weeks their actions set in motion a wave of non-violent sit-ins which spread to 15 cities in five southern states. Within two years the non-violent protests engulfed the entire South and engaged students at most HBCUs. At Virginia State, Mary joined the protesters and marched in Petersburg against the city's segregated public facilities. Unexpectedly, she received a phone call from her mother who "wanted to know how I felt about the Civil Rights Movement." Somewhat surprised, she told Josephine how great it was for the country, to which her mother replied, "Well, Mary Alice, you know I did not send you down there to go to jail." Later Mary learned that a television news broadcast in Lynchburg had shown film of her in the Petersburg marches.[21]

Josephine's rebuke to Mary for her civil rights involvement must be understood in the context of her own life, and the sacrifices she had endured—white water fountains; restraint in expressing any complaints to her white employers; inferior segregated accommodations and facilities; acceptance of her place in society, and a lifetime of working long hours—had all been for one purpose: to provide the best possible education for her daughters. Nothing was acceptable if it interfered with or jeopardized Josephine's American dream. Josephine's call had been a close and personal conversation with Mary about caution, but, just as the faculties of other HBCUs had influenced their students' activities, the Virginia State faculty had come to master Mary's balancing act of social activism and academic excellence.

The faculty at Virginia State was intent on providing leaders, and it nurtured the students both in the classroom and on the campus. In matters purely academic, the teachers were firm, holding high expectations of the students, and monitoring their activities with the vigilance of security officers. Like Professor Henry Higgins transforming Eliza Doolittle in George Bernard Shaw's play *Pygmalion*, the professors at Virginia State "were committed to making us anything we could aspire to be." When Mary's faculty advisor noticed how much time she was spending with a fellow, he motioned her aside for a one-on-one talk. "He told me straightforwardly that if I did not become serious and devote more time to my courses, he would give me an orange, a funny book, and a one-way ticket—an orange to eat, a book to read, and a bus ticket back home," laughed Mary years later. That episode was a signal experience because it forced her to make a personal decision about the seriousness with which she would approach her college studies. Although she barely survived that semester academically, she proceeded to make the Dean's List in each subsequent semester during her undergraduate studies.[22]

Overall, the Virginia State experience prepared Mary well, despite facilities far inferior to those of the University of Virginia, where no blacks had ever been admitted to the undergraduate school, though owing to the legal work of Thurgood Marshall, Charles Houston, and William Hastie of the NAACP Legal Defense Fund, the Law School and Graduate School had been ordered in 1950 to admit a black to each of their programs. Coincidentally, the graduate student admitted to UVA was Walter Ridley, a 41-year-old professor and head of the Psychology Department at Virginia State, who had received his Ph.D. degree in 1953, five years before Mary Alice Hatwood entered Virginia State. He was well-known to NEA, having served several years as president of the American Teachers Association.[23]

The Virginia State faculty, despite campus deficiencies, demanded excellence without excuse, preparing students with the intention of enabling them to compete anywhere. The buy-in for Mary was natural because the faculty's position bore out the lessons and values she had learned from her mother and teachers in Lynchburg. Apart from her academic achievement, Mary matured, gained confidence, made lifelong friendships, and joined Delta Sigma Theta Sorority.

While she was a coed at Virginia State, her sense of social justice became more focused through experiences such as collecting books to send to the Virginia county of Prince Edward, where, to avoid integration, officials closed all public schools from 1959 to 1964, depriving black students of schooling, while white students continued their education in "private" free academies. One memory of college for Mary ranks above all the rest, and that was the visit of Martin Luther King, Jr. to Virginia State. He had been invited to the campus to speak to the faculty, administrators, and student body, as well as the Petersburg community. This was relatively early in his career, and though already well-known, he was nowhere near the national figure he was to become after his March on Washington, his "I Have a Dream" speech, and his acceptance of the Nobel Peace Prize. In fact, Mary had taken her notebook to the assembly to complete homework should the speech be boring. After he started to speak, however, she asked, "Who in the world is that?" His voice and message held the audience spellbound. "I put down my notebook; I listened to every word he said. He talked about us marching and standing up for freedom; he talked about dignity, about us being human beings; he talked about us giving back to the community; and about us getting out there to help the next generation."[24] In effect, that speech became a first draft of the blueprint that would guide the career of Mary Hatwood Futrell.

Mary graduated from college with honors in 1962, with her mother sitting proudly in the audience at the commencement exercise. She had overcome tremendous odds, proving wrong the doubters and detractors of Lynchburg. By not allowing anyone to define her boundaries, she had exceeded the perimeters of expected achievement. Her sister Ann traveled with Josephine by bus to the graduation, proudly cheering Mary when she crossed the stage as the first college graduate in the family. Persistence had prevailed, and now she turned her attention to getting a job.

When Mary applied for a teaching position in Fairfax County, Virginia, one of the Virginia Beach families for whom she had worked as a maid in the summers, paid for her airline ticket—her first plane trip—to Northern Virginia to interview for the job. She had also applied for a job with the most dependable employer of black college graduates other than public schools, the federal government. When she was turned down by the Fairfax schools, she accepted a position as a clerical secretary at the U.S. Department of Housing and Urban Development in a division in which grievances were filed. Her Washington, D.C. office was located near NEA. "I remember walking around the corner, and there was the NEA," she said, "but never did I imagine that I would end up there one day." On occasion she would even have lunch in the NEA building.[25]

After about a year at HUD, Mary was contacted by Flora Chase, the teacher who had supervised her when she had done her student teaching stint at the all-black Parker Gray High School in Alexandria, Virginia. Her former supervisor informed her about an upcoming vacancy, and encouraged her to apply for the teaching position. Shortly thereafter, she was offered the position and accepted it. Soon after arriving at Parker Gray, she gained hands-on experience with the meaning of separate and unequal in a segregated black school where the typewriters and other business equipment were outdated, malfunctioning, and grossly inferior to those supplied to the all-white schools.[26] She was outraged and disappointed but determined not to let it interfere with the expectations she set for her students. Adversity was nothing new to Mary; she had lots of personal experience in making the best out of bad situations.

In 1965, there was local tension when the Alexandria schools were desegregated, and Mary became irate over the assignments given to black teachers at predominately white schools, where they were disproportionately placed in vocational and physical education programs. She was among those selected for "white" George Washington High School, and on reporting to work, she was met with a cold reception by an assistant principal who boldly asked her if she could teach. "I told her I thought I could, since I had a teaching certificate from the State of Virginia," said Mary, remembering that she had replied with a stern face and direct eye-to-eye contact. Eventually, she won the respect of her colleagues and became chair of the business education department at the school. Still, accepting desegregation for many was a slow process, and interracial riots at her school were not uncommon, some of them instigated by the Ku Klux Klan whose members marched outside, and others by single tragic events such as the assassination of Martin Luther King, Jr. These incidents flared for two or three years before calm was restored.[27]

In 1965, the black and white local teachers' associations had merged, and her mentor, Flora Chase, explained the importance of joining the union if she wanted a voice in the district. With that guidance from a veteran teacher and trusted friend, Mary joined the Education Association of Alexandria (EAA), in which she served as a faculty representative and as treasurer during a time when the primary goal of EAA was to bring black and white members together. In the process, her credibility, trustworthiness, and visibility were increased among both whites and blacks. Predictably, there were ebbs and flows in the membership, but as the members came to know each other, personal bonds were forged and integrity and ability came to replace racial distrust in local decision making.

By 1973, she was elected president of EAA, with the backing and full confidence of the majority of members. By then, she had also earned a graduate degree at George Washington University. In the years since she had come to Northern Virginia, she had become active in the Virginia Education Association (VEA), speaking out against the demotion of black teachers to non-teaching positions, as well as about issues regarding compensation and conditions of practice. Believing her views demanded more attention and corrective action in the state, in 1967 she had decided to campaign for a seat on the VEA Board, running against a formidable opponent. She had become irate when, after complying with all the required campaign procedures, she found her biography and campaign statement deliberately left off the ballot. With only her name on the ballot, she lost her bid for the Board. "I felt cheated, and I protested," she said, but VEA officials refused to consider another election as a remedy. Irritated by the violation, she challenged the election; it was the first time in the history of the VEA that such a challenge had been brought. Taking her case all the way to the VEA convention, she went to the floor of the assembly to explain her protest. Her appeal was visibly sincere and compelling, and though the delegates did not vote to place her on the Board, they refused to seat her opponent who had won more votes in the suspect election. Several years later, in 1971, she did win a seat on the VEA Board in a "fair" election, and in 1976, when she had become president of VEA, "many members came up to me and told me the reason they voted for me was because of the stand I took in 1967, and their belief that I would stand up and fight for them."[28]

Over 40 years later, Mary spoke about how that challenge had branded her as a fighter who would stand for principle at all costs:

> "I was nervous and my knees were shaking, but I had to give my rationale as to why I was challenging the election, and though I knew my cause was justified, I thought I was going to lose. After my speech to the delegates, I went outside and got down on the floor and covered by head…I then heard a roar, and members came rushing out of the convention floor saying, 'Mary you won, Mary you won, your opponent was unseated.'"[29]

That single act of courage had lessons that remained with Mary and reminded her of the adage so often repeated by her mother and her teachers to stand up for what she believed, and to let no one define her boundaries. Even when she made a decision to run for the presidency of VEA, she was criticized by many black members for not being ready, not having paid sufficient dues, and not deferring to a black man running first. By that time, Mary had attended NEA Representative Assemblies—she went to her first in 1968 as a substitute—and had been active in the Virginia Black Caucus; she had also served as a local president, as a state board member, and as a member of several committees. "I felt I was ready and ignored those who felt otherwise," she said, "but when they called to tell me I had won, I refused to believe it. I thought they were playing a trick on me because their criticisms had been vicious." She hung up the phone in disbelief, but after state association officials had called her principal with the election results, and he confirmed the decision, it all sank in. It was gratifying that her message of unity had prevailed, given that the NEA and ATA affiliates (the Virginia Education Association and the Virginia Teachers Association) had only recently merged.[30]

Mary took a leave of absence from George Washington High to serve as VEA president, from 1976 to 1978, and she was so impressive and engaging in union advocacy and consensus building during her years in office that VEA expressed its satisfaction by changing its constitution and allowing her a second year in office, thus making her its first multiyear president.

When asked what she thought she would most be remembered for as VEA's president, Mary replied, "For inspiring the teachers to believe in themselves and what could be achieved with unity, and for making them believe that students could learn, regardless of their race or economic background."[31] Her former colleagues at VEA and EAA continue to remember her for those very reasons.

In 1975, J. Rupert Picott wrote *A History of the Virginia Teachers Association*, a book that highlighted the significance and contributions of VTA, which by that time no longer existed. Cautiously optimistic about the merger and what impact it might have on the tradition of developing black education leaders in the state, he listed near the last pages of the volume a set of 14 recommendations that would assist VEA in addressing the issues and concerns of former VTA members. He had once served as executive secretary of VTA and as a dual affiliate delegate to NEA's Representative Assembly, and was recognized as a long-time activist for blacks. Sanguine about the prospects of the state merger, but uncertain of its implications for black leadership, he pointed to "one development that augurs well for the future," the election of Mary Hatwood Futrell as the first black president-elect of VEA. A full page photo of Mary was included in the book, and Picott wrote, with barely suspended belief, that she had defeated a white male teacher by almost double his vote count.[32]

By his surprised observation on Mary defeating a white member in a statewide election, J. Rupert Picott unwittingly disclosed a dynamic of progress on race relations unfolding at the local and state association levels of VEA. With increasing frequency, the maturation of outlook and behavior on race was being replicated in other states, as well as at the national level. That same year, John Ryor of Michigan, with the support of large numbers of black members, defeated the black incumbent, James Harris, for the office of NEA President. The sword cut both ways and blacks, too, were demonstrating the capacity to elect officers whose abilities and platforms, and not necessarily race, were considered best for the contested positions.

Returning to the classroom following her successful term of office in VEA, Mary Hatwood Futrell prepared for the next stage, and she was elected to the NEA Board of Directors as a Minority-at-Large representative, a position in which she developed close relationships with NEA Executive Director Terry Herndon, and Sam Ethridge, NEA's only black executive staff member. In June 1977, her personal life had also changed when she married Donald Futrell, an educator and graduate of Hampton University. She remained professionally active in NEA while assuming the new roles of wife and stepmother of twins, Kristopher and Kimberly. While on the Board, she was appointed to chair the Human Relations Commission, whose work was highly valued by Herndon and Ethridge and broadly publicized by NEA.

Both were impressed with Futrell and each took a personal interest in her Association growth. "I learned a lot from all of those who had been involved at the national level before I arrived. Sam, Gene Dryer, Ester Wilfong, Leon Felix, and others made me understand what the issues were, and made sure I knew what was going on. Black staff and leadership worked together, looked out for each other, and shared respect. Among ourselves we had no tensions, and there was no distrust," she said, in describing the NEA black network she met as she emerged on the national scene.[33]

The Minority-at-Large Board position had been created as part of NEA's minority guarantees to assure that the Board would have adequate numbers of minority members. After serving two years in that capacity, in 1980 Futrell ran for Secretary-Treasurer, the third highest elective office in the Association. Significant, but not exclusive, among her organizational concerns during that period was maintaining the leadership training programs for minorities and women, because she believed NEA was a stronger association when its leadership and programs reflected all of its members. She believed that she had learned much about NEA's history and personalities when she attended the annual meetings of past NEA and ATA presidents and personally met the earlier generation of leaders. For the first few years after the 1966 merger, those meetings did not include former ATA presidents, until Don Morrison became NEA president in 1971 and insisted they be invited to the gatherings.[34] Morrison's decision was important because it linked the then current NEA leadership to the past leaders and legacy of ATA, and the accumulated wisdom and insights of those former presidents. The sharing of their experiences and information proved immeasurably valuable. It was a moment in time that can never again be repeated—the old and new, segregated and integrated, past and future. Because of age, the numbers of those past ATA leaders were slowly dwindling until there would soon be none.

Once again, Futrell faced a white male opponent who waged an aggressive campaign with a strategy claiming that she was unsuited for the position of Secretary-Treasurer, was divisive and too political, and would advance an agenda that would only address ethnic minorities. That style of politics had not won in Virginia when she had run for state president, and it would not win at NEA. The 1980 Representative Assembly in Los Angeles was full of progressive delegates who decided she was the superior candidate.

Three years later, in 1983, when she chose to run for the presidency of NEA, her popularity had risen to such an extent that she ran unopposed. At that time, during an era in which critics often pointed to teachers as impediments to improving education standards in the country, NEA needed a strong leader to provide direction for the organization and establish it as a creditable entity in the education reform movement. Union laws, some argued, provided protection for poorly performing teachers, making it difficult for school boards and administrators to fire them, a view that found traction with disgruntled parents and those adverse to unionized school personnel.

Although collective bargaining may not previously have been Futrell's forte, according to NEA's general counsel Bob Chanin, she knew that it was a vital asset in NEA's arsenal. "It was not her strongest suit," Chanin said, "but she listened and learned until she became comfortable. With Keith Geiger as the vice president—who was strong on collective bargaining—they were a great team."[35] In facing union critics, Futrell earned a reputation for the frankness of her statements in defense of teachers who would not be the scapegoats for declining education standards. "Teachers are easy prey," she told *The New York Times*, "we're easy people to blame. If we should be blamed for anything, though, it should be for not standing up to protest all the burdens that society puts on us."[36]

The defense of the teaching profession became the overarching theme of Futrell's presidency. The national conversation on educational reform had been escalating with the challenges placed on school systems by the social revolution that had begun with *Brown v. Board of Education*. That decision of the U.S. Supreme Court had caused mayhem when blacks entered historically segregated schools in search of stable learning environments and better education, only to create chaos by their mere physical presence and to cause "white flight" to the suburbs and too often to private schools. When busing had been mandated as a remedy for integrating blacks in schools located outside of their neighborhoods, the flight continued. The result was that black and other economically disadvantaged students had found themselves in school districts where diminished property taxes, political upheaval, and deteriorating conditions led to a general de-emphasis on teaching and learning. In those districts the callous practices employed in keeping the schools open and staffed superseded concerns for providing quality education.

Following *Brown*, not only teacher unions, but also many groups with special issues, including the disabled, students with limited English proficiency (LEP), ethnic minorities, women, and, to a lesser extent, gay, lesbian, bisexual and transgendered people (GLBT), began to demand fair treatment in schools. With collective bargaining and strikes, teachers exercised political muscle, and representatives of the profession began to be recognized— often reluctantly—as legitimate stakeholders, equal to administrators, policymakers, school boards, and elected officials. Still, public education for disadvantaged students had deteriorated rapidly from the late '60s and early '70s on.

The public debate on education for disadvantaged minorities had caught fire in 1966 when James S. Coleman released a study reporting that socio-economic status was the primary determinant of academic achievement. In his book *Inequality*, Christopher Jencks reaffirmed Coleman's findings by stating that academic achievement was inherent in student characteristics. Both discounted the effect of schools, teachers, and resources on learning.[37] In language better understood outside of ivory towers, their message was that all children could not learn, but that some would likely learn pending changes in their socio-economic status and, possibly in settings removed from their racial heritage. Neither argument was conscionable to Mary, because not only did she dismiss such studies as politically convenient at best and racist at worst; to the contrary, she was her own best example, and none of it made any sense to her. It was the mother-wit learned from Josephine and the knowledge gleaned from her educational and professional experiences that prepared her to enter the discussion with confidence.

The conversation on educational reform, which had begun in the late '60s in academic think-tanks, in education advocacy organizations, on school boards, and among community and social activists, had, by 1983—Futrell's first year in office—become part of the national dialogue. That year the National Commission on Excellence in Education issued a study, entitled *A Nation at Risk*, that warned of "a rising tide of mediocrity in public education." The report, issued by Secretary of Education Terrence Bell, shook the nation and galvanized the demand for the reformation of education in America. The report stated, "Our nation is at risk….If an unfriendly foreign power had attempted to impose on America the mediocre education performance that exists today, we might well have viewed it as an act of war."[38] Ronald Reagan adopted the report as his own.

Within weeks after Futrell became NEA's President, Reagan spoke at the AFT's national convention and blasted NEA for encouraging multiculturalism and conflict resolution in school curriculums, and he announced his approval of the findings of *A Nation at Risk*. Later, he pointed to those aspects of the report that called for more rigorous teacher accountability.[39] Neither Futrell nor NEA found much to admire in Reagan's education initiatives, proposals, and programs. It was Futrell's habit to rise above political partisanship in defense of quality education. Although NEA had supported Democrats in both elections, Futrell's decisions and judgments were based on sound educational philosophy and effective programs, not on personalities or partisan politics. In 1989, when George H. W. Bush succeeded Reagan and appointed Lauro Cavazos as Secretary of Education, she was quick to acknowledge that she and Cavazos were in agreement on many aspects of school improvement issues—encouraging more minorities to enter the teaching profession, fighting drug abuse among students, and sharing the effective school movement's credo, "All children can learn." She was always balanced enough in her approach to salute a good idea put forth by the opposition, and she also saw promise in Cavazos' successor, Lamar Alexander.[40]

In press interviews following the issue of *A Nation at Risk*, Futrell conceded that some teachers —perhaps as many as 10 percent—were not doing their jobs and noted that underperformers were common to many fields and every profession, "even at the White House." Mary Hatwood Futrell was one of America's premier union proponents, and Reagan was notoriously anti-union, as he demonstrated when he fired all the members of the air traffic controllers' union in reprisal for their going out on strike to improve working conditions that would guarantee greater safety for air travelers. With that action Reagan had drawn a line in the sand, and Futrell would hold her own in defending NEA against the criticism of the President of the United States.

A Nation at Risk was followed by a series of other critical reports on education issued by such organizations as the Committee for Economic Development, the Education Commission of the States, the National Governors' Association, and others. As the leader of NEA, Futrell became highly adept at protecting the Association's image. She became famous as an exponent of implementing solutions, an avoider of instinctive reactions to criticism of teachers, and an expert in crafting the Association's message that teachers would and should be accountable, but only within a framework of fair and balanced assessment and professional respect.

Education is a broad field of study, larger than most, and Futrell—though competitive with the best—had no pretensions to omnipotence. During the period of reform reports, Sharon Robinson, a talented staffer, was director of NEA's Department of Instruction and Professional Development. Futrell was savvy enough to recognize Robinson's genius and smart enough to use it. Sharon assisted Mary in weighing NEA's interests against the reform reports and became one of NEA's most visible spokespersons on the reform issue. A characteristic of Mary's shrewdness was her capacity to acknowledge the strengths and abilities of others and to share the stage with them. She consulted with staff on most crucial issues before interviews and major presentations. "I would not have been effective" she said, "had I not utilized the skills and knowledge of our great staff—Sharon, Nelson Canton, Chuck Williams, Gary Watts, Bob Chanin, and Carl Luty deserve some credit for my success."[41]

She was invited to serve on a 14-member task force of the Carnegie Forum on Education and the Economy, which issued in 1986 a report on the teaching profession. It called for higher compensation and a revamping of the certification process. Reaction to the report was strong and mixed, with most observers applauding the objective of attracting and maintaining the best teachers, while others, such as U.S. Secretary of Education William Bennett, favored the call for higher certification standards, more liberal arts training and higher pay for outstanding teachers, though he cautioned against the task force's exclusion of principals from the report. Futrell agreed with the general goals but was skeptical about the report's suggestion of a differentiated pay system, fearing it would become a merit pay or career ladder plan, both long viewed as "one-dimensional responses to multi-dimensional problems." She approved of the report, however, and was pleased with its teacher-centered thrust. Ezra Bowen of *Time* magazine noted that "experts like Futrell may be the key to the Carnegie program's success or failure. . . . Teachers are central to the study's implementation, they will also determine whether the program will be accepted or rejected." Bennett conceded Futrell's influence. "If NEA decides to play," he said, "there's a game. If not, forget it."[42] Ultimately, her doubts prevailed, and NEA prevented any wide-scale implementation of merit pay as outlined in the report.

Mary Hatwood Futrell's passion, energy, courage, and resonating voice of advocacy, caused the members to re-elect her for a second term in 1985, and following that, the rank and file approved her serving for an unprecedented third term. Thus, she became the only person to have had term extensions as both a state and an NEA president. At the Association level, this was, in large part, an expression of appreciation for her leadership in protecting member interests, and for positioning NEA as a preeminent force in the education reform movement. The ancient adage, "All roads lead to Rome," is applicable in a way to Futrell's position in the education scene of the late 20th century. Under Mary's helm, conventional wisdom had it that all roads traveling to education reform must pass through NEA, where she operated the toll booth.

A Nation at Risk not only forced the response from the Carnegie Commission, but it also pressed NEA and AFT to address student achievement issues with the same zeal both had brought to basic collective bargaining. With increased public and political pressure for teacher accountability, the unions had to reconsider the usefulness of traditional industrial models of unionism, which had established quality product control mechanisms as part of the responsibility of management. NEA had long been involved with issues of professional development, though the teacher revolution of the 1960s, collective bargaining, and con-con had balanced unionism and professionalism as primary Association values. The education reform movement revived professionalism and NEA began to place more of its resources and emphasis on student achievement and teacher quality issues. Futrell consequently became quite versatile in explaining to the public the complexities of teaching and schooling, defending teachers against unwarranted attacks and criticisms, and establishing collaborative relationships with other education stakeholders. More than any other single personality in the Association, she created space for NEA to become less instinctively defensive and more proactive on education reform. Collective bargaining had been essential to NEA survival in the 1960s, as noted by Don Cameron, former NEA executive director, and by the 1980s, Futrell had come to accept that NEA's well-being was dependent upon its embracing and shaping the contours of education reform.[43] The concept of the "new unionism" which gained wide currency in the mid-1990s with NEA President Bob Chase, could trace its origins to Futrell in the 1980s.

In 1984, *NEA Today* reported that a new state law passed "at the urging of Governor Bill Clinton and his wife, Hillary, would require [the] Arkansas" teaching force to be tested for reading, writing, and math skills, and that anyone who did not pass, faced loss of certification. The debut of this law made Arkansas the first state to mandate such a test for practicing teachers, though Houston, Texas—a school district—had already begun testing in-service teachers a year earlier. Only a year after *A Nation at Risk* was issued, the Arkansas legislation was a measure some state politicians calculated to be synchronized with public opinion on school performance and stiffer teacher standards. The political miscalculation backfired. The Arkansas Education Association (AEA) revolted in protest against the law which required practicing teachers to pass tests as the sole determining condition of employment, a process which could not find a parallel in any other profession.[44]

Futrell joined the AEA chorus of opposition, appointing a special investigative team of the Executive Committee to work with AEA to evaluate the effects of the teacher testing law. Odetta Fujimori led the team and summarized the group's findings that the test "was a formula for demoralization" and was "totally contrary to what a fair evaluation system would do." Futrell went on the offensive, lambasting the test and spearheading AEA's counter-offensives which included a statewide information campaign arguing that teacher competency could be assessed and, for those deemed inadequate, improvement procedures could be implemented in a much more acceptable manner. The test was a calamity, resulting in terminations disproportionately affecting minorities, and ultimately public pressure stirred by vigorous AEA efforts caused the law to be repealed. NEA and AEA had won a single battle in Arkansas, but the war over teacher accountability and education reform raged throughout the nation.[45] Along the way, Futrell concluded that teacher credibility would be dependent on NEA embracing those elements of reform that called for improved teacher quality but added the caveat that teacher professionalism would involve teachers as the primary arbiters of change.

The Carnegie Commission's 140-page report, *A Nation Prepared: Teachers for the Twenty-First Century*, was intended to be a direct response to *A Nation at Risk*, and the two reports were decidedly different. Carnegie's sought to place resources in the hands of educators and their constituent groups, and the Excellence Commission's appeared comfortable with the "civilian control" arrangements which traditionally characterized the governance of schools. Carnegie recommended a shift of power and emphasis, enabling teachers to be key decision-makers and central figures in the shaping of school improvement. The teacher revolution that began in the 1960s, had now matured sufficiently to redefine the nature of schooling itself and to package and market it as essential to education reform. *Education Week* wrote:

> "In 1986, a landmark report issued by a task force of the
> Carnegie Corporation of New York called for radical changes
> in teaching to make it a true profession. The authors
> envisioned a different kind of teacher—flexible, up-to-date,
> and able to lead children into deeper learning. The next
> step was for teachers to be mentors and coaches rather than
> dispensers of facts. Students would take more responsibility
> for their own education, and teachers would collaborate with
> them in a search for knowledge and understanding. The
> school structure would change so that teachers would be
> deeply involved in decision making: within broad curricular
> frameworks, teachers would decide how best to meet their
> goals. They would participate in the development of new
> performance-based assessments. They would be empowered
> to make decisions that affect instruction, budget, personnel,
> and scheduling... at the same time, though, the teachers would
> be much better educated and would be eased into their jobs
> with help from experienced mentors."[46]

A stamp of general public approval followed the report whose credibility was enhanced because of Carnegie's stellar historical background in education reform and the diverse range of experience, talent, and ethnicity on its 14-member task force. Some of the recommendations such as the elimination of the undergraduate degree in education failed to gain traction; but the proposal for the establishment of a private, non-governmental National Board for Professional Teaching Standards (NBPTS), became the key recommendation. It called for a board operated by teachers, which would certify excellent teachers who passed a teacher-administered evaluation and review process, which would lead to higher compensation.

The proposal for an NBPTS posed a challenge for Futrell and it was, perhaps, the stiffest test of her leadership. Since the recommendation was issued in May on the eve of NEA's Representative Assembly, she faced an Executive Committee, Board of Directors, and RA delegates philosophically opposed to the concept of a National Board process, viewing it as a way to establish merit pay. Futrell also knew that AFT and other education stakeholders supported the tilt of public opinion toward NBPTS, and that NEA's image as a progressive organization would be tarnished if it flatly opposed. At the RA in early July she devoted her entire speech to NBPTS and made a passionate plea to delegates—whom internal polls had shown opposing it by an 80 to 20 percent margin—to endorse it. Arguably, it was her finest performance as NEA president, and one that Keith Geiger, NEA vice president, saw as an important moment in Association history.[47]

Futrell's shrewdness at that moment foreshadowed her entire philosophy on and approach to education reform. Teachers were closer to the learning process than politicians and policymakers, and, therefore, had to become leaders in proposing, approving, and responding to education reform initiatives. The power of teachers to control their own destinies had been her message since she had become a leader in the local education association of Alexandria. For Futrell it was as applicable and relevant on the national as it had been on the local level. On that philosophy she wrote:

> "Along with thousands of my teaching colleagues throughout the United States, I have watched, listened, and responded to the avalanche of education reform reports that have emerged during the 1980's...I am not worried about a lack of interest in the improvement of public education....I am not worried by the fact that some of the reports have blamed teachers (and their organizations) for the shortcomings of the public schools. Indeed, they have given us some positive proposals to enhance teacher education, induction, and practice. What does concern me is the absence within the education community itself...of any real consensus on some professional issues and objectives that are essential to education reform. I am concerned that unless educators themselves assume the right and responsibility for establishing high, meaningful standards for preparation, entry, and practice, the governance of our profession will remain the province of legislators, bureaucrats, and other non-educators."[48]

The education reform movement and the Association's constitutional change of the 1970s which created longer presidential terms and the possibility of reelection, combined to increase Futrell's visibility and stature in NEA, the larger education world, and the nation. One of her predecessors, John Ryor, had been enormously popular and had strengthened presidential identity at NEA as a result of the longer terms and the augmented role of the office as defined by con-con. But Ryor, who was charismatic and had photogenic appeal, was not fortunate enough to have had a platform as powerful as the education reform movement to showcase his skills. Largely because of it and the political and media attention it demanded, Futrell's visibility was pronounced and she emerged as one of the leading figures in public education, sharing the limelight with Al Shanker. Wayne Urban, a scholar on NEA, argues that her persona as a black female and the Association's successful and publicized desegregation of the formerly segregated affiliates established NEA in the public forum as a leader in the movement for equity in American education and American society.[49] The fact that she was the fourth minority president in 16 years, the minority guarantees of con-con, and the commitment to affirmative action at the national office also promoted NEA beyond AFT as the stronger organization in supporting the interests of minorities.

NEA's prominence as an organization advocating equity, civil rights, and social justice grew under Futrell, while AFT became noticeably more conservative on those issues. In the 1970s when NEA had supported affirmative action in the Bakke case, AFT had supported the plaintiff who claimed he was denied admission to the University of California Medical School in favor of less qualified minority applicants. On bilingual education, NEA sided with those who supported it because of its potential for improving academic achievement and self-esteem for language minorities. AFT saw it as contributing to the separation of cultural and ethnic groups and not proven to promote learning. On policies designed to protect women's interests in schools and society, NEA had become a leading advocate, yet AFT was selective on women's issues and on special education initiatives. NEA consistently called for mainstreaming those students into regular classes while AFT cautioned against the effect of such policies on the academic achievement of regular students. But on no single issue did NEA distance itself farther from AFT than on its minority guarantees, which AFT thought represented "reverse discrimination." Shanker felt such policies were inconsistent with a colorblind society. Futrell, on the other hand, was less sanguine about minority progress on an unlevel playing field and uncomfortable with the notion that it could correct itself without assistance.[50]

All of these differences came to define the two organizations, NEA being much more willing and flexible in considering alternatives to status quo arrangements without compromising the integrity of unionism, and AFT more conservative and traditional in its approach to trade union principles of seniority rights, which often clashed with policies advancing minority interests.[51] Politically, AFT's positions were more congruent with the views and policies of Ronald Reagan's administration, than those of NEA. The visibility of Futrell—a female and black president—and the policies of NEA on minority issues, made her and the Association popular with minority and disadvantaged populations. Thus, when Reagan criticized the policies of NEA, the response came from Futrell who became an even more formidable spokesperson and national personality.

When Reagan spoke at the AFT's national convention in the summer of 1983, charging that NEA's new curriculum plans for students amounted to "brainwashing" because it included multiculturalism and conflict resolution, Futrell responded that Reagan's bitterness toward NEA was politically motivated because NEA had not endorsed his presidential campaign or supported his anti-union action in 1981, when he fired all members of a national union of striking air traffic controllers.[52] NEA had also opposed his plans to abolish the U.S. Department of Education and his notion about merit pay for teachers, and she challenged the appropriateness of his reforms for standards for accountability and the operation of schools based on a business or industrial model, rather than union negotiated contracts with school districts. Futrell flexed the muscle of NEA, vowing to fight any Republican cut-backs to education, and proposals which undermined teacher unionism. "If we sit back and do nothing," she said, "they will push us around.

Teachers are no longer going to be passive little old ladies who accept what is handed to them."[53]

Reagan's criticisms of public education were unrelenting, and for the media Futrell was equal to the task with the frankness of her responses, and for the metaphors and satirical tone of her extemporaneous sound bites. In February of 1984, Reagan gave a speech before the National Association of Secondary School Principals about the virtues of "good old fashioned" discipline, which did not sit well with many educator groups. Futrell was upset with the tone and message of the speech and responded that the "public schools are not blackboard jungles" and orderly schools were not to be achieved by "throwing kids out on the street."[54] In 1987, she expressed disappointment with cut-backs in education funding. Noting that after Presidents Eisenhower, Kennedy, Nixon, Ford, and Carter all agreed on the importance of education to the nation's future, Reagan had slashed the federal education budget by $5.4 billion. "For the seventh time in seven years," she said, "this President seeks to gut public education." She concluded that Reagan's cuts, unlike those of his predecessors, were tantamount to "skydiving lessons" instead of lessons which "lift us towards the lofty ideas" of quality education for all the people.[55] Futrell also became highly skilled at analyzing and explaining to the public the impact of the federal cuts, and the mathematics and logic of programs the main intention of which was political posturing. For example, that same year Congress conceded the urgency in the need to educate homeless children by passing the Stewart B. McKinney Homeless Assistance Act and appropriating five million dollars to fund it. In her column in *NEA Today*, Futrell revealed the legislation for its cruelty when she wrote that if each of the seven hundred thousand homeless children in America was given an equal share of those funds, each portion would be about a $7.14 slice of "the five million dollar pie."[56] Throughout Reagan's term, Futrell took exception to his policies which "treated education like a doormat," and being the teacher, she gave him failing grades for his determination to dismantle the Department of Education, for supporting tuition tax credits, and for the massive cuts he proposed for the federal education budget.[57]

Reagan's policies on education proved to be an anathema to NEA, but in November of 1983, Futrell was thrilled when he signed into law a bill making Martin Luther King, Jr.'s birthday the nation's tenth official holiday. NEA, which had contributed annually to the King Center for Non-Violent Social Change, had been actively seeking a holiday in honor of King since 1969. In fact, though the celebration was to begin only in 1986, NEA and many of its affiliates had long been celebrating his birthday and furnishing teachers with suggestions and plans for activities to help students better appreciate his achievements. King had been an inspiration for Futrell since he visited Virginia State College when she was a student, and she was overwhelmed with delight with the passage of the bill by wide margins in both the U.S. Senate and House of Representatives. She spoke solemnly when she said, "It was symbolic of Americans' continued belief in the principles Dr. King taught—and proof of the progress we have made as a nation toward the dream he envisioned."[58] The ability to sense the importance of something good, and proceed to make it even better was a Midas touch that Futrell came to perfect. Within NEA change is constant and inevitable, and she was careful that the changes she initiated resulted in improvement, rather than change for the mere sake of change. Futrell suggested streamlining the HCR Awards Dinner which made it an even more attractive annual event. The idea of each member contributing one dollar to NEA's National Foundation for the Improvement of Education provided an untapped source of revenue for NFIE to provide grants to teachers to implement innovative and promising proposals for pedagogy and school improvement. In the mid-1980s an Executive Committee member recommended that NEA conduct a comprehensive study on public education and Hispanics that would offer recommendations for all education stakeholders to bring about improvement. Futrell brought the proposal to the attention of Chuck Williams, Director of Human and Civil Rights, requesting that research be initiated with the object of developing a design for such a study, with plans for its implementation and the distribution of data gathered through it. Williams thought the idea was a good one, but felt it would be enhanced if a comparable study were also done for blacks. Futrell agreed and countered with the suggestion that a study be done for each ethnic minority group, including Asians and

Pacific Islanders and American Indians and Alaska Natives.[59] Politically, it was a stroke of genius, and the ethnic minority constituent groups and the Minority Affairs Committee collaborated with NEA staff in 1988 to produce *And Justice for All*, a compendium of reports unprecedented in scope and comprehensiveness. *And Justice for All* became a core reference on education and ethnic minorities, often cited in research literature. "It was right before our eyes," said Williams, "but until Mary saw the value of the whole, we had not grasped the importance of doing each group and releasing the reports at once."[60] Up to that time, no other education advocacy organization had attempted anything as comprehensive as *And Justice for All*, and it placed NEA on center stage with ethnic minority advocacy and professional groups, organizations, and institutions.

Futrell's rescue and revival of the semi-dormant and voluntary National Council for Accreditation of Teacher Education (NCATE), may have been her best effort in transforming the old to the new. Founded in 1954, NCATE was created through a joint relationship of NEA, the National School Boards Association (NSBA), the American Association of Colleges for Teacher Education (AACTE), the Council of Chief State School Officers (CCSSO), and the National Association of the State Directors of Teacher Education and Certification (NASDTEC). NCATE's purpose was to improve teacher education by developing standards, policies, and procedures for accrediting teacher education programs. By 1974, NEA had become a more dominant partner, and a larger percentage of teachers were constitutionally authorized to be on its governing council. By 1979, 85 percent of institutions preparing teachers were accredited by NCATE. Futrell saw that NEA was well positioned to leverage influence in NCATE, and contributed to making it an active agent of the education reform movement by, among other changes, upgrading its standards for student admission to teacher education programs and developing more rigorous examinations prior to graduating. The buy-in from teacher education institutions and state departments of education was tremendous, and NEA launched an initiative requiring all teacher preparation programs to obtain NCATE certification. Soon accreditation became mandatory so that nearly every state had a partnership with this accrediting organization, and in over half of the states NCATE had power to determine which teacher training programs obtained approval for teacher certification. This process began with Futrell's determination that teachers play a greater role in teacher professionalism.[61]

Futrell's monthly column in *NEA Today* is an excellent index for tracking the issues of the education reform movement, and those that she felt merited the attention and action of NEA members. The issues she selected were also written in a language and style of advocacy that never veered from the basic principle that educators could not be neglected in the search for solutions. The articles can be grouped into seven categories of commentary: the drop-out rate, school resources, computers for schools, childcare programs, expansion of Head Start, drug prevention programs in schools, funds for college loans, and the policies of Ronald Reagan.

In her first column, titled "Promises to Keep," which appeared in October of 1983, she skillfully merged race, gender, and the teaching profession to personalize her commitment to the Association.

> "...I made a promise—to all of you, but also to myself. I would, I pledged, no longer allow the exploitation and denigration of our nation's most dedicated servants—our public school employees. As a black child, I learned early the meaning of the words *exploitation* and *denigration*. As a woman, I learned those meanings again. And as a public school teacher, I learned them once more...I made a second promise—we will tolerate no longer the federal government's cruel abandonment of our nation's children. We care too much. Our professional lives are the expression of that caring. Quality education is every child's right. And that right is not negotiable."[62]

On dropouts Futrell was brave enough to write "only when we have the courage to call them push-outs will we begin to solve their problem, which is our problem." Dropouts troubled Futrell, and she hastened to point out that linguistic minorities and poor children were the most likely victims, urging

NEA members to rescue the classroom exiles by demanding relief for push-outs and "in-school discrimination."[63]

The urban education issues that Helen Bain and others transformed into a movement at NEA in the early 1960s in the creation of NCUEA, and continued through Braulio Alonso, Libby Koontz, and James Harris during their presidential terms, also appeared in her column. The flight of the affluent from the large cities "left behind a trapped people—the poor, the destitute, the desperate," she wrote in making the case that urban school districts suffered far more than their share of Reagan's federal budget slash. She also blamed those cuts for handicapping Head Start, the federal preschool program for poor children, and child care for young and poor families. Citing the facts, Futrell said:

> "Six out of 10 American women with children under the age of six are employed outside the home. Over half the mothers with children less than a year old are in the labor force. Two out of every three working women are either their families' sole providers or married to men who earn less than $15,000 a year. One-fifth of mothers of pre-school children…are not working because they cannot find good, affordable child care; lack of child care is the major reason women on welfare don't have jobs…and last but not least, every dollar invested in pre-school programs saves nearly $5 in later costs for special and remedial education."[64]

One theme reigned throughout most of the articles in her column and it was that education reform required adequate funding, and that the involvement of teachers as equal partners and lead collaborators could not be undervalued and was crucial to its success. The term "teachers" rather than school personnel was the operative language of the education reform reports and dialogue, but near the end of her term, Futrell could not ignore that NEA's "ESP membership had increased from 10,000 to 120,000 members in eight years," or the roles educational support professionals played in public education. From that point forward she wrote and talked about the overall importance of bus drivers, cafeteria workers, custodians, teacher aids, counselors, secretaries, and nurses in public schools. "You have reminded us all," she told education support professionals, "that education is not confined to the classroom, that it is at best, a school-wide endeavor."[65]

Futrell's last column was given the same title, "Promises to Keep." In that farewell article, she spoke of the world as a global village and challenged members not to be content with an education framework that was not "intertwined with the destiny of the human family." Referring to a recent plan of the United Nation's Educational, Scientific, and Cultural Organization (UNESCO) that aimed to bring about a massive reduction in worldwide illiteracy, she urged NEA members to join the initiatives.

> "...As we move forward we cannot forget our responsibility
> to our neighbors in the global community. For we seek, not
> merely a more democratic nation, but a more democratic
> world. We seek the 'universalization' of the ideals that have
> guided our Association for 132 years: quality education for all,
> human rights for all, economic justice for all."[66]

Over a quarter of a century after becoming President of NEA, Futrell is still fondly remembered when appearing at various NEA venues. On being introduced at the annual Human and Civil Rights Awards Dinner and whenever she speaks from the floor of the Representative Assembly, she receives a thunderous round of applause. Many give her acclaim in appreciation for the leadership she provided the Association and out of respect for her continuing stature in the education community. Others cheer and applaud because of positive personal experiences shared with her. And, then, some who have joined NEA since she was president stand and applaud her out of respect for her legacy. As Futrell moves through NEA crowds and audiences, shaking hands, signing autographs, having her picture taken, and reminiscing with friends, she never loses the common touch and remains oblivious to the celebrity of it all. Keith Geiger affectionately refers to her as the "Queen," and says that at every RA someone will invariably approach him and ask, "Where is the Queen?"[67]

Joe Reed, E. B. Palmer, Jackie Gilmore, former Black Caucus chairperson, and others make note of her amazing memory and ability to resume a conversation at the precise point where it was months and even years earlier. "She will ask about your children, your family, and personal incidents in your life," said Gilmore, "and never once will you ever doubt her sincerity." The "folksy" quality of her personality, claim Bob Muñoz and Eleanor Coleman, both active members during her presidency, humanized the aura of her unsolicited celebrity and made her authentic and approachable.[68]

The magic of Futrell was at once obvious and elusive, because of the complex layers of its simplicity. Her only predictable qualities were her confidence in school personnel to make responsible decisions on school policies, and her unwillingness to retreat from any position in which she deeply believed, even when risks were involved. Futrell was a black female and fiercely proud of her heritage, but her appeal was universal for reasons above race or gender. She was warm and friendly, but firm, and no-nonsense when attending to Association business. She politely demanded much from governance and members, and expected excellence from staff, though she understood human frailties and was not reserved in pointing out her own. Eugene Dryer recalled how Futrell "had the ability to chuckle at herself when she made a mistake on stage, and the audience loved it."[69] It made her human, someone that everyone could relate to, and the President of NEA became the girl next door. Marnell Moorman, former president of the Kentucky Education Association once said, "Mary could introduce an idea, ask for your support, and motivate you to promote it with a passion as if it were your very own creation."[70]

Through her life experiences, character, moral fiber, and compassion for those disadvantaged by class, race, and other distinctions, Futrell cultivated a unique sense of what members felt, thought, believed, wanted, and needed. For many older Association members, she was all that Lauri Wynn might have been, though a more restrained and refined version. And for Lauri, Futrell was the minority to whom was handed the baton for the next generation. From the sidelines Lauri applauded the Association's continuing progress toward inclusion at all levels.[71]

Linda Pondexter-Chesterfield, a member of the NEA Board and Executive Committee during Futrell's presidency, and later president of the Arkansas Education Association, provides an eloquent and fitting tribute to her leadership:

"When I first saw Mary Hatwood, she was the President of the Virginia Education Association. An issue was being hotly debated on the floor, and Mary was about to speak to the issue. Sid Johnson [of AEA] turned to me and said, 'You just wait until Mary speaks; the whole issue is going to be decided.' And, it was.

"I'm not sure when I went from inexperienced delegate to being Mary's friend, but being her friend has allowed me to grow as a person and as a leader in this Association.

"Mary did not just talk about service to the members; she showed that service in everything she did. If you were invited to Mary's room, she served you coffee. If you went to the office of the President, Mary didn't sit behind the desk and talk at you, she came from behind the desk and talked to you. Mary did not ride first-class on airplanes, although she could have. She said she never wanted the members to think that she did not value their hard work and the dollars that they spent on their membership. Mary always carried her own bags.

"During NEA Board meetings, Mary always had an agenda that would not only inform you about education, but she had an agenda that would change education. She challenged us to give an extra dollar to fund the National Foundation for the Improvement of Education. She challenged us to be a part of the Martin Luther King, Jr. Center for Non-Violent Change. She led the fight to make the ethnic minority chairpersons members of the NEA Board of Directors so that a board that sometimes had to depend on special elections to have minority representation would have a continuing minority presence. She led the fight to try to get the Equal Rights Amendment passed, and she challenged us to join the fight....

"There were also the fun times when we saw Mary dance at our Back-to-Work dance which marked the beginning of the fall board agenda. It allowed us to get to know each other socially as well as politically. She danced at our prom which marked the end of our board season in May....

"Mary created the first *And Justice for All* study. She sent Executive Committee members to barrios, reservations, ghettoes, urban and rural America, to see what we needed to provide to our members to help them help our children. It was not done on the cheap, but it was done with the idea in mind that the Association could and should make a difference in the lives of children.

"She is a special woman, she is a brilliant leader, she is a better friend of public education."[72]

Mary Hatwood Futrell was such an important and popular president that the Board of Directors extended the length of her term in office, as had the Virginia Education Association. When J. Rupert Picott, stalwart of the Virginia Teachers Association wrote about her rapid rise in the newly integrated VEA, he spoke of her as "one development that augurs well for the future." At that time in the mid-1070s, he was cautiously optimistic about her prospects for leadership in a largely white state association. As he moved toward retirement following a stellar career with the VTA and NEA, he spoke of Mary as the hope for the future, and conceded that her ability to lead white and black teachers would be "a matter for future judgment." Slightly more than a decade later, he could hardly have comprehended how much this single person had transformed the culture and politics of NEA. Not only did she redefine Association presidential identity, but she also led the movement which empowered teachers to responsibly take charge of their professional destinies, while increasing union membership from 1.6 million to just under 2 million. The visibility of teachers in education reform under her watch was unprecedented. More importantly, she brought a new brand of commitment and passion to the corridors of NEA.

Of her presidency, NEA general counsel Bob Chanin said, "Of all the presidents, none believed more sincerely in the mission of NEA. When a tear came to her eye it was real, she really cared—as did the others—but her caring was special."[73]

After leaving NEA, Futrell remained active in Education International and served on the boards of a number of national organizations dealing with education. She was the recipient of over a dozen honorary degrees. While completing her doctorate at George Washington University, she was associate director of the Center for the Study of Education and National Development. Since 1995, she has served as dean of the Graduate School of Education and Human Development at the institution; and she continues to attend NEA's annual Representative Assembly and the Human and Civil Rights Awards Dinner, at which an award has been named in her honor.

Timing is essential for greatness and Futrell's presidency coincided with the education reform movement, which brought unprecedented attention to the head of the nation's largest combined labor union and professional organization. She was the major contributor to the creation of NEA's role in that movement. If luck is defined as the precise point where preparation meets opportunity, then Mary Hatwood Futrell may be the luckiest President the National Education Association has ever had. Most say she was the best and her record provides compelling evidence to confirm that judgment.

Reginald (Reg) Weaver

2002-2008

Reginald (Reg) Weaver
2002-2008

No Child Left Behind,
Great Public Schools, and Team NEA

No two campaigns or elections for the presidency of the National Education Association have been the same. Each has been different, largely due to the personalities and backgrounds of the candidates, and the internal dynamics and politics of the Association, as well as how the campaigns are aligned with the current issues in public education. Reg Weaver's election at the Dallas Representative Assembly (RA) in July of 2002 is notable for two distinct reasons: he was the first black male to become president since NEA's constitution of the early 1970s had been fully implemented, allowing for longer presidential terms and defining the president as the Association's principle spokesperson. And, secondly, it was the first NEA presidential election in which both candidates were black. Thirty-five years had passed since Braulio Alonso had become NEA's first minority president, and perhaps nowhere had the continued growth and progress of NEA on racial inclusion been better demonstrated. Weaver defeated Denise Rockwell-Woods, a black female from California, and the delegates and media paid little attention to the historical nature of the election, nor did the media notice that NEA, the nation's largest combined union and professional organization, had elected its fifth minority president since its 1966 merger with the American Teachers Association (ATA). By comparison, the American Federation of Teacher (AFT) had yet to have a minority member run for its leading elected position.

Much had changed in the politics and culture of NEA since 1966, but the organizational memory of the Association, which had tripled its membership since the 1960s, was such that, after only one generation, few Dallas RA delegates remembered Braulio Alonso, Libby Koontz, or James Harris. "I could hardly believe," said Eleanor Coleman, an Arkansas delegate, "that so many in the Assembly did not know about the merger or those earlier minority presidents."[1] Very quietly, NEA had made a transition from one generation to the next, and a changing of the guard was taking place, with the result that a rapidly shrinking number of members and new leaders had had any personal experience of dual affiliates, the merger, or the pre-Constitutional Convention (con-con) NEA that lacked minority guarantees. Actually, most delegates in Dallas had not been members during the era of the mergers, and many of those who had been active during that period were now inactive or retired. Yet, the NEA of those in attendance in Dallas was unmistakably one that had profited from the merger, the minority guarantees of con-con, NEA's minority leadership training program, the ethnic minority affairs committee, the ethnic minority caucuses, and the policies whose origins sprang from a long tradition of liberal and progressive Association leadership. Over the years, the membership had witnessed hundreds of minorities on the NEA Board of Directors, thousands on local and state boards, and dozens serving on every NEA committee. Several states had minority executive directors and high ranking staff, and scores of minority members had served as state presidents. At the national headquarters, minority staff members were in every department, many of them serving on the executive staff. Even when the reactionary climate of the larger society introduced the concept of reverse discrimination, causing unprecedented litigation on minority employment, promotion, and admission decisions, NEA had never retreated from its affirmative action goals. In short, the phenomenal Association practice of inclusion from top to bottom had been so sweeping that it partially eclipsed the memory of the past and of those whose efforts had brought full integration to the organization. One NEA staff person was staggered when, during a training exercise with minorities, a youthful participant stood and asked in earnest, "Did you mean it when you said the Mississippi Education Association was once segregated?"[2]

From 1989 to 2002, the period between the presidencies of Mary Hatwood Futrell and Reg Weaver, the Association and the nation had made remarkable progress toward diversity and inclusion. Minorities continued to be elected to the Executive Committee and Iona Holloway, a black female from Louisiana, had become the first education support professional (ESP) to serve on it. Weaver himself had been a member of the Executive Committee and had been elected NEA vice-president during that interim period. In the nation during that time, ethnic minority *firsts* continued to diminish as lead news headline material, mainly because of the sheer volume of minority appointments. Some, however, captured more attention than others. The Congressional Asian, Black, and Hispanic Caucuses continued to grow in membership and influence, and NEA developed meaningful collaborations with each. Douglas Wilder had been elected Governor of Virginia. David Dinkins in New York City, Willie Herenton in Memphis, Wellington Webb in Denver, and Emmanuel Clever in Kansas City along with others had been elected mayors. Carol Moseley Braun had become a U.S. Senator from Illinois, Marguerite Barnett had been appointed President of the University of Houston, Clarence Thomas had been confirmed for a position on the U.S. Supreme Court, and Thurgood Marshall had died. Joycelyn Elders had become Surgeon General, Toni Morrison had won the Nobel Prize in literature, the *Bill Cosby Show* and *Oprah* had become two of television's all-time highest-rated programs. Most major cities had hired at least one minority school superintendent, and President Bill Clinton had appointed the largest number of minorities and women ever to Cabinet positions.

During the 1990s, NEA had released a study showing that public school teachers were becoming overwhelmingly white and female, while public school students were becoming increasingly minority. And, shortly before Reg Weaver became president, the Harvard Civil Rights Project had released a study on the re-segregation of American schools.[3] On the eve of his election, NEA needed sustained leadership on student academic achievement; the fight against vouchers and privatization; professionalism issues concerning school personnel; school funding; elevating the

Association's image with the public—particularly minorities; and maintaining its critical role in the education reform movement.

When the NEA presidential vote count was announced in Dallas, Reg Weaver assumed the position for which he was exceptionally well prepared and eminently qualified. He had been a local president, state vice-president and president, Executive Committee member, and NEA vice-president. No previous NEA president had brought more significant elective experience to the position. Ann Davis, a close friend of Weaver and a former Illinois Education Association president, rejoiced over the announcement and saw it as the culmination of his hard and dedicated work to bring greater respect to teachers and other school personnel. She thought his election was made possible through an Association "which had been transformed by the spirit of NEA minority guarantees which filtered down to the state and local levels," that years earlier had infiltrated Danville, Illinois, where he had begun his teaching career.[4] As Reg walked down from the podium, shaking hands with friends and supporters who literally swamped him with congratulations, the soul music of McFadden and Whitehead, "Ain't No Stopping Us Now," blared from the speakers through the Dallas Convention Center. This moment had been more than a quarter century in preparation, a time during which he had refined his advocacy skills, bridled his passions, developed composure as a leader, and mastered Association politics. Supporters danced in the aisles in jubilation at his victory, and the words and music of the song echoed throughout the convention hall.

> *Ain't no stoppin' us now!*
> *We're on the move!*
> *Ain't no stoppin' us now!*
> *We've got the groove!*
>
> *There's been so many things that's held us down.*
> *But now it looks like things are finally coming around.*
> *I know we've got a long, long way to go,*
> *And where we'll end up, I don't know.*
> *But we won't let nothing hold us back,*

We're getting ourselves together,
We're polishing up our act!
If you've ever been held down before,
I know that you refuse to be held down any more!

Don't You Let Nothing, Nothing
Stand in Your Way!
I Want Ya'll to Listen, Listen
To Every Word I Say, Every Word I Say![5]

Those lyrics had particular meaning for Reg *apropos* of his personal and professional journey in overcoming challenges and obstacles in the unionization and empowerment of school personnel, and prophetic for the opportunity of placing his trademark on the efforts of organized educators. Over time, the song would become a motivational vehicle for his Association audiences, and highly effective in energizing and rallying members for Association causes.

For Reg, so much of what culminated that day began in the Danville, Illinois of his childhood and earlier generations of his family, where the sting of prejudice and discrimination were not unfamiliar to the black residents. Looking back to his past, he could reflect on where it had all started. His hometown had produced famous actors Jerry and Dick VanDyke, Donald O'Connor, Gene Hackman, and astronaut Joe Tanner. One black, Bobby Short, had gained celebrity as a sophisticated world-famous singer and supper club entertainer. But no famous son or daughter of Danville had come as far in public education as NEA's new president.

Reginald Weaver was born in Danville, on August 13, 1939, near the end of the Great Depression. His tight-knit family, however, had escaped many of the hardships of the economy by securing blue-collar jobs at General Motors and General Electric, the major employers for blacks in the city of roughly 40,000 population, 10 percent of whom were black. He was the second child of Carl and Mary Alice Weaver. His mother had remarried when he was young and had two other sons, Dewey and Mike Buchanan. The three generations of his family who lived in the neighborhood included his grandfather, the family patriarch, Dewey General Robinson. All of the members of the family were employed, belonged to the same church, and were determined that Mary Alice's children would be the first in the family to attend college. In his early years, Reg, as he became known to his friends, learned that his family's expectations required a level of discipline and respect for schooling that were not always required by other blue-collar parents. Education was the gateway to better opportunities, and the family would not entertain any other alternatives for its children. "We knew how much it meant to our mother and we never questioned it," he recalled. Mary Alice, who did not have college training, had found employment at the "white only" Danville Country Club, at the Laura Lee Fellowship House for Colored People, and at General Electric. Her income contributed to a stable home environment, and in the 1940s and '50s it helped provide the middle class standard she maintained and the positive values and self-esteem she promoted for her children.[6]

Although Reg was a good student from his earliest school days, he was never encouraged or guided by local educators into courses beyond the basic requirements. His mother placed all of her faith in Jackson Elementary School to educate her sons to their greatest potential, but the teachers at that school and the school district did not hold sufficiently high expectations for the large number of black students enrolled there to ensure them an appropriate learning environment. Reg's third and fourth grade classes, for example, had been merged into one, and by the end of the fifth grade, his mother had exhausted her patience. After complaining to the principal, she demanded that Reg be transferred to a school that might better prepare him for college. That transfer, brought about by Mary Alice's sheer determination, changed the trajectory of her son's life.[7]

By the time Reg entered Danville High School, he noticed that only a handful of his black friends from elementary school had made it that far, and the numbers of his cohorts diminished with each advancing year of high school. It was at that point that the term "dropout" first began to take on new meaning in his life. Having only had two black teachers throughout his entire public schooling, he learned first-hand what condescending white teachers could do to a black student's morale, hopes, and dreams. Because of several white teachers who had taken a special interest in his academic and personal growth, however, he concluded that effective teaching could be racially neutral if teachers cared and believed all children could learn. "Miss Dorothy Sturm inspired me to learn Spanish, and helped me to become good enough at it that I wanted to become an interpreter," Reg remembered. "My wrestling coach, Don Pittman, thought enough of me that he helped me to secure an athletic scholarship, as he had done for my older brother; and my homeroom teacher, John Saunders, insisted that I take chemistry courses." Yet, it was advice that he did not take from "Miss Helen Watkins," his history teacher, that stuck with him over the years. She was in charge of the Speech Club and approached him about becoming a member, extolling the benefits of public speaking. "I thought about it for a quick minute before dismissing the idea as not one appropriate for the image of the kid," he later laughed, when remembering that ill-advised decision. Just as contemporary black students are often chastised and subjected to the contemptuous ridicule of their peers, who label them as "acting white" for speaking proper English, in Reg's youth joining academic clubs and taking rigorous advance placement courses were jeered at by other teenagers That peer pressure prevented him from joining a school group that would have allowed him to practice what would become unquestionably one of his strongest skills—public speaking.[8]

Reg was 15 years old when the ruling in *Brown v. Board of Education* was issued by the U.S. Supreme Court; 16 when Rosa Parks refused to give up her seat on a Montgomery, Alabama bus; and 18 when President Dwight D. Eisenhower ordered federal troops to protect the Little Rock Nine who were integrating Central High School. Like Mary Hatwood Futrell's high school years, his coincided with the nascent Civil Rights Movement that would shape his world view and his sense of social justice. The center stage for the movement was in the South where segregation, discrimination, and prejudice were more pronounced than they were in Danville, but blacks in Illinois during that period were not removed from injustices attributable solely to race. Yet white Illinoisans would not have done to a black Mississippi youth what white Mississippians did to Emmett Till, a black 13-year-old from Illinois, visiting his family in Money, Mississippi in the summer of 1955. He was abducted and brutally murdered by white men for allegedly "wolf-whistling" at a grown white woman. The killers bragged of the killing, knowing that no white Mississippi jury would ever return a guilty verdict for the murder of a black youth. During the Civil Rights Movement some crimes were more troubling than others, and in Illinois, where more black former Mississippians lived than in any other state, this crime hit particularly hard. Reg was only 16-years-old when it occurred, and it sobered him to a realization of the fragile and often precarious position of young black males in society, reinforcing the lessons he had already learned from his grandfather, Dewey General Robinson.[9]

While Illinois was a much different world from the segregated South, it was not utopia for blacks. During the 1950s, the state had more "sundown towns"—all white towns where blacks were not allowed to reside—than any other state, despite the fact that the practice had been banned by a 1948 decision of the U.S. Supreme Court that invalidated laws maintaining restrictive covenants. Because of clever real estate manipulations, the ruling was largely unenforceable, and when, in 1956, sociologist William H. Whyte examined efforts to keep blacks out of Park Forest, a Chicago suburb, he coined the phrase "sundown suburb" in his classic, *The Organization Man*. Whyte wrote:

> "Several years ago there was an acrid controversy over the possible admission of Negroes. It threatened to be deeply divisive—for a small group, admission of Negroes would be fulfillment of personal social ideas; for another, many of whom had just left Chicago wards which had been "taken over," it was the return of a threat left behind. But the people who were perhaps most surely vexed were the moderates. Most of them were against admission too, but though no Negroes ever did move in, the damage was done. The issue had been brought up, and the sheer fact that one had to talk about it made it impossible to maintain unblemished the ideal egalitarianism so many cherished."[10]

The social and psychological dynamics of the sundown suburbs Whyte described was also the subject of Lorraine Hansberry's award-winning play of the same era, *A Raisin in the Sun*. Its setting was Chicago, where the black Younger family spurned financial offers from the leaders of a sundown suburb as an incentive to prevent the family from integrating an all-white community. This was the climate of Reg's youth in Illinois, and when he graduated from Danville High, only three blacks in his class would continue their education by enrolling in college.[11] By comparison, Libby Koontz, NEA's first black president, had graduated from a segregated North Carolina high school in 1934, which had more black students in her class attend college than did Reg's entire "integrated" Illinois high school over two decades later.

In the fall of 1957, Reg left home to attend Illinois State Normal College (now Illinois State University). Mary Alice and the Weaver family were pleased as he followed on the college path chosen by his brother Carl, who had enrolled two years earlier at Northern Illinois University. "There were not more than 100 of us," said Weaver, estimating the number of blacks on the Illinois State campus. At that time his professional ambition was to become a physical therapist, but since that major was not offered at Illinois State, he chose Special Education for the Physically Handicapped, with a minor in Elementary Education. He earned high grades, competed on the wrestling team, and made many lasting friendships. Ann Davis and Pearl Mack, black women at the college, became two of his closest friends. "Everybody on the campus knew Reg, and though he was an upperclassman, he took the time to make sure that we made good adjustments from high school to college and life away from home," remembered Ann Davis.[12]

In the spring of 1961, the Weaver family traveled the 95 miles from Danville to Normal for Reg's graduation; he was the second in his family to attend college, but the first ever in the family to receive a college degree.[13] The persistence of Mary Alice had paid off, and the family was proud. Reg secured an interview for a special education teaching position in the Galesburg, Illinois School District. "I did well on the interview," he recalled, "but did not get the job because they preferred a woman rather than a man to work with the special education students." The disappointment was erased when he interviewed for and was offered a teaching position in the Harvey, Illinois School District at a salary of $5,100 a year.[14] Harvey was the only district in which he was ever employed, and it was there that he first began to show exceptional teaching ability and union leadership skills that separated him from others. Most of the students at Riley School where he taught were black, though most of the teachers were white. "There were only three black men at the school, the principal, the janitor, and Mr. Weaver," recalled Sandra Lamb, who was a student in Reg's first class. At that time, Harvey was undergoing a dramatic demographic transition in which the black population rose from seven to 66 percent between 1960 and 1980. Full of energy and optimism, "he made an immediate impression on all of us, and our community where he developed a trust with the parents," said Lamb. In that fifth grade class was another student, Lolita Dozier, who remembered his rule "that performing better than expected was a requirement for all students, and he drilled that message daily."[15]

Interracial tensions in the community ran high and were exacerbated by black assertiveness and white resistance to the change threatened by the Civil Rights Movement. "You could feel the uneasiness in the community and it was not uncommon, even in Illinois, to be called 'nigger' when going outside of the black neighborhood," recalled Lamb.[16] Those tensions, unfortunately, sometimes had a tendency to transfer to the school, where some black students complained of being academically short-changed by some of the teachers. "The reason Reg was so important at that time was that he forced fairness," she continued, "by making us, our parents and the school more aware of what should be expected for all students." Other teachers soon learned that Reg would be vigilant in both monitoring attitudes and encouraging fairness at Riley, which contributed to changing the school culture.[17]

The Civil Rights Movement and its goals were of interest to his students, and Reg responded by talking about it in his classes and by displaying posters and photographs of its leaders on the walls of his classroom. Soon there were new expressions of pride among the students, and one female came to school with a new hairstyle, the "Afro." The students were in awe of her appearance and some made derisive remarks. "I remember Mr. Weaver rescuing that student from shame and teaching all of us the importance of cultural expressions," said a former student. He often talked to his class about Martin Luther King, Jr. and the protest strategy of non-violent civil disobedience, but "after his say, he reminded us of the importance to think on our own."[18]

Of all the states outside of the South, Illinois was most notorious for racism and discriminatory housing practices. In the summer of 1966, the state was chosen for the most ambitious civil rights campaign in the North. What Reg and other Illinois citizens knew, the nation was soon to discover. Cicero, another Chicago suburb, was selected as a site for a demonstration against residential and employment discrimination. The Cicero sheriff warned Martin Luther King, Jr. that a march would be suicidal, and would make "other civil rights disturbances look like a tea party."[19] He was correct. King and several hundred protesters met the most violent resistance to any previous civil rights march when whites attacked the marchers, hurling bricks, bottles, rocks, and other objects at them. As many as 54 were injured in Cicero, which, 15 years earlier had been the site of a fierce race riot caused when a black man moved into an apartment there in 1951; the disturbance had been quelled only after 3,000 National Guardsmen moved in to restore order. Since that time, no black had sought residence in the town. As Jesse Jackson once remarked when talking about the Cicero protest, "It was real, blatant, ugly, and violent."[20]

The anxiety created by the changing racial demographics in Harvey spilled over into the schools. Sandra Lamb, who went on to become a successful lawyer, recalled an incident at the city's Thornton Township High School when a counselor suggested that Sandra pursue a vocational career, despite the fact that she was an honor student and in the college preparatory program. "When I asked why he made such a recommendation, he replied that all I was going to do was get pregnant," said Lamb. "Mr. Weaver had taught all of us about boundaries, and when the line was crossed, and because of those lessons, I successfully challenged my counselor with confidence."[21] Regrettably, interracial relations deteriorated at the school, leading to racial violence and race riots in 1969. All of it, however, shaped Reg's views on social justice, and affirmed his conviction that teachers and schools were obligated to promote fairness and to prepare students to live peacefully in a multicultural, pluralistic, and democratic society.

When Reg reported to work at Riley School in 1962, he was surprised to learn that Pearl Mack had accepted a teaching position at Riley, and one year later, Ann Davis also began teaching there. The employment of Reg and his two Illinois State friends at Riley was the beginning of the rise of each of them to the highest levels of educational leadership. Of her first day at Riley, Ann Davis said, "Reg met me at the door, made me feel welcome, and, like Pearl before me, he insisted we join the local Harvey Education Association." The principal was the person who had asked Reg to join, "and with a record of 100% membership in his building, "I had no choice but to join," Reg said later.[22] Riley was an ideal school building for the three friends; it was innovative, creative, and on the minority side of town. Parents were involved in the school and, after Reg's first year, more black teachers taught there than in any other school in the district. The race demographics of Harvey were being expressed in the hiring of more black teachers to work in a school where the student enrollment was becoming increasingly black.

Reg served as a building representative for the local, and, after Pearl and Ann came on board, his activism intensified as he came to appreciate the potential of the union to improve the conditions of practice for the teachers. At Riley, he also taught students to respect the dignity of the education support professionals. "Mr. Weaver was the first teacher who demanded that we respect Mr. Taylor, the school janitor, as we did all other adults," recalled one student.[23] As his reputation spread from the school to the district, Ann and Pearl encouraged him to run for vice president of the local. He won in an election in which he was unopposed, and when the president unexpectedly resigned, he moved into the top position. The primary source of his appeal, according to Ann, "was that he was not afraid to speak out even when he knew it would not be popular with the administration."[24]

In 1963, Reg married Betty Moppin, a nurse, and settled into the Harvey
community where they raised two sons, Reginald Von and Rowan Anton.
Being the father of two boys, being a husband, teaching school, coaching
basketball, and being active in the local, placed demands on his time. But
for his student Lolita Dozier, Reg found enough time to become a surrogate
parent, counselor, and advisor. Lolita became pregnant, dropped out
of school, and drifted into a downward spiral leading to self-pity and
dependency. Visiting the homes of parents had become one of Reg's routines,
and though Lolita was a dropout, he visited her home, hoping to salvage
some of the hopes and dreams she had had before leaving school. "What
are you going to do?" was the refrain he left with her every time he came by.
Lost, disappointed, and disillusioned, she had no answer. "If you go back
to school," he promised, "I'll take you to any restaurant in the world." The
fact that "he would not give up on my future eventually persuaded me to
return to school and, true to his word, he took me to a seafood restaurant,"
she remembered. Later, as an adult, Lolita graduated from college, became a
teacher, and of course, at his urging, joined the local. When Reg was elected
to the National Education Association's Executive Committee, she became his
teaching partner and he continued to groom her. Later she became a delegate
to the RA, a member of the Board of Directors of the Illinois Education
Association (IEA), and "because of Mr. Weaver, Ms. Mack, and Ms. Davis,"
she encouraged her own children to become teachers; and was pleased when
her eldest also became active in IEA.[25]

As Reg spoke out about teacher issues in the district, ranging from decision-
making to textbooks and curriculum, the local he led became stronger.
In 1964, he attended his first delegate assembly of the Illinois Education
Association. It was an eye-opening experience. "I could not believe" he
recalled, while shaking his head in wonder, "that of the 700 to 800 delegates,
practically every one of them was white and most were administrators."[26]
Rather than resign in indignation over IEA's apparent indifference to race, he
absorbed as much knowledge as he could about how business was conducted
at the state level. His determination was to be an agent for bringing about
change to the racial composition of that body. His challenge was to chart a

course that would result in that change. Returning to Harvey, he became even more determined to continue his active involvement.

Along with Pearl and Ann, he started attending IEA regional council meetings and soon parlayed his local presidency into the office of chairperson of the region. At that level, during a period of pre-collective bargaining in the district, he built relationships with the superintendents in the region. In 1965, the Harvey superintendent approached Reg and asked if the local might want a professional negotiations agreement. That conversation began a process that led to the first professionally negotiated contract for Harvey. Reg's participation in the process was exemplary, and he gained members' respect for monitoring and maintaining the contract, which, in turn, increased his credibility, reputation, and visibility. He was appointed to several state committees and became a member of the IEA Board of Directors. His rise was rapid, and it was impressive enough for John Aurand of NEA's UniServ to encourage Reg to run for state president in 1971. After huddling with Pearl, Ann, and a close-knit group of colleagues, he placed his hat in the ring, and, though he made a respectable showing in a field of four candidates, he lost the election. There was some modest consolation on that election weekend, however, when he received his master's degree at the Roosevelt University commencement ceremony.[27]

Losing is as much a part of learning as it is of life, and as soon as the election was over, he thought the time was right to build a base within IEA. Reg joined Patty Brown, Patricio Perez, Tony Vasquez, Pearl Mack, and Ann Davis to form a state Black and Hispanic Caucus. "We first met on the University of Chicago campus and agreed that we could collectively have an impact on IEA," Reg recalled. The caucus members attended the 1973 IEA representative assembly, and in the spirit of the minority guarantees first formulated at NEA's 1971 con-con, they secured representation on the state board. After that, the pace of inclusion accelerated at IEA, much as it did to the same degree at NEA following its 1966 merger with ATA and con-con.[28]

What happened in Illinois during the late 1960s and early 1970s was typical of the flurry of activity spreading throughout NEA's affiliates around the goal of broader representation for minorities. Minority guarantees, the minority caucus movement, and, equally important, the willingness of whites to elect quality minority candidates to Association offices were operating simultaneously and efficiently enough to cause a quiet revolution in the racial composition of Association leadership. When Thomas Bicknell in 1884 billed the National Education Association's annual convention as "the greatest educational show on earth" he could not have envisioned NEA's Representative Assemblies of the 1970s, which had become the best reflection of "all the people"—a truer reflection than that of any other organization of its size and influence in the nation.

The timing could not have been better for Reg, and in 1977, according to Ann Davis, his campaign manager, "he learned from the election he had lost, and this time he truly believed he was ready."[29] Indeed he was, and he was elected IEA's vice-president, in which position he served two terms. Thus, in 1981, it was without surprise to anyone that he became the first member of a minority to become president of IEA. Several of his team members also began to rise within Association politics. Jeremiah Floyd and Pearl Mack won seats on the NEA Board of Directors, Floyd being the first black from Illinois in that position. Pearl went on to be elected to NEA's Executive Committee. Ann became a member of the Illinois Teachers Retirement System, and her leadership trajectory continued until she, too, was elected IEA president.

As IEA president, Reg was popular and effective in working with the state legislature in passing Illinois' first comprehensive collective bargaining bill in 1983, and an education reform bill in 1985. Stan Johnson, who would go on to become a state president of the Wisconsin Education Association, remembered meeting Reg at a Minority Leadership Training Seminar, when he first became active in the Association. "I was excited to meet a minority in the mid-west region who, like Lauri Wynn of my state, had beat the odds and become a state president," said Johnson. "He became a mentor for me," he continued, "and taught me that nothing was a given, but the Association's progressive culture would allow me to become a leader if I was willing to work twice as hard as my competitors."[30] IEA membership increased under

Reg's leadership, enhancing his state profile. Because of term limitations he could not run again after his second term ended. Illinois Governor James Thompson, however, thought enough of his abilities and political acumen to appoint him to a job with the Illinois Department of Employment Security, in which capacity he served from 1987 to 1989. He had considered making a bid for vice-president of NEA in 1989, but, instead, he ran unopposed for an at-large position on the Executive Committee. While serving two three-year terms on the Executive Committee, he learned "more about the elected leaders, the influence and impact of staff, and the timing for speaking out on what is right." He made a concerted effort to reach out to the members, measuring his progress by the large numbers of requests he received to participate in the activities of local and state affiliates.[31]

After his years on the Executive Committee, Reg decided that the time had now come for him to set his sights on the office of NEA vice-president, for which office he emerged victorious despite spirited opposition from another minority member, Susie Jablinski of Maryland. "The National Education Association is incredible," said Stan Johnson. "Can you imagine both leading candidates for a position of that magnitude being minorities, and nobody even blinking an eye?"[32] When the election results were announced, President Bill Clinton was preparing to speak to the 1996 RA, and was in the holding room with Reg and other NEA officials. Outside on the convention floor, Tamara Blair, a Secret Service Agent and member of Clinton's detail, also heard the announcement. She rushed to the Illinois delegation, to find out if the name she had heard was indeed that of a former teacher in Harvey. When delegates confirmed that Reg Weaver was the new Vice-President, she went backstage to meet her former teacher and to express her delight in sharing the excitement of the event. Reg became fond of recalling the incident, "Because" he said, "it reminded me of who I really am, and what I really am, a teacher from Harvey, Illinois."[33]

During his two terms as Vice-President, Reg understood his role in supporting NEA President Bob Chase, exerting much of his energy on promoting the proposed merger of the National Education Association and the American Federation of Teachers. "I often traveled with Reg when he talked to our members about the advantages of merging with AFT," said Bob Chanin, NEA general counsel. "He gave it everything he had, did everything he was asked to do, and understood his role as Vice-President." Ann Davis recalled that when members challenged him on his home turf of Illinois, where opposition to the merger was significant, Reg told them "that as Vice-President he represented all 50 states, and while he appreciated the pushback, he believed the merger was best for all of the National Education Association." The delegates to the 1997 RA in New Orleans decisively rejected the merger proposal, but Reg never regretted nor second-guessed himself for taking a position at odds with many in Illinois. "I held a position elected by all of our delegates, and I did the best I could for what I thought was right."[34]

"When I became President of the National Education Association at the 2002 RA in Dallas, my top priority was the one that had sustained me since I took my first teaching assignment in Harvey, the education of our kids," Reg said.[35] Others, too, including President George W. Bush, placed public education as a top priority. In 2001, Bush had signed the legislation reauthorizing the Elementary and Secondary Education Act (ESEA), known as No Child Left Behind (NCLB), making the bipartisan law the cornerstone of his education reform policy. Reg Weaver and George W. Bush fundamentally agreed on the stated goals of NCLB—to improve student achievement and to close achievement and skill gaps in the nation's primary and secondary schools. But their disagreement began over the means of achieving those goals. NCLB touted increased standards of accountability for states, school districts, and schools. Parents were to be given more flexibility in choosing their children's schools, and an increased focus was to be placed on reading.

NCLB was grounded in standards-based education reform or outcome-based education, proponents of which believe that defining high expectations and establishing measurable goals could improve individual outcomes in education. The Act, however, made federal funding to the states dependent on the states developing assessments of basic skills to be administered to all students in certain grades. Reg led NEA, and other critics joined, in the assertion that a one-size-fits-all assessment approach—as opposed to providing schools the resources and support they needed for improvement—was inappropriate for the diversity of the student population; and that the punishment of schools that failed to measure up to the law's accountability requirements was cruel and inappropriate. Teachers would be forced to teach to the test, based on a narrow imposed curriculum, and the standardized testing would be biased against minorities. Moreover, critics maintained that NCLB had a punitive effect on the students it sought to help, particularly low-income students. Still nothing about NCLB was more galling than the federal government's failure to fulfill its financial responsibility.[36]

The bipartisan nature of the NCLB legislation and the general consensus of the American public on the desirability of its goals required NEA to launch an awareness campaign designed to reveal the utterly impractical implementation requirements. Leading NEA in forging working partnerships with other education groups such as the American Association of School Administrators (AASA) and community-based organizations, including the Public Education Network (PEN); the National Council of La Raza; the League of United Latin American Citizens (LULAC); NAACP; ASPIRA, the national organization devoted solely to the educational leadership development of Puerto Rican and other Latino youth; and the Association of Community Organizations for Reform Now (ACORN), Reg launched the theme of "fix it and fund it" in speeches and addresses to members and advocacy groups throughout the nation. Soon, local and state school officials, education advocates, and notable politicians joined NEA in challenging the legislation.

In addition to highlighting NEA's strongest argument, that NCLB constituted unfunded mandates, Reg continued to hammer at the pedagogical view that it demanded that all students meet the same level of achievement in the same period of time, and that it defied "everything both administrators and teachers know about quality teaching, and meeting the individual needs of our students." When providing testimony on the law before congressional committees, Reg presented fact-by-fact evidence of its demoralizing impact on the teaching profession and its troubling implications for student achievement. Utilizing a low-keyed, subdued, and professional style, he was highly effective in expressing to policymakers all of the "confusion, frustration, and yes, anger" he was hearing from NEA members.[37] By contrast, the methodical, measured, detached, and analytical approach Reg employed for Congress changed when he spoke on NCLB before NEA constituency groups. There he developed a unique and innovative style of witty sarcasm about the absurdity of the legislation's simplistic approach, which had the effect of making members think more deeply about policies that made no logical sense, and were disconnected from the everyday realities of their professional lives. Whenever questions arose about funding for public education, he took delight in pointing out federal pork-barrel spending and controversial financial bailouts. "Don't ask me where the money is going to come from when schools need more resources and school personnel better compensation," he would ask rhetorically when questioning federal spending priorities. "Just go find it from the same place you find money to bail out the savings and loan scandals, to subsidize failing but politically affluent corporations; and from the same place where you find billions upon billions to fund an undeclared war," and he worked hard to perfect different styles for different audiences—but always with the same message.[38]

In his *NEA Today* column, "President's Viewpoint," he reduced the complex NCLB law to the essentials that teachers and educational support professionals (ESPs) needed to know to understand the urgency of uniting against its shortcomings. Careful to endorse its goals, while challenging its implementation flaws, he wrote:

> "At the same time that the federal government is requiring improved student performance on standardized tests, our class sizes are ballooning, our qualifications for a highly qualified teacher and professional development have been reduced, and school funding and construction to accommodate the growing number of students is being put on hold.

> "If we are to survive this storm with our professional integrity intact and our jobs secure, we are going to have to strategize,

organize, and mobilize like we have never done before.
What's more, we must re-energize ourselves as we recruit
new members who are committed to our profession, children,
students, and public education.

"We must champion the goals that we have long advocated--
many of which are embodied in the reauthorized Elementary
and Secondary Education Act (ESEA)—while fighting to
change how those goals are implemented. And to this fight,
we must bring a passion, an intensity, and a high level of
member participation that is unrivaled.

"Under ESEA, as it is currently crafted, your best efforts in
the classroom, and your students and school, can be judged
a failure—based on a single number on one of either of two
tests.

"Under ESEA, if the students in your school do not score
higher on the standardized tests every year for four straight
years, you could face serious consequences.

"Under ESEA, your school's lack of resources will not prevent
you from being labeled a failure.

"Under ESEA, successful, experienced teachers will have
to demonstrate their subject matter competency, either
by passing a test or by meeting a 'high objective uniform
statewide standard of evaluation.'

"I have yet to meet a professional educator who is not angered
once he or she learns about the fine print in ESEA. We must
help teachers and ESPs channel their anger and frustration in a
manner that will support our plight in this fight."[39]

Between 2002 and 2008, Reg wrote specifically about NCLB, using variations
of this theme in over 30 percent of his articles in *NEA Today*. During that
period NEA would also file a lawsuit challenging the unfunded mandates
of NCLB. The basis for the lawsuit was Section 9527(a) of the law, which
states that "nothing in this Act shall be construed to authorize an officer or
employee of the Federal Government to…mandate a state or any subdivision

thereof to spend any funds or incur any costs not paid for under this Act." Working closely with NEA general counsel Bob Chanin, Reg galvanized support from some of the state affiliates, and nine school districts in Michigan, Texas, and Vermont that joined in the lawsuit. A federal district judge in Detroit dismissed the suit in 2005, and it languished in the Sixth Circuit U.S. Court of Appeals until early 2008 when a three-judge panel for that circuit affirmed that the federal government could not require a state or a school district "to spend funds or incur any costs not paid for under this Act."[40] When the Sixth Circuit Court returned the case to the district court for further proceeding, the larger question then became what did the ruling mean in practical terms for states and school districts? The court had been vague on that point. Whatever the ultimate outcome, which was not known before the end of Reg's term in office, any meaningful changes in NCLB will be credited, in large part, to NEA's "fix it and fund it" campaign which began under his leadership.

The effectiveness of the campaign Reg led, which called for substantive changes in NCLB and made NEA members and the public more aware of the most egregious weaknesses in the law, proved unsettling for the Bush Administration. Angered over NEA's message gaining traction with an increasingly skeptical public, Secretary of Education Rod Paige, now on the defensive, answered a question raised about NEA and NCLB at a White House meeting of the National Governors Association in February of 2004, by casually referring to the NEA as "a group of terrorists." Coming only two and a half years after 9/11, his metaphor, which could not have been more offensive, immediately deepened the divide between Paige and Reg, respectively, the nation's top education official and the head of its largest professional union. In an apology explaining his poor choice of words, Paige made a bad situation worse when attempting to make a distinction between the union and its members. NEA, he argued, often acted at odds with the wishes of its rank and file teachers regarding school standards and accountability, and he noted that the spirit of his remarks was directed at NEA, but not its members.[41]

"He called me that same afternoon about the blunder," said Reg. "He apologized, but we both understood the magnitude of the mistake." It was too late. When the story broke that day and became the nation's lead news story the next day, Reg issued a press release calling Paige's comments "absolutely pathetic" and "not anything to joke about," yet it was "the kind of rhetoric we have come to expect from this administration" whenever its views were challenged.[42] Rather than being offered an apology from Paige, Reg indicated that what he preferred was "a commitment from the Department of Education to work with NEA to fix and fund" NCLB, and that "President Bush express his regret to the nation's teachers and demand Secretary Paige step down." Some members clamored for a confrontation between Reg and Paige. "I decided," he recalled, "not to make a spectacle by arguing with a black man in public, because of the signal it might send and how that might come across as personal when in fact it was all about competing ideas."[43]

Both Paige and Reg were black and both had personal education experiences in inferior segregated schools of which their parents had disapproved. Both remembered the day the U.S. Supreme Court had ruled that separate and equal schools were inherently unequal, and both agreed on the goals of NCLB. But Paige represented the Bush Administration and Reg the National Education Association: the divide over how to accomplish those goals could not have been wider. Philosophically, they were operating from competing frames of reference that their common experience could not reconcile. Paige understood his role in satisfying the Bush administration and its constituency, and Reg made certain that NEA was a cohesive force in bringing all of its issues and concerns to the NCLB table and to the court of public opinion. NEA members responded to the claim that the union and its members were separate entities by distributing and proudly wearing buttons proclaiming, "I AM THE NEA."

In retrospect, the Paige incident caused a surge of interest in NCLB among educators and the public, and NEA members bonded more tightly to the "fix it and fund it" campaign. Reg's popularity soared, while Paige's federal career went into a tailspin from which he was unable to recover. Shortly after the incident involving Paige's unfortunate words, *60 Minutes* broadcast an investigative report about Paige's term as superintendent of the Houston, Texas schools that exposed fraud in the claims of student-achievement record keeping in that district. His credibility was further weakened when the General Accounting Office determined impropriety in his awarding a federal contract to conservative commentator Armstrong Williams, for the specific purpose of promoting NCLB. In November of that year, Paige resigned from his federal post.[44]

Nothing occupied NEA more during Reg's term in office than NCLB, and though it dominated his writings in *NEA Today* while updating the 3.2 million members on the Association's scorecard on "fixing and funding it," he did not ignore or neglect other important top-tiered education and social issues. His other notable articles dealt with teacher shortages, education support professionals, parental involvement, safe schools, dropouts, pay for performance proposals, and Hurricane Katrina.

On teacher shortages, which resulted in teacher mis-assignments—where educators had to teach in subject areas or work with students at age levels different from those for which their college trained them—and on teachers entering the classroom with emergency credentials, Reg explained that such practices were much more common in schools populated with poor children than in those in affluent school districts. To reverse the shortage, Reg argued that the profession needed to be made more attractive and that was to begin with professional pay competitive with other fields. Thus, he offered a plausible remedy for the shortage:

> "Is there really a shortage of qualified teachers? I would say so. And why? Because there is a 'shortage of respect.'

> "Each year, America's colleges of education could produce enough new teachers to replace retiring teachers and meet the needs of growing student enrollments. The problem is not that too few men and women desire to come into the profession. The problem is that there are too many sacrifices that must be made to realize success in the profession. And the solution is not to develop alternative routes of entry into

the profession or to increase the supply of recruits by allowing prospective teachers to skip "burdensome" education courses or student teaching. The solution is to show a little R-E-S-P-E-C-T, and show us the money.

"We are short of qualified teachers because education and educators have not been given the respect that we deserve. Respect that is reflected in our work environment—modern schools, small class sizes, and adequate resources. Respect that is reflected in our compensation—educators should not have to sacrifice the desire to pursue an honorable profession in order to provide a decent standard of living for their families. Change those conditions and the teacher quality, recruitment, and retention issues will vanish."[45]

When making the case for higher teacher salaries, Reg made certain that education support professionals were a part of that dialogue. But, more than compensation, he wanted ESPs to be "comfortable, confident, and secure" in knowing they were important and appreciated members of the school team. "One minute a school secretary might be trying to get the principal organized, and the next minute she may be comforting a feverish child who is waiting for his mother to pick him up from school," he wrote. "At the same time that a cafeteria worker serves lunch, she might be coaxing a smile out of a sad-faced child. A custodian may go from fixing a broken boiler to helping a student fix a broken bike. And when not behind the wheel, a bus driver might very well be collecting warm winter clothes for children who do not have them."[46] Reg's sincerity on ESPs' value to public education was unassailable, and it was also an acknowledgment of NEA's membership base in which the ESP category of members was its fastest growing. One ESP member, Iona Holloway, had served on the Executive Committee during Bob Chase's term, and the numbers of ESPs on the NEA Board of Directors were greater during Reg's term of office than they had been under any previous NEA president. Reg grasped the importance of this dynamic, and he was rarely remiss in incorporating language and message that spoke to both ESPs and teachers, at the same time that he appointed unprecedented numbers of ESPs to NEA standing committees. It was also during his term that the official designation of ESP was changed from "education support personnel" to "education support professionals," indicating their increasing influence in the Association and a reconsidered respect for the services they offered to public education.

The salary and living wage campaign of NEA, for example, represented a combination of the compensation issues of both teachers and ESPs. On this subject, he wrote:

> "No one who dedicates a life to driving, nourishing, counseling, or teaching our nation's students should be forced to live at or below the poverty line. But all too often, teachers and ESPs who choose a life of public service must trade away their right to a decent standard of living.
>
> "NEA is fighting to change that with a nationwide salary campaign to win a $40,000 starting salary for all teachers, an appropriate living wage for all education support professionals, and appropriate professional pay for higher education faculty and staff.
>
> "As the national voice for public school employees, we know that too many teachers and ESPs have been denied professional pay for too long. Working in public schools is not an act of charity, and educators should not have to sacrifice their families' needs when they choose a career in public education."[47]

Making safe schools a national priority became even more of an education issue following highly publicized incidents, including those at Columbine and Virginia Tech University, among others. The specter of student violence threatened the confidence of many parents as schools were being challenged to assuage public concerns about maintaining safe and orderly environments for learning.[48] While the incidence of students' threats against each other and against educators never reached epidemic proportions, every publicized incident was considered one too many. Reg urged all stakeholders—the community, administrators, parents, school staff, and students—to come together to ensure safe schools. The NEA Health Information Network in 2007 revised the *School Crisis Guide: Help and Healing in a Time of Crisis*, to provide educators, school district administrators, and principals with a resource for keeping schools safe. Reg also spoke often about violence and intimidation in schools, as evidenced in racial prejudice, sexual harassment, and bullying, and in discriminatory practices and physical and psychological assaults against those of different sexual orientation. "Our parents must talk to their children more and pay closer attention to early warning signs well in advance of potential violence," he admonished the readers of *NEA Today*. "Teachers must communicate more effectively with parents and administrators, and create classrooms that are free of bias and encourage freedom of thought. And our students must be willing to avoid confrontation and to notify school staff of the suspicious behavior of other students."[49] On a much smaller stage, some 40 years earlier, he remembered giving a similar lecture to his students at Riley in Danville, when a female student in his classroom was chastised and intimidated because of her preference for an Afro hairstyle. Throughout his career, Reg was uniformly consistent and adamant in his position that there must be zero tolerance for violence, discrimination, and intimidation in schools.

When Reg first began his teaching career, his signature approach to teaching was that the parents and the community had to be involved. "Mr. Weaver," recalled one of his first students, "was as well known among the parents as he was among the teachers."[50] Drawing on his personal experiences in Danville, he reminded NEA members that "the message we must send to parents is that we can't replace you, we can't do it for you, but together, we can make a huge difference for your child." The strategies he suggested for getting parents involved, were those that had worked well for him, and that he hoped would serve as a prescription for success. On this he shared his personal thoughts and experiences when he wrote:

> "Ideas include meeting parents on their turf through home
> visits; parent meetings in neighborhood centers, restaurants,
> and other locations that are close and comfortable for
> community members; and family resource centers in schools

with flexible hours so parents can attend informal gatherings
or workshops during the day, at night, or on weekends.

"Wishing for more parent involvement won't make it happen.
Sometimes we need to go the extra mile to connect with
parents so they can see that we, like them, are dedicated to
their children succeeding. We can also help improve public
education because parents who get involved in their child's
school are more likely to become advocates for schools in their
neighborhoods and communities.

"As partners, parents and educators have forced politicians
to address the class size issue. And it has been parents and
educators who have fought for up-to-date textbooks and
materials, and fought against harmful policies that divert
scarce resources from public schools."[51]

Since the publication of *A Nation at Risk,* education reformers had toyed with
the idea of basing teacher pay on performance. Mary Hatwood Futrell, Keith
Geiger, and Bob Chase all had argued persuasively that the larger question
should not be how to differentiate between teachers in compensating them
for their work. Rather, the central question should be paying all teachers
salaries commensurate with their educational background and experience,
and competitive with those of other professionals. When speaking, Reg was
at his absolute best in making the case that school employees were generally
underpaid. Speaking in a vernacular understood by practitioners, he would
ask rhetorically how many policymakers would accept a teacher's salary
for dealing daily with students like "Little Ray-Ray," a name he used to
personify "your worst classroom nightmare."[52] Then he would proceed to
present a laundry list of all the things that were expected of a teacher and
have his audience nodding in agreement with each one, confirming that
they understood the professional challenges they faced. Reg's writings on
pay for performance, though pushed to capture the energy of his public
speaking, were equally eloquent in making his case that "too many teachers
and educational support professionals have been denied professional pay for

too long." Highly effective in connecting the dots between compensation and quality education, he wrote:

> "Our members have always felt a responsibility to help students achieve, be successful, and compete in an interdependent world. We accomplish that by making public schools great places for teaching and learning—a goal that requires paying professional salaries that truly attract and retain quality educators.
>
> "As the national voice for public school employees, we know that too many teachers and education support professionals have been denied professional pay for too long. To attract more dedicated, committed professionals into these fields, we need salaries that are literally "attractive." That is the principle behind NEA's salary campaign, which is gaining traction and securing fair and competitive compensation for teachers, ESPs, and higher education employees. Bit by bit, this strategic goal is helping local communities recruit and retain the kind of education professionals that students need and parents want."[53]

Mark Twain once said, "There are lies, damn lies, and then there are statistics." Reg liked to use statistics for dramatic effect when making presentations, but he frequently resorted to personal experiences from his past that were easily identifiable to educators. Whether from coaching basketball and building character in young men, or from interactions with students and colleagues, he relied on that with which he was most familiar. "I grew up in the Midwest, where many people used to work in factories," he wrote in an article on the high cost of dropouts. "Today, many of those manufacturing jobs are gone. And the new jobs that have replaced them require new skills that we never even thought about when I was in school," he stated. "Today, a high school diploma is absolutely essential for anyone who wants an opportunity to succeed. For the most part, our schools are serving the needs of students who go on to college, but we are failing the ones who never make it to the finish line."[54] Using that as an introduction to the sobering fact that over a million students drop out of school each year—one every 26 seconds, ranking the United States among the highest in the industrialized world in the number of its students who failed to finish school—Reg wrote about the heavy financial price that students who drop out will pay for the remainder of their lives, and the price incurred by all of society. He continued:

> "We will pay a price in lost tax revenue, because these young people will be unable to earn a decent living. We will pay the cost of incarcerating those who turn to crime because they cannot find a good-paying job. And our society will pay an awful price for squandering the human potential of millions of young people."[55]

Looking back at his own life and remembering the attrition rate of his childhood friends from elementary school who never completed high school, Reg had a personal feel for the "human toll" on society of dropouts and the wasted lives of many who never recovered from the economic consequences of failing to obtain a high school diploma.

"I don't think anything bothered Mr. Weaver more than a student dropping out of school," recalled one of two former students, who, having dropped out of school was saved by Reg in a life-altering rescue.[56] It was with his passion for education and from his own personal experience that he led NEA to unveil its 12-point action plan to reduce dropouts. Introduced in 2006, the plan drew acclaim from congressional leaders, progressive organizations, and allies from minority communities such as ASPIRA, NAACP, the National Indian Education Association, and the National Association for Asian and Pacific American Education. The plan called for more emphasis on vocational and technical training and for offering relevant skills training in schools for students who had elected not to pursue higher education. The plan also called for early identification of potential dropouts by providing educators with the training and resources to spot generic dropout indicators: poor grades, poor attendance, poor family support, and lack of interest. Mandating high school graduation for everyone below the age of 21, making it a federal priority; maintaining more accurate dropout reporting; encouraging family involvement in students' learning at school and home;

and establishing high school graduation centers for older students—all were features of the plan for reducing school dropouts.[57]

Reg's commitment to relieving those needing help was never more evident than it was in the summer before the dropout campaign was initiated. In August of 2005, Hurricane Katrina—one of the five deadliest hurricanes in the history of the United States—reached shore along the Gulf Coast, devastating cities in its path. Causing severe loss of life and property damage across the entire Mississippi coast and into Alabama, it breached every levee in New Orleans, Louisiana, flooding 80 percent of the city. At least 2,836 people lost their lives in the storm and subsequent floods. The hurricane is estimated to have been responsible for $81.2 billion in damage, making it the costliest natural disaster in U.S. history. The catastrophic failure of emergency assistance and relief wreaked havoc on those in the disaster areas, and created bedlam, particularly in New Orleans, where the mayor ordered the first-ever mandatory evacuation of the city. Some citizens, mostly the poor, were unable to leave, and several relief centers of last resort were hastily established, including one in the massive Louisiana Superdome, which sheltered approximately 26,000 people. The social impact was beyond calculation, and disaster relief assistance was needed on an almost unimaginable scale. "I have to give special credit to Reg for understanding from the beginning that NEA should be involved in the relief efforts," said Joe Reed of the Alabama Education Association.[58] Teachers were without classrooms, citizens without homes, students without schools, and workers without jobs. Reg personally visited the disaster areas, witnessed the destruction close-up, and proceeded to lead NEA's Hurricane Relief Fund, which raised over $1 million and provided financial assistance to thousands whose lives had been abruptly uprooted by the devastation. Michael Marks of the Executive Committee was from Hattiesburg, Mississippi, where the damage was great. "Reg's response to Katrina may have been one of his finest hours as President of NEA," said Marks. "He gave NEA an identity in my area that will not be soon forgotten."[59] Many others considered NEA's Hurricane Relief Fund to be one of the finest initiatives of his presidency, when both he and the organization rose to new heights in the mind of the public and the Association reached a peak in its illustrious history of assisting those with the greatest need. Reg's article entitled "Katrina: We Are Family" spoke poignantly about the tragedy, and revealed NEA's compassion for humanity and its enduring commitment to social causes. He wrote:

> "No natural disaster in American history has displaced America's school children in such a way as Katrina. It left 372,000 of them with no school to attend; it closed 700 schools, 100 damaged beyond repair; and it means thousands of NEA members have no jobs.

> "Across the country, the NEA family knew what to do when people hurt. We mobilized. We set out to raise $1 million to help all the public school employees get back on their feet, and to support those who are taking in the displaced children.

> "As soon as the money started coming in, I went on a trip to the Gulf Coast to start handing it out, because the need is now.

> "We set up a helpline, and there have been days when more than a thousand teachers and education support professionals have called asking for emergency aid, be it to pay for medication or rent an apartment. One call was from a husband and wife, both NEA members, who had their house, their car, and their school all under water.

> "We set up an adopt-a-school program, and hundreds of organizations have called, saying count us in, we want to assist. And we are asking some NEA staff to go to the area because an extra hand never hurts."[60]

The gradually changing role and identification of the Association in education reform, which began with Mary Hatwood Futrell's appointment to the task force of the Carnegie Forum on Education and the Economy and the subsequent NEA endorsement of the National Board for Professional Teaching Standards (NBPTS), had been sustained by Keith Geiger and defined by Bob Chase in the "new unionism," continued with Reg and was promoted with the popular phrase, "Great Public Schools for Every Child." The simplicity of that visionary statement served as an excellent trademark for NEA, which sought as much brand identify for its work on student achievement as had been sustained by its traditional image as a well organized union whose purpose was to protect and advance educators' rights and interests. The NEA budget had substantially reflected the "new unionism," but the public relations value of the phrase Reg had created made for an easier introduction of NEA to parents, public education advocates, minority communities, and other non-member groups. Eventually it was incorporated into NEA's logo.

Perhaps one of Reg's most significant contributions was the improvement of NEA's relationships and identity with ethnic minority communities, where outreach programs broached new ventures and opened new doors much more receptive to the NEA message. It was in those communities—not only of blacks, but also of Hispanics, American Indians and Alaska Natives, and Asian and Pacific Islands of lower socio-economic standing—where NEA and other progressive forces were losing ground on the issues of vouchers and privatization to conservative organizations, politicians, policy makers, and critics of education. Reg wrote about the importance of building relationships with ethnic minorities, and exposed the threat of the conservative movement to public education for "all the people," explaining that saving a few students from poorly performing public schools was not nearly as good an investment as was an unconditional commitment to improve all public schools. The notion that a zip code or parental income and educational background should be determining factors in the quality of education a student received was totally rejected by Reg as counter to the ideals of democracy and social justice. His writings, however cogent and persuasive they might be, fell somewhat short of equaling his public speaking engagements in which he was always excellent and sometimes extraordinary. The size of the audience or the location bore no relation to his preparation and enthusiasm of the moment. "It never mattered whether there were 50, 500, or a thousand" said Stan Johnson of Wisconsin, "he always gave every speech as if it were the most important of his life." Joe Reed of Alabama was also impressed by Reg's willingness to travel to remote locations to share the NEA message. "He wanted each member to know how much their membership was valued," reflected Reed.[61]

Reg's strength came from ground-level with the members, "because he listened to the smallest voice, leaving them to feel they were heard and understood," Johnson said when summarizing his leadership. Though comfortable on the stage, he was even more relaxed on the floor and wanted to convey that to each member.[62] And though his presentations and style of delivery often varied, one of his favorite, frequently used techniques was to enter from the rear of the room, one hand on his cane and the other extended to shake hands with the audience as he made his way to the podium. On closing, it was not unusual for him to reverse that route from the stage to the floor with the same routine, imploring members in the words of Sir Winston Churchill to "never give up." For those hearing him for the first time, it was a moving experience, and for those familiar with his style, it was the fulfillment of what they had come to both hear and see. His personal introspection and awareness that Reg on the page and in the media, could not match Reg in person, might have been what drove him to maintain such a demanding schedule of speaking engagements throughout all six years of his presidency. He understood and had confidence in his strengths and accepted the source of his appeal. In all areas of presidential expectations, he was adequate, and in some remarkable. But when at the podium and on the stump, he was, as one member said, "worth the price of admission."[63] "Hey baby!" "You got that right!" "That's what I'm talking about!" became his signature phrases for seamless transitions into often intricate discussions of the full range of education issues which he presented with ease, skill, and dexterity. His use of the vernacular was only a vehicle for humor and comic relief which demonstrated that, despite his stature as NEA President, he was not removed from the culture of regular people, who were also owed the same opportunities, resources, and quality of education as individuals from the most affluent backgrounds. The connection to the members was transparent, and it was effective.

When appearing before and speaking to members, Reg made it a regular practice to acknowledge the value of every component of the organization.

Just as the African proverb "It takes a village to raise a child" had caught fire with educators, his insistence that it took all of "TEAM NEA" for the Association to be effective caught the spirit of the members; no single part of the organization held a greater value than any other. The impact of his concept on member and staff morale is difficult to measure, but it cannot be ignored that NEA's membership rose from 2.7 to 3.2 million members on his presidential watch.

Outside of NEA, Reg became vice president of Education International, a 348-member organization representing over 29 million teachers and educators in 166 countries. He served as a board member of the National Council for the Accreditation of Teacher Education (NCATE), the Joint Center for Political and Economic Studies, and the National Board for Professional Teaching Standards, among many other organizations. He was the recipient of three honorary degrees and received awards from scores of organizations and groups, including the Congressional Black Caucus, the U.S. Hispanic Leadership Institute, and the National Conference of Black Mayors. In 2006, he traveled to Lincoln Cathedral in England, where, in recognition of his commitment to democracy and the fundamental freedoms laid down in Magna Carta, the Cathedral unveiled a stone column in his name. None of the national and international awards however, meant more to Reg than the honor of being named on the Danville High School Wall of Fame, because that recognition—among all others—was the most closely connected to the world of his roots and his upbringing.

Reg's legacy, opined Stan Johnson, "will be the doors he opened for countless members, the coalitions built with external partners, the new venues pursued, the attention given to the achievement gaps, steering the NEA ship through NCLB, and his understanding that NEA could make a decided difference in public education, but could not do it alone." Bob Chanin echoed, "He may have been the best cheerleader for the NEA we have seen." Cheerleaders in the organizational context motivate crowds, inspire followers, rally members, and promote esprit de corps. A cheerleader is an adulator, one who expresses hope for the outcome of the future. For school personnel, Reg was not just another cheerleader on the sidelines rooting for Team NEA—he was the captain of the squad.[64]

On July 4, 2008, at the final RA of his presidency, Reginald Weaver had the pleasure of announcing NEA's endorsement of Barack Obama's bid for the office of President of the United States. A few weeks later, on August 25, he stepped on one of the most powerful stages in America when on behalf of NEA he spoke about the prospective nominee at the Democratic National Convention in Denver. He talked about access to early childhood education, small class sizes, parental involvement, increased higher education, financial assistance for lower income students, accepting and treating school personnel as allies and professionals, and of school accountability absent of summative student judgments based on single assessment instruments. Those were the issues for NEA, and their solutions were promised by Obama. "That, my friends," said Reg, "is why the 3.2 million members of the NEA are organized, energized and mobilized to help elect Barack Obama as the next president of the United States of America."[65] It seemed fitting that his term should draw to a close with another example of NEA members voicing an expression of the organization's enduring commitment to social justice and the legacy of inclusion, which began in 1857 when Robert Campbell, a black Philadelphia teacher, was counted among the founding members of the organization that has become the National Education Association.

Epilogue

In 2006, the National Education Association's Representative Assembly adopted a statement of its vision, mission, and values. Framed with a vision of a great public school for *every* student, the mission called for advocacy for education professionals and uniting NEA's members to prepare every student for a *diverse* and *interdependent* world. The core values guiding the work of the Association include *equal opportunity* to take advantage of the *human* and *civil rights* of a quality education. Public education is essential to establishing *a just society* where respect for the *worth*, *dignity*, and *equality* of *every* individual in our *diverse* population is assured. Public education is articulated as a cornerstone for building an involved, informed, and engaged citizenry for a *representative democracy*. Moreover, the statement maintains that the highest professional standards are critical to student achievement and worthy of the status, compensation, and respect due *all professionals*. Further, members are encouraged to enter into partnerships with *parents*, *families*, *communities*, and *other stakeholders* to achieve student success. And, finally, the *collective actions* of education professionals are extolled as essential for promoting the *common good*.

The liberal use of terms and expressions of inclusion contained in NEA's statement of vision, mission, and values may be unparalleled in the foundational positions of major organizations in America. But, with a commitment considerably greater than lofty language on parchment, NEA holds itself fully accountable for inclusive practices and policies, and it incorporates those principles into organizational culture and politics. Indeed, it gives a tangible structure to what Mary Hatwood Futrell meant when she called NEA an organization "with a soul."

The elections of Braulio Alonso and Elizabeth Koontz to the presidency of NEA are remarkable milestones in the Association's history. Those elections were directly attributable to the merger of NEA and the American Teachers Association in 1966, and to the rise of the NEA constituent group, the National Council of Urban Education Associations in the 1950s and early '60s. Both presidents were linked to the changes in America resulting from the Civil Rights Movement, the urban crisis, and the advent of collective bargaining for teachers. Together they saved NEA, they transformed NEA, and they ushered NEA into the modern era.

Prior to Alonso and Koontz, only a few minorities had ever been elected to the top offices in predominantly white professional organizations, and none ever in an organization of the size and influence of NEA. To demonstrate those elections were not token gestures or expressions of fleeting interest, NEA proceeded to elect Harris, Futrell, and Weaver between 1974 and 2006, the year in which it issued its statement of vision, mission, and values. The impetus for electing minorities to leadership positions came in sequence from the bottom up in the Association, beginning with NCUEA and the NEA/ATA merger, and escalating after the Constitutional Convention (con-con) with its bold provisions for minority member guarantees. During that same period, the sharing of power and decision-making at the local and state levels resulted in countless numbers of minorities and women becoming actively involved and being elected to office in the local and state associations. It would require an encyclopedia to list all of the names of those minority and female members who hold or have held local and state leadership positions since the 1960s. Emerging from that huge membership, minorities are now serving or have recently served in all of the highest positions of NEA, including the Executive Committee, the Board of Directors, and as delegates to the Representative Assembly.

Only in relation to the historical perspective can there be a full appreciation of and respect for a human organization, which—though having had the courage to allow a black man to be among its founders in 1857—would not elect a minority to the Board of Directors or any significant leadership post until 1954, nor a single one to its Executive Committee until the early 1960s, and then proceed with dispatch to elect five minority presidents in 32 years, and become the largest and most progressive non-governmental force in public education. Historian Roy Nichols stated in his autobiography, *A Historian's Progress*, that "if you erase the 'r' from any 'revolution' you will find that it is none-tenths 'evolution.'" That cogent analysis is relevant in understanding NEA's legacy of inclusion. The longest journey begins with a single step, and for NEA that step was taken when Robert Campbell, the black Philadelphia teacher, placed his signature on its initial charter. From that point forward, NEA never allowed the issue of educating minorities with public funds to be removed from the table of its concerns. In an era of aggressive white supremacy, it had the courage to invite black speakers to its annual conventions and maintain a race-neutral membership policy at the national level. It not only agreed in 1926 to assist the ATA in securing accreditation for black high schools, but it also established a Joint Committee of the two organizations and allowed that group a national forum to sustain the dialogue on black education through the Great Depression, World War II, and the Civil Rights Movement. Over time, the Joint Committee gained stature and influence in the Association and guided it through the merger of 1966.

By 1967, the Association's monthly publication, the *NEA Reporter*, followed the Civil Rights Movement more than did the periodicals of any other educational organization. Even before con-con, NEA elected three minority presidents, and two afterwards. The minority guarantees of con-con distanced NEA from all its competitors for minority loyalty. And, when the education reform movement came to dominate discussions on education policy, NEA embraced social justice for the disadvantaged in ways best expressed in its vision, mission, and values statement.

The infrastructure of NEA continues to identify, develop, and promote minority leaders at all levels. To be sure, the election of five minority presidents—Alonso, Koontz, Harris, Futrell, and Weaver—since the merger is an accomplishment that may be difficult to match. But NEA has demonstrated both the will and the capacity to maintain its commitment to the legacy of inclusion for "all the people," and if the past is truly prologue to the future—others will follow.

Notes

The Origins of the Legacy of Inclusion, 1857-1966

1. Edgar B. Wesley, *NEA: The First Hundred Years* (New York: Harper and Brothers, 1957), 3-19.

2. Thelma D. Perry, *History of the American Teachers Association* (Washington, D.C.: National Education Association, 1975), 29; Henry A. Bullock, *A History of Negro Education in the South: From 1619 to the Present* (Cambridge: Harvard University Press, 1967); James Anderson, *The Education of Blacks in the South, 1860-1935* (Chapel Hill: University of North Carolina Press, 1988).

3. Wesley, *NEA*, p. 4: John W. Blasingame, The Slave Community (New York: Oxford University Press, 1972).

4. John Vishneski, "What the Court Decided in Dred Scott v. Sandford," *The Journal of Legal History*, 32 (4), 1988, 373-390.

5. Albert C. Norton, "Founders of the National Education Association," NEA Research Memo 1960-3, Archive of the National Education Association, 20.

6. Richard Blackett, *Beating Against the Barriers* (Baton Rouge: Louisiana State University Press, 1986), 139-41.

7. Blackett, *Beating*, 143.

8. Blackett, *Beating*, 146-47; W. E. B. Du Bois, *The Philadelphia Negro, A Social Study* (Philadelphia: University of Pennsylvania, 1899), 88.

9. Blackett, *Beating*, 144-49.

10. Wesley, *NEA*, 20.

11. Wesley, *NEA*, 21.

12. *Philadelphia Press*, August 26, 1857.

13. Wesley, *NEA*, 24.

14. Wesley, *NEA*, 25-30.

15. See *Journal of Proceedings and Addresses of the National Education Association (1858-1877)*.

16. *Philadelphia Press*, August 26, 1857.

17. R. J. M. Blackett, "Return to the Motherland," *Phylon, 40, No. 4 (4ᵗʰ Quarter, 1979)*, 375-86.

18. Robert Campbell, "A Pilgrimage to My Motherland: An Account of a Journey Among the Egbas and Yorubas of Central Africa in 1859-60," in Howard Bell (ed.), *Search for a Place: Black Separatism and Africa* (Ann Arbor: University of Michigan Press, 1971), 170-71; Richard Blackett, "Martin Delaney and Robert Campbell: Black Americas in Search of an African Colony," *Journal of Negro History*, LXII (1977), 1-25.

19. Perry, *History of the American Teachers Association*, 13-23; Perry Murray, *History of the North Carolina Teachers Association* (Washington, D.C.: National Education Association, 1984), 11-34; James F. Potts, Sr., *A History of the Palmetto Education Association* (Washington, D.C., National Education Association, 1978), 15-40; Vernon Mc Daniel, *History of the State Teachers Association of Texas* (Washington, D.C., National Education Association, 1977), 21; W. J. Hale, "Purpose and Program of the National Association of Teachers in Colored Schools," *The Bulletin* 1 (November 1928), 6, Luther P. Jackson, *A History of the Virginia Teachers Association* (Norfolk: Guide Publishing Company, 1937) 2,11-15, 32; Adam Fairclough, *A Class of Their Own, Black Teachers in the Segregated South* (Cambridge: Harvard University Press, 2007).

20. NEA *Proceedings* (1865), 297; Wesley, *NEA*, 38.

21. NEA *Proceedings* (1865), 235-249.

22. *Ibid.*

23. Wilson J. Moses, *Alexander Crummell: A Study of Civilization and Discontent* (Amherst: University of Massachusetts Press, 1992).

24. Wesley, *NEA*, 39.

25. NEA Proceedings (1865), 297; Wesley, *NEA*, 38-39.

26. Wesley, *NEA*, 255-261.

27. In 1943, the NEA's Representative Assembly passed a New Business Item saying it would not chose cities for its conventions which discriminated in "housing, feeding, seating at the convention, and general welfare of all delegates and teachers regardless of race, color, or creed." In 1950 the selection of St. Louis, Missouri as the convention site caused uproar because of the segregated hotels of that city. After that episode, NEA never again held its convention in cities with segregated hotel accommodations. See Carol F. Karpinski, *African Americans and the National Education Association During the Civil Rights Movement* (New York: Peter Lang Publishers, 2008), 55-61; Wesley, *NEA* 255-261.

28. NEA Proceedings (1884), 125-130.

29. NEA Proceedings (1884), 130; Louis Harlan (ed), *The Booker T. Washington Papers, Volume 2: 1860-89* (Urbana: University of Illinois Press, 1972) 266-262; Louis Harlan, Booker T. Washington, *The Making of a Black Leader*, New York: Oxford University Press, 1972).

30. NEA *Proceedings* (1884), 85, 76-95.

31. NEA *Proceedings* (1886), 230.

32. NEA *Proceedings* (1884), 114.

33. NEA *Proceedings* (1896), 216.

34. NEA *Proceedings* (1890), 267-276.

35. The NEA conventions of the late 19th century encouraged open debate on the "race question" and regularly issued reports on the educational status of minorities. The majority of leading NEA leaders and personalities deplored racism and discrimination,

though their declarations had little impact on public policy, during a period when race relations deteriorated and the conditions of minorities, particularly blacks, worsened with the introduction of black codes, segregation and other unfair practices. See Rayford Logan, *The Betrayal of the Negro: From Rutherford B. Hayes to Woodrow Wilson* (New York: Collier Books, 1954); C. Vann Woodward, *The Strange Career of Jim Crow* (New York: Oxford University Press, 2001), Quoted in I. A. Newby, *Black Carolinians* (Columbia: University of South Carolina Press, 1973), 84.

36. NEA *Proceedings* (1890), 506.

37. Perry, *History of the American Teachers Association*; Bullock, *A History of Negro Education in the South*.

38. NEA *Proceedings* (1890) 497-505; (1890) 505-521; (1865) 535-549; (1884) 76-95; (1886) 229-232; (1884) 117-120; (1893) 35; Perry, <u>ATA</u>, 14-15; Bullock, *Negro Education*.

39. NEA *Proceedings* (1894) 561-562.

40. *Ibid*.

41. The deficiencies of black schools were too great to be compared in any equitable way to white schools. The buildings, resources, length of school term and per pupil expenditures were uniformly inferior to those of whites. "It is not a wonder that [pupils] do not learn more, but the real wonder is that they learn as much as they do" remarked one South Carolina state education agent during this period. Quoted in I. A. Newby, *Black Carolinians: A History of Blacks in South Carolina from 1895 to 1968* (Columbia: University of South Carolina Press, 1973), 88. One of the most exhaustive studies on the disparities in black and white school expenditures in the early 20th century is Louis Harlan, *Separate and Unequal: Public School Campaigns and Racism in the Southern Seaboard States, 1901-1915* (New York: Athenaeum, 1968); James Anderson, "Black Rural Communities and the Struggle for Black Education During the Age of BTW," *Peabody Journal of Education*, 67, No. 4 (1992), 46-62.

42. Perry, *A History of the ATA*, 11-22.

43. *Ibid*; Murray, *History of North Carolina Teachers Association*, 15-34.

44. Perry, *A History of the ATA*, 13-14.

45. Perry, *NEA*, 146-55, 348-49.

46. Charles M. Christian, *Black Saga: The African American Experience* (New York: Houghton Mifflin Company, 1995), 267.

47. Perry, *A History of the ATA*, 22.

48. *Ibid*, 111-131.

49. *Ibid*, 14-22.

50. *Ibid*, 45-46.

51. *Ibid*, 32.

52. *Ibid*, 47-50.

53. NEA *Proceedings* (1900), 490.

54. Logan, *Betrayal of the Negro*. The life and philosophy of Wright receives excellent scholarly treatment in June O. Patton, "And Truth Shall Make You Free: Richard Robert Wright, Sr., Black Intellectual and Iconoclast," *Journal of Negro History* (81) (January 1996), 573-589.

55. Perry, *ATA*, 104-05; LeRoy Davis, *A Clashing of the Soul: John Hope and the Dilemma of African American Leadership and Black Higher Education in the Early Twentieth Century* (Athens: University of Georgia Press, 1998).

56. Perry, *ATA*, 189-206.

57. The legal sanctioning of segregation crushed hope for an integrated society. Consequently, blacks formed their own organizations for the professions, and between 1900 and 1930, virtually every white professional group had its counterpart in black society.

58. Perry, *ATA*, 163-186; Wesley, *NEA*, 317-319; Allan M. West, *The National Education Association: The Power Base for Education* (New York: The Free Press, 1980), 23; Wayne Urban, *Gender, Race, and the National Education Association: Professionalism and Its Limitations* (New York: Routledge Falmer, 2000), 213; Susan Lowell Butler, *The*

National Education Association: A Special Mission (Washington: National Education Association, 1987), 43.

59. Perry, *ATA*, 163-189, 209-222.

60. Wesley, *NEA*, 318.

61. NEA *Proceedings* (1928) 217-220.

62. Perry, *ATA*, 163-188, 209-222.

63. NEA *Proceedings* (1929), 107.

64. *The New York Times,* January 30, 1937, 20; Rolland Dewing, *The National Education Association and Desegregation,* Phylon, 30, No. 2 (Second Quarter, 1969), 110-111.

65. NEA *Proceedings* (1935) 884; Karpinski, *African-Americans and the NEA,* 42-43.

66. Elizabeth Ihle, "The Teacher Salary Equalization Movement in Virginia: The NAACP and the Virginia State Teachers Association, 1935-1941," paper presented at the Annual Meeting of the American Educational Research Association (New Orleans, April 4-8, 1994); Richard Kluger, *Simple Justice: The History of Brown v. Board of Education* (New York: Random House, 1975); Hazel Davis, a former NEA research staffer, left NEA an oral interview in which she noted in the early 1940's how Thurgood Marshall researched NEA records relating to the inequities in the salaries of black and white teachers   NEA did not publish the information but allowed Marshall unrestricted use of its salary data. See Hazel Davis interview [June 17, 1988] box 3117, in NEA Archive, Washington, D.C.

67. Perry, *ATA*, 237-240.

68. Glenda Elizabeth Gilmore, *Defying Dixie: The Radical Roots of Civil Rights, 1919-1950* (New York: W. W. Norton, 2008); Al-Tony Gilmore, "The Black Southerner's Response to the Southern System of Race Relations: 1900 to Post World War II," in Robert Haws (ed.), *The Age of Segregation: Race Relations in the South* (Oxford: University of Mississippi Press, 1978), 89-116.

69. NEA *Proceedings* (1934), 664.

70. NEA *Proceedings* (1938), 821-822.

71. Kluger, *Simple Justice;* Genna Rae McNeil, *Charles Hamilton Houston and the Struggle for Civil Rights Movement* (Philadelphia: University of Pennsylvania Press, 1983).

72. Gilmore, *Defying Dixie,* 225-264; Pater Wallenstein (ed.) *Higher Education and the Civil Rights Movement* (Gainesville: University Press of Florida, 2008).

73. Gilmore *Defying Dixie,* 247-296.

74. Kluger, *Simple Justice;* Mark Tushnet, *The NAACP's Legal Strategy Against Segregated Education,* 1925-1950 (Chapel Hill: University of North Carolina Press (1987); Jack Greenberg, *Crusaders in the Courts* (New York; Basic Books, 1994).

75. Karpinski, *African-Americas and the NEA,* 96.

76. Lawrence P. Scott and William Womack, Sr., *Double V: The Civil Rights Struggle of the Tuskegee Airmen* (East Lansing: Michigan State University Press, 1994); Nat Brandt, *Harlem at War: The Black Experience in WWI* (Syracuse: Syracuse University Press, 1996); an interesting account of the Double V campaign is also contained in R. J. Smith, *The Great Black Way: L. A. in the 1940's* (New York: Public Affairs Books 2006), 52-54, 60-206.

77. William Beatty, "What Makes an American," *NEA Journal,* 12 (February, 1943) 55-58.

78. West, *The National Education Association,* 112-114.

79. NEA *Proceedings* (1942), 527.

80. Karpinski, *African Americans and the National Education Association,* 45-53.

81. Most of the major black press took notice of the 1943 NEA resolution against discrimination of its members at the conventions. See Norfolk *Journal and Guide, Pittsburgh Courier, Chicago Defender* and *Baltimore Afro-American* for August and September 1943.

82. Christian, *Black Saga*, 367; Beth Tompkins Bates, *Pullman Porters and the Rise of Protest Politics in Black America, 1925-1945* (Chapel Hill: University of North Carolina Press, 2001).

83. Michael R. Gardner, *Harry Truman and Civil Rights* (Carbondale: Southern Illinois University Press, 2002), 43-64, 174-177.

84. Karpinski, *African Americans and the National Education Association*, 55-69.

85. *Ibid.*

86. NEA *Proceedings* (1951).

87. Karpinski, *African Americans and the National Education Association*, 62.

88. Interview with Don Morrison, June 13, 2008.

89. Interview with Eugene Dryer, May 14, 2008; West, *NEA*, 140.

90. Karpinski, *African Americans and the National Education Association*, 65; Civil Rights Documentation Project, Mississippi Department of Archives and History, Oral History Transcript N. R. Burger.

91. West, *NEA*, 89.

92. NEA *Proceedings* (1954).

93. West, *NEA*, 319.

94. Rolland Dewing, "The NEA and Minority Rights," *Journal of Negro Education*, 47, No. 4. (Autumn 1978); Wayne Urban, *General Race and NEA*, 173.

95. Interview with Eugene Dryer, May 17, 2008.

96. Jo McGuire, *NCUEA: An Agent of Change*, 1986, a report on the origins of the *National Council of Urban Education Associations*, papers of Helen Bain. Interviews with Helen Bain, July 9, 2008, and July 24, 2008.

97. Interview with George Fischer, June 5, 2008; Interview with Joe Reed, May 23, 2008.

98. Interview with Braulio Alonso, July 24, 2008.

99. Perry, *ATA*, 298-301.

100. Interview with E. B. Palmer, March 6, 2008; Interview with Julius Chambers, June 27, 2007; Michael Fultz, "The Displacement of Black Educators Post Brown," *History of Education Quarterly*, 44, No.1 (Spring 2007), 4-45; National Education Association, *Report of the Task Force Survey of Teachers Displacement in Seventeen States* (Washington, D.C.: December 1965); Sam Ethridge, "Impact of the 1954 Brown v. Topeka Board of Education Decision on Black Educators," *Negro Educational Review*, 30:4 (October 1979), 217-232.

101. West, *NEA*, 103-104.

102. Interview with Joe Reed, May 23, 2008.

103. Perry, *History of ATA*, 330; Urban, *Gender, Race and the NEA*, 217.

104. Interview with E. B. Palmer, March 6, 2008; Interview with Lois Edinger, March 4, 2008.

105. Excerpt from speech by Joe Reed to the NEA Southeast Regional Minority Leadership Training Seminar, Memphis, Tennessee, October 4, 2001.

106. West, *NEA*, 159.

Braulio Alonso: 1967-1968 – The Teacher Revolution, the Urban Movement, and the Merger

1. United States Census, 1970, Census Bureau of the U. S. Government.

2. Interview with Braulio Alonso, February 7, 2008.

3. Interview with Alonso, February 7, 2008; Braulio Alonso, "The Ybor I Remember," from the personal papers of Alonso; Interview with Alonso by Angela Reeder, July 17, 2001, possession of author.

4. "Historical Perspective—Ybor City: An Island of Immigrants" a publication of the Ybor City Folk Festival 1986 by the Ybor City Centennial Committee, Tampa, Florida, 4-6.

5. Interview with Braulio Alonso, February 7, 2008.

6. Interview with Braulio Alonso, February 7, 2008.

7. Interview with Braulio Alonso, February 7, 2008.

8. Interview with Braulio Alonso, February 7, 2008; Gary R. Murmino and George E. Pozzetta, "The Reader Lights the Candle: Cuban and Florida Cigar Workers' Oral Tradition," *Labor's Heritage,* Vol.5, No 1. (Spring 1993); "Life in the Cigar Factories of Ybor City" in brochure produced by the Ybor City Museum Society, n.d., in papers of Braulio Alonso, "The Lector" an unpublished paper by Braulio Alonso; copy in author's possession.

9. Alonso, "The Ybor I Remember," 1.

10. Reeder Interview, 4.

11. Alonso, "The Ybor I Remember," 10.

12. Interview with Alonso, February 7, 2008; Cleo Cabrera, "An Educator's Educator," *Tampa Tribune*, November 7, 2000, 2.

13. Paul Guzzo, "Silhouettes," *La Gaceta,* September 29, 2000, 12.

14. *Ibid.*

15. Interview with Alonso, February 7, 2008; Reeder Interview, 7.

16. Guzzo, "Silhouettes," 12.

17. Interview with Alonso, February 7, 2008.

18. Ben Green, *Before His Time: The Untold Story of Harry T. Moore, America's First Civil Rights Martyr* (Gainesville: University Press of Florida, 2005).

19. Cabrera. "An Educator's Educators," Gary R. Murmino, "Tampa's Greatest Living Person," *The Tampa Tribune*, October 8, 2006, 12.

20. Reeder Interview, 6.

21. Interview with Braulio Alonso, February 7, 2008.

22. *Ibid.*

23. Interview with Bain, 7/9/08; Palmer 3/6/08; Edinger 3/4/08; Chanin 7/15/08; and Reed 5/23/08.

24. Cabrera. "An Educator's Educators," 2; Murmino, "Tampa's Greatest," 12.

25. Richard Kahlenberg, *Tough Liberal: Albert Shanker and the Battles Over Schools, Unions, Race, and Democracy* (New York: Columbia University Press, 2007).

26. *Ibid*; Alan West, *The National Education Association* (Washington, D.C.: NEA 1980), 39-87; Wayne Urban, *Gender, Race, and the National Education Association* (New York: Routledge Falmer, 2000) 171-181.

27. Interview with Helen Bain, July 9, 1908; Interview with Alonso February 7, 2008, Jo McGuire, *NCUEA: An Agent of Change*, 1986, A Report on the Origins of the National Council of Urban Education Associations, papers of Helen Bain.

28. Michael Makowsky, "The 1968 Florida Teachers' Strike and the Emergence of Teacher Unionism," a paper presented at the Annual Meeting of the Florida Conference of Historians, Orange Park, Florida, March 11-13, 1994 in *Annual Proceedings*, Volume 2 (September 1994), 162-183."

29. NEA *Proceedings* (1967), 39-44; *NEA Reporter*, December 15, 1967, 1. Interview with Alonso, February 7, 2008; West, NEA, 224; Makowsky, "1968 Florida Teachers' Strike."

30. Makowsky, "1968 Florida Teachers' Strike."

31. West, *NEA*, 67, *NEA Reporter*, March 15, 1968, 2.

32. *NEA Reporter*, September 15, 1967, 1; Makowsky, "1968 Florida Teachers' Strike."

33. *NEA Reporter*, January 19, 1968, 3, and October 6, 1967, 7.

34. Interview with Alonso, February 7, 2008;

35. *Ibid*; *NEA Reporter*, April 19, 1968, 1; Makowsky, "1968 Florida Teachers' Strike."

36. Makowsky, "1968 Florida Teachers' Strike."

37. West, *NEA*, 225-226.

38. *NEA Reporter*, October 20, 1967, 6; West, *NEA*, 223.

39. Interview with Bob Chanin, July 15, 2008.

40. Interview with Braulio Alonso, July 24, 2008; *NEA Reporter*, March 15, 1968, 3.

41. Cabrera. "An Educator's Educators," 2; Murmino, "Tampa's Greatest," 12.

42. Interview with Alonso, February 7, 2008.

43. NEA *Proceedings* (1968), 40.

Elizabeth (Libby) Duncan Koontz: 1968-1969 – Human and Civil Rights, Decentralization, and Black Power

1. "A Fighting Lady for NEA," *Time*, July 12, 1968.

2. Wayne Urban, *Gender, Race, and the National Education Association: Professionalism and Its Limitations* (New York: Routledge Falmer, 2000), 226; Interview with Lois Edinger, March 4, 2008; Interview with E. B. Palmer, March 6, 2008.

3. NEA *Proceedings* (1968),267-275.

4. *Time*, July 12, 1968.

5. Interview with Craig Phillips, March 7, 2008.

6. Interview with Harold Webb, June 21, 2i008; Interview with E. B. Palmer, March 6, 2008.

7. *Ibid*; Interview with Craig Philips, March 7, 2008.

8. Interview with Lois Edinger, March 4, 2008, Interview with Eugene Dryer, June 21, 2008.

9. Interview with Craig Phillips, March 7, 2008.

10. *Time*, July 12, 1968.

11. Peter Wallenstein, "Black Southerners and Nonblack Universities: The Process of Desegregating Southern Higher Education, 1935-1965," in Wallenstein (ed.) *Higher Education and the Civil Rights Movement* (Gainesville: University Press of Florida, 2008), 17-59; Glenda Elizabeth Gilmore *Defying Dixie: The Radical Roots of Civil Rights, 1919-1950* (New York, W. W. Norton, 2008), 255-260.

12. Gilmore *Defying Dixie*, 258.

13. *Ibid*.

14. Janet Sims-Wood, "Elizabeth Duncan Koontz," in Jesse Carney Smith (ed.), *Notable Black American Women* (Detroit: Gale Research, Inc., 1992), 639.

15. Interview with E. B. Palmer, March 6, 2008; Perry Murray, "Elizabeth Duncan Koontz," in Darlene Clark Hine (ed.), *Black Women in America* (Brooklyn: Carlson Publishing, 1993), 683.

16. *Time*, July 12, 1968.

17. Allida Black, *Casting Her Shadow: Eleanor Roosevelt and the Shaping of Postwar Liberalism*, (New York: Columbia University Press, 1996), 123-125.

18. Interview with Harold Webb, June 21, 2008; Interview with E. B. Palmer, March 6, 2008.

19. Percy Murray, *History of the North Carolina Teachers Association* (Washington, D.C.: National Education Association, 1984), 62-65; Interview with Harold Webb, June 21, 2008.

20. Murray, *History of the North Carolina Teachers Association*, 46-48.

21. *Ibid*, 62-65.

22. *Ibid*; Murray, *Black Women in America*, 683; Interview with Lois Edinger, March 4, 2008.

23. Interview with Braulio Alonso, February 7, 2008 and July 2, 2008.

24. Murray, *History of the North Carolina Teachers Association*, 62-64, 106-107, 151.

25. Interview with E. B. Palmer, March 6, 2008.

26. Urban, *Gender and Race*.

27. Interview with Lois Edinger, March 4, 2008.

28. *Ibid*.

29. *Ibid*.

30. Interview with E. B. Palmer, March 6, 2008.

31. Interview with Braulio Alonso, February 7, 2008; Interview with Helen Bain, July 9. 2008, and July 25, 2008.

32. Interview with Eugene Dryer, June 21, 2008; Urban, *Gender and Race*, 226; Michael J. Schultz, Jr., *The National Education Association and the Black Teacher* (Coral Gables: University of Miami Press, 1070), West, *NEA*, 133, 226.

33. Interview with George Fischer, June 5, 2008; David Seldon, *The Teacher Rebellion* (Washington, D.C.: Howard University Press, 1985), 137.

34. *NEA Reporter*, April 19, 1968, p. 3.

35. *NEA Proceedings* (1968), 29-44.

36. *Ibid*, 40.

37. *Ibid*, 43-44.

38. West, *NEA*, 106-107; *NEA Reporter*, October 4, 1968, 1.

39. Richard Kahlenberg, *Tough Liberal: Al Shanker and the Battle Over Schools, Union, Race, and Democracy* (New York: Columbia University Press, 2007, 67-124.

40. *Ibid*; Selden, *The Teacher Rebellion*, 144-156.

41. Kahlenberg, *Tough Liberal*, 73.

42. *Ibid*, 69.

43. *Ibid*. 93-11. Also see Don Cameron, *The Inside Story of the Teacher Revolution* (Lanham, Maryland: Scarecrow Education, 2005).

44. Kahlenberg, *Tough Liberal*, 66-124.

45. Kahlenberg, *Tough Liberal*, 111.

46. *NEA Reporter*, February 28, 1969, 1; "The Seeds of Reform," *The Circle*, Vol. 5, No. 9, February 7, 1969, 5, a publication of Marist College, Poughkeepsie, New York.

47. *Ibid*, 1-3.

48. *NEA Reporter*, October 4, 1968, 1, and September 20, 1968, 5.

49. *Ibid*, 1-3.

50. *NEA Reporter*, October 4, 1968, 1.

51. West, *NEA*, 133. *Time*, July 12, 1968.

52. Selden, *Teacher Rebellion*, 137-138; West, *NEA*, 235.

53. Dean Kotlowski, *Nixon's Civil Rights* (Cambridge: Harvard University, Press, 2001), 242-243.

54. Interview with E. B. Palmer, March64, 2008; Interview with George Fischer June 5, 2005.

55. Interview with Lois Edinger, March 4, 2008.

56. Interview with Reed 6/12/08, Fischer 6/5/08, Palmer 3/6/08.

57. *NEA Reporter*, February 28, 1969, 2.

58. *Ibid*, "Black Woman and Double Discrimination," *Sepia* 18 (September, 1969), 18.

59. Jane Simms-Wood, "Elizabeth Koontz," 641.

60. *Ibid*.

61. Interview with Lois Edinger, March 4, 2008.

62. *Ibid.*

63. "A Symposium: What's Right in American Education," *Education Horizons*, 54 (Spring 1976), 144-145.M

64. Interview with Craig Phillips, March 7, 2008.

65. Molly Meijer Weitheimer and Nicholas D. Gertgold, *Elizabeth Hanford Dole: Speaking from the Heart* (Westport, CT: Greenwood Publishing Group, 2004), 77.

James Alexander Harris: 1974-75 – Project Urban Neglect and the Constitutional Convention Transition

1. Interview with George Fischer, June 6, 2008.

2. Allan West, *The National Education Association* (NEW York: Free Press, 1980), 227.

3. Interview with Lauri Wynn, April 23, 2008.

4. Interview with James Harris, January 23, 2008.

5. *Ibid.*

6. *Ibid.*

7. *Ibid.*

8. *Ibid.*

9. *Ibid.*

10. Interview with George Fischer, June 6, 2008.

11. Interview with James Harris, January 23, 2008 and June 10, 2008.

12. *Ibid.*

13. Lawrence P. Scott and William H. Womack, *Double V: The Civil Rights Struggle of the Tuskegee Airman* (East Lansing: Michigan State University Press, 1994).

14. *Ibid*; R. J. Smith, *The Great Black Way: L. A. in the 1940's* (New York: Public Affairs, 2006), 53.

15. Interview with James Harris, January 23, 2008.

16. Interview with James Harris, January 23, 2008 and June 10, 2008.

17. "The Johnny Bright Story," The Drake Heritage Collections, Cowles Library at Drake University, Des Moines, Iowa, Adam Cohen, "The Mugging of Johnny Bright," in David Wiggins and Patrick Millers (ed.) *The Uneven Playing Field* (Urbana: University of Illinois Press, 2003) 250-254.

18. *Ibid*.

19. Interview with James Harris, January 23, 2008, and interview with George Fischer, June 5, 2008.

20. Interview with James Harris, January 23, 2008.

21. *Ibid*.

22. Interview with Joe Reed, May 23, 2008, and interview with E. B. Palmer, March 6, 2008.

23. Interview with James Harris, January 23, 2008, and interview with Braulio Alonso, February 7, 2008.

24. Interview with Joe Reed, May 23, 2008, and interview with E. B. Palmer, March 6, 2008.

25. Interview with James Harris, January 23, 2008 and June 10.

26. Interview with E. B. Palmer, March 6, 2008.

27. Interview with Lauri Wynn, April 23, 2008, Interview with Don Morrison, June 13, 2008.

28. West, *NEA*, 105; Interview with Joe Reed, May 23, 2008, E. B. Palmer, March 6, 2008, and Interview with Lauri Wynn, April 23, 2008.

29. Interview with E. B. Palmer, March 6, 2008; Perry, *History of ATA*, 327-342.

30.   Interview with Helen Bain, July 9, 2008, Selden, *The Teacher Rebellion*, 201-202.

31.   Interview with E. B. Palmer, March 6, 2008.

32.   Interview with Lauri Wynn, April 23, 2008.

33.   West, NEA, 232-233; Kahlenberg, *Tough Liberal*, 161.

34.   Kahlenberg, *Tough Liberal*, 161.

35.   *Ibid*.

36.   Interview with Eugene Dryer, June 21, 2008.

37.   *NEA Reporter*, October 1973; Interview with George Fischer, June 6, 2008, Interview with James Harris, January 23, 2008; Selden, *The Teacher Rebellion*, 185.

38.   NEA *Proceedings* (1974), 17-24.

39.   *NEA Reporter*, April 4, 1975, p. 13-15.

40.   *Ibid*.

41.   *NEA Reporter*, October 1974, 11; Interview with James Harris, June 10, 2008.

42.   *NEA Reporter*, December 1974, 3.

43.   *NEA Reporter*, April 4, 1975.

44.   Speech by James Harris "The Role of the Teacher in Bilingual Bicultural Education: A National Perspective: presented at the National Bilingual Bicultural Institute, Albuquerque, New Mexico, November 29, 1975. Papers of James Harris.

45.   Interview with James Harris, January 23, 2008.

46.   Interview with Keith Geiger, July 11, 2008.

47.   *NEA Reporter*, September 1975, 9.

48.   Interview with James Harris, June 10, 2008.

Mary Hatwood Futrell: 1983-1989 – The Education Reform Movement and the Rise of Presidential Identity

1. Interview with Chuck Williams, June 5, 2008.

2. Interview with Eugene Dryer, June 21, 2008, and January 17, 2008.

3. Interview with Ann Davis, June 9, 2008.

4. Interview with E. B. Palmer, March 6, 2008; Interview with Joe Reed, May 23, 2008.

5. Interview with George Fischer, June 5, 2008.

6. Allan West, *History of the NEA*, 230-232.

7. Charles Christian, *Black Saga*, 463-497.

8. Interview with Mary Hatwood Futrell., January 29, 2008.

9. *Ibid.*

10. *Ibid.*

11. *Ibid.*

12. Mary Hatwood Futrell, "Mama and Miss Jordan," *Readers Digest* (July 1989), 75-80.

13. *Ibid, 78.*

14. *A History of Dunbar High School"* a brochure developed by the Lynchburg, Virginia Public Schools. www.1csedy.net/schools/dms/default.html.

15. Interview with Mary Hatwood Futrell, January 29, 2008.

16. *Ibid.*

17. *Ibid.*

18. *Ibid.*

19. *Ibid.*

20.   *Ibid.*

21.   *Ibid.*

22.   *Ibid.*

23.   Erwin L. Jordan, Jr., "Dr. Walter Ridley-UVA's First Black Graduate," a paper prepared for the website of the University of Virginia's Office of African American Affairs. www.virginia.edu/oaaa/his_ridley.html.

24.   Interview with Mary Hatwood Futrell., January 29, 2008.

25.   *Ibid.*

26.   *Ibid.*

27.   *Ibid.*

28.   *Ibid.*

29.   *Ibid.*

30.   *Ibid.*

31.   *Ibid.*

32.   J. Rupert Picott, *A History of the Virginia Teachers Association* (Washington, D.C.: National Education Association, 1975), 228.

33.   Interview with Mary Hatwood Futrell, January 29, 2008; Interview with Eugene Dryer, January 17, 2008.

34.   Interview with Don Morrison, June 13, 2008; Interview with Helen Bain, July 9, 2008.

35.   Interview with Bob Channing, July 15, 2008; Interview with Keith Geiger, July 11, 2008.

36.   *New York Times*, July 3, 1983.

37.   Both reports fueled the debate on the most important factors contributing to learning and divided the political and education leaders and communities of America. The Congressional Black Caucus torpedoed Marshall Smith's bid to become Commissioner

of Education when it was learned he had contributed to Jencks'
book which devalued the contribution of integration to education.

38. Gerald Holton, "An Insider's View of "A National At Risk" and Why It Still Matters," *The Chronicle of Higher Education, the Chronicle Review, Vol. 49, Issue 33, B-13.*

39. Kahlenberg, *Tough Liberal*, 245-249, 265-666.

40. *NEA Today,* February 1989, 2.

41. Interview with Mary Hatwood Futrell, January 29, 2008.

42. Ezra Bowen, "Putting Teachers Up on Top," *Time*, May 26, 2989, 58.

43. *NEA Today,* November 1986, 2; December, 1982, 2; December, 1986, 2; May 1988, 2; Futrell's monthly column "President's Viewpoint" in NEA *Today* is an excellent source for tracking the evolution of her thinking on NEA and education reform.

44. *NEA Today,* April 1984, p. 3.

45. *Ibid,* Interview with Linda Pondexter-Chesterfield, March 24, 2008.

46. *Education Week,* May 29, 1985.

47. *Interview with Keith Geiger, July 11, 2008.*

48. *NEA Today,* May, 1986, 2.

49. Wayne Urban, *Gender, Race, and the NEA,* 261.

50. Kahlenberg, *Tough Liberal,* 161; Interview with Mary Hatwood Futrell, January 29, 2008.

51. Kahlenberg, *Tough Liberal,* 112-124.

52. Virginia Wilson-Wallace, "Mary Hatwood Futrell," in *Notable Black American Women* (Detroit: Gale Research, Inc., 1992), 278; Futrell interview with *People,* July 25, 1983, 54.

53. *Ibid.*

54. *New York Times,* February 12, 1984, 05.

55. *NEA Today*, March 1987, 2.

56. *NEA Today*, April 1988, 2.

57. *NEA Today*, March 1989, 2.

58. *NEA Today*, November 1983, 2.

59. Interview with Chuck Williams, June 5, 2008.

60. *Ibid.*

61. *NEA Today*, December 1986.

62. *NEA Today, October* 1983, 2.

63. *NEA Today*, March, 1988, 2.

64. *NEA Today*, March 1989, 2.

65. *"Especially Imperfect," NEA Today*, November 1989, 2.

66. *NEA Today*, May 1989, 2.

67. Interview with Keith Geiger, July 11, 2008.

68. Interview with Gilmore, Munoz, and Coleman, February 16, 2008.

69. Interview with Eugene Dryer, January 17, 2008.

70. Speech by Marnell Moorman to NEA MLT Seminar, October 4, 2987, in flies of the author.

71. Interview with Lauri Wynn, April 23, 2008.

72. Letter from Linda Pondexter Chesterfield to Al-Tony Gilmore, March 5, 2008. Author's personal files.

73. Interview with Bob Chanin, July 15, 2008.

Reginald (Reg) Weaver: 2002-2008 – No Child Left Behind, Great Public Schools, and Team NEA

1. Interview with Eleanor Coleman, February 12, 2008.

2. Observation of the author at the Minority Leadership Training, October 6, 1997, Charleston, South Carolina.

3. Christian, *Black Saga*.

4. Interview with Ann Davis, June 9, 2008.

5. McFadden and Whitehead, "Ain't No Stopping Us Now." Published by Warner/Chappell Music, Inc. Permission requested.

6. Interview with Reg Weaver, February 22, 2008.

7. *Ibid*.

8. *Ibid*.

9. *Ibid*; Stephen Whitefield, *A Death in the Delta* (Baltimore: Johns Hopkins Press 1988.).

10. William H. Whyte, *The Organization Man* (New York: Simon and Schuster, 1956), 311; John Coggeshall, "Carbon Copy Towns: The Revitalization of Ethnic Folklore in Southern Illinois' Egypt," in Barbara Allen and Thomas Schlereth, (eds.), *Sense of Place* (Lexington: University of Kentucky Press, 1990), 103-119.

11. Interview with Reg Weaver, February 22, 2008.

12. Interview with Ann Davis, June 9, 2008.

13. Interview with Reg Weaver, February 22, 2008.

14. *Ibid*.

15. Interview with Lolita Dozier, March 5, 2008.

16. Interview with Sandra Lamb, July 19, 2008.

17. *Ibid*.

18. Interview with Lolita Dozier, March 5, 2008.

19. "Crossing the Red Sea," *Time*, September 2, 1966.

20. "Eyes on the Prize" America's Civil Rights Movement 1954-1985," A special presentation of American experience, Public Broadcast Service, Washington, D.C.

21. Interview with Sandra Lamb, July 19, 2008.

22. Interview with Reg Weaver, February 22, 2008.

23. Interview with Sandra Lamb, July 19, 2008.

24. Interview with Ann Davis, June 9, 2008.

25. Interview with Lolita Dozier, March 5, 2008.

26. Interview with Reg Weaver, February 22, 2008.

27. *Ibid*.

28. *Ibid*. Interview with Ann Davis, June 9, 2008.

29. *Ibid*.

30. Interview with Stan Johnson, April 16, 2008.

31. Interview with Reg Weaver, February 22, 2008.

32. Interview with Stan Johnson, April 16, 2008.

33. Interview with Reg Weaver, February 22, 2008.

34. *Ibid*.

35. *Ibid*.

36. Interview with Bob Chanin, July 15, 2008.

37. Interview with Reg Weaver, February 22, 2008.

38. *Ibid*.

39. *NEA Today*, October 2003.

40. "Major Court Ruling on No Child Left Behind: States and School Districts Not Required to Spend Own Funds to Comply with Low," Press release, National Education Association, January 7, 2008.

41. *USA Today*, September 24, 2004, 1.

42. NEA Press release, September 24, 2004.

43. Interview with Reg Weaver, February 22, 2008.

44. Press release, US. Department of Education, November 15, 2004; 60 Minutes, "Transcript on Houston / Texas Miracle," August 25, 2004, *USA Today*, January 1, 2005.

45. *NEA Today*, March 2007.

46. *NEA Today*, January, 2003.

47. *NEA Today*, October 2005. See also *NEA Today*, March 2007.

48. By 2004, both NEA Human and Civil Rights and Health Information Network were developing a variety of materials, workshops, and presentations on safe schools.

49. *NEA Today, February* 2008.

50. Interview with Lolita Dozier, March 5, 2008.

51. *NEA Today*, September 2007.

52. Weaver used this approach and theme in speeches and presentations throughout his term as president.

53. *NEA Today*, March 2008.

54. *NEA Today*, April 2007.

55. *Ibid.*

56. Interview with Lolita Dozier, March 5, 2008.

57. "Nation's Educators Sound the Alarm on School Dropout Crisis: NEA's Plan for Reducing School Dropouts," NEA Press release, October 3, 2006; *NEA Today*, April 2007.

58. Interview with Joe Reed, May 23, 2008.

59. Interview with Michael Marks, January 14, 2008.

60. *NEA Today*, November 11, 2005.

61. Interview with Stan Johnson, April 16, 2008.

62. *Ibid.*

63. Interview with Al Llorens June 7, 2008.

64. Interview with Bob Chanin, July 15, 2008; Interview with Stan Johnson, April 16, 2008.

65. Press release by the Democratic National Convention Committee, August 25, 2008.

Index

~A~

AASA. See American Association of
School Administrators
"Address to the Friends of Colored
Schools," 27
AFL. See American Federation of Labor
African Methodist Episcopal Zion
Church
Livingstone College founding, 90
AFT. See American Federation of
Teachers
Agricultural Workers Organizing
Committee
merger with the National Farm
Workers Association to form
the United Farm Workers, 73
Alabama
teacher loyalty oaths, 43
Alabama State Teachers Association
formation of, 28
Trenholm's leadership, 38
Alexander, Lamar
appointment as Secretary of
Education, 176
Alonso, Braulio
accomplishments, 80
Adult Education director job, 68
attendance at Martin Luther King,
Jr.'s funeral, 79
childhood experiences, 62–64, 158
committee to investigate Tate's
charges against the Georgia
Association of Educators, 47
conversation with Carr, 54
educational background, 65–66
el lector at the cigar factory and,
64–65
Florida Education Association
presidency, 70–71
Florida teacher strike and, 75–78
high school principal career, 69–70,
78, 79, 81
Hillsborough County Teachers
Association presidency, 68–69
Hispanic heritage, 61
honorary degrees, 82
On the Job Training for Veterans
job, 68
Koontz as president-elect and, 101
Koontz's appointment to head the
Women's Bureau and, 114
meetings with Pres. Lyndon
Johnson, 82
military career, 67–68
minority members and, 135
NEA International Relations director
career, 82
NEA president career, 61, 71–82, 156,
189, 234, 235
one-year term limit of the NEA
presidency, 72
parents' background, 62, 64, 67
personal reflections, 83
personality and style of, 69–70, 81–82
relationship with Carr, 76
relationship with Sam Lambert, 156

relocation from Florida to
Washington, D.C., 71–72
retirement, 82–83
school lunch program and, 134–135
support of NCUEA, 76
American Association of Colleges for
Teacher Education
National Council for Accreditation
of Teacher Education and, 187
American Association of School
Administrators
No Child Left Behind Act and, 214
teacher strikes and, 75–76
American Colonization Society
Pan African Movement and, 10
American Federation of Labor
discrimination against black porters
and, 45
American Federation of Teachers
AFL affiliation and, 142–143
collaboration with NEA on specific
projects, 51–52
collective bargaining victories, 73
competition with the NEA, 51–52, 72,
78, 112–113
Harris's concerns about, 142–143
merger with ATA proposal, 143
merger with NEA proposal, 51–52,
112–113, 139, 213
New York teachers strike and, 51
Ocean Hill-Brownsville controversy
and, 105–107
policy differences with NEA, 183–
184
urban interests, 51
American States' Rights Association
Brown v. Board of Education and, 49
American Teachers Association
delegate representation in the RA,
46 "Double V campaign," 42–43,
129–130
election of blacks to serve as officers
at the local and state levels and,
56–57
identification with the NAACP, 41
Joint Committee leader selection and
characteristics, 39–40
merger with AFT proposal, 143
merger with NEA, 1, 55–58, 71, 89,
109, 123, 234
name change from National
Association of Teachers in
Colored Schools, 37
North Carolina Teacher's
Association and, 96
Prince Edward (VA) Free School
Association and, 54–55
relationship with the NEA, 37–38
teacher wage lawsuits, 42–43
And Justice for All, 187
The Anglo African (Campbell), 11
Arkansas Education Association
teacher certification and, 179–180
ASPIRA
No Child Left Behind Act and, 214
school dropout reduction plan,
225–226
Association for the Study of Negro Life
and History
black professionals and, 33
Association of Community
Organizations for Reform
No Child Left Behind Act and, 214
Association of Teachers of Negro Youth
of Arkansas
formation of, 28
ASTA. *See* Alabama State Teachers
Association
ATA. *See* American Teachers
Association

~**B**~

Back-to-Africa Movement
Campbell's efforts, 10–11
Bain, Helen
National Council of Urban Education
Associations leadership, 52–53

NEA president career, 124, 155
urban education issue and, 189
views on Alonso, 71
views on Wynn, 138–139
Barrett, Catherine
NEA president career, 124, 155
NEA's Political Action Committee
and, 143
Bartholomew, W.H.
convention address, 19
Beecher, Agnes W.
National Teachers' Association
founding and, 5, 9
Bell, Terrence
A Nation at Risk study and, 176
Belton, Howard
first wave of NEA minority hires
and, 142
Bennett, William
teacher certification views, 178
Berry, Mary Francis
U.S. Civil Rights Commission and,
157
Bethune, Mary McLeod
Spingarn Medal recipient, 32
Better Regulation Act of 1826
provisions, 6
Bicknell, Thomas W.
convention of 1884 and, 15–16, 211
Bilingual Education Act, 75
Billups, Larry
first wave of NEA minority hires
and, 142
Bingham, Robert
"New South" views, 18–19
Black Caucus, 109, 136–140
Black Codes
impact of, 26
Black educators. *See also specific*
educators
Civil Rights Movement and, 54–55
convention attendance problems,
13, 25

criticism of the industrial education
option for blacks, 31
early black teachers' associations,
26–29
early focus of, 25
early working conditions, 25
election of blacks to serve as officers
at the local and state levels and,
56–57
employment opportunities in the
early 1900s, 33
Gibbs v. Board of Education case
and, 42
Historically Black Colleges and
Universities and, 22
Jim Crow laws and, 32–33
local and state teachers' associations
and, 25–26
perceived value of black teachers
instructing black students, 13–15,
19, 23–24
Plessy v. Ferguson and, 28
respect for, 24–25
salary issues, 25, 28, 42–43, 97
shortages of, 22–23
Black Power movement, 105–108
Blackmon, Fredrika
first wave of NEA minority hires
and, 142
Blair, Tamara
relationship with Weaver, 212
Board of Directors
Alonso's role, 71
Byers' leadership, 48
committee to investigate Tate's
charges against the Georgia
Association of Educators, 47
decision-making power, 72
Futrell's role, 172–173
Harris's career, 134–135, 140
Mack's election to, 211
minority representation, 141, 154, 234
NEA's mission and, 1

Bolden, Charles
first wave of NEA minority hires
and, 142
Bowen, Ezra
views on Futrell, 178
Bowser, Vivian
Black Caucus and, 137
Bradley, Tom
campaign for governor of California,
157
elected to the Los Angeles City
Council, 88
Bright, Johnny
football game incident, 131–132
Brimmer, Andrew F.
appointed to the Board of Governors
of the Federal Reserve, 88
Brooke, Edward
elected Attorney General of
Massachusetts and then U.S.
Senator, 88
Brotherhood of Sleeping Car Porters
anti-discrimination case, 45
Brown, William, II
Nixon's appointment to Chairperson
of the EEOC, 116
Brown v. Board of Education
NEA integration of black affiliates
and, 46
NEA's response to, 48–50
segregation issue, 19
Virginia's response to, 163
Warren's majority opinion, 48
Browne, Pat
Black Caucus and, 137, 138
IEA's Black and Hispanic Caucus
and, 210
Bundy, McGeorge
Connection for Learning, 106
Burger, N.R.
NEA Resolutions Committee
membership, 48

Burke, Yvonne Braithwaite
elected to the California state
legislature, 88
Bush, Pres. George H.W.
appointment of Cavazos as Secretary
of Education, 176
Bush, Pres. George W.
No Child Left Behind Act and, 213
Butler, George
Black Caucus and, 137
Harris's first campaign for NEA
president and, 135
Byers, Walter
NEA Board of Directors leadership,
48
Byrd, Rep. Harry F.
resistance to the *Brown vs. Board of
Education* decision, 163

~C~

Cameron, Don
Futrell's relationship with, 156, 179
NEA/AFT competition and, 108
Campbell, Robert
The Anglo African, 11
biographical background, 5–6
integration of Philadelphia's schools
and, 6
National Teachers' Association
founding and, 6–7, 10, 47, 231, 234
Pan African Movement and, 10
A Pilgrimage to My Motherland, 11
Canton, Nelson
relationship with Futrell, 177
Carmichael, Stokely
Black Power movement and, 105–108
Carnegie Forum on Education and the
Economy
Futrell's role, 178, 179, 227
*A Nation Prepared: Teachers for the
Twenty-First Century*, 180–181
Carr, William
anti-union views, 75, 76

executive secretary role, 48–49, 50, 53–54, 154

relationship with Alonso, 76

Carswell, Harrold

U.S. Supreme Court nomination, 57

Carswell, Lillie

views on Wynn, 138

Carter, Pres. Jimmy

blacks in Cabinet-level positions, 157

increase in the number of black federal judges, 157

Cavazos, Lauro

appointment as Secretary of Education, 176

Chambers, Julius

teachers rights case, 54

Chanin, Bob

No Child Left Behind Act and, 217

relationship with Futrell, 177

views on Alonso, 71, 80

views on Futrell, 174, 194

views on Weaver, 212–213, 230

Chase, Bob

NBPTS and, 227

NEA president career, 179

relationship with Weaver, 212–213

Chase, Flora

mentoring of Futrell, 168–169

Chavez, Cesar

United Farm Workers and, 73

Cherry, Billie

comments on Harris's second-term election bid, 148

Chisholm, Shirley

elected U.S. Representative from New York, 89

Civil Rights Movement

American Teachers Association identification with, 50

Black Power movement, 105–108

black teacher involvement, 54

"Fit to Teach, Fit to Vote" voter registration campaign, 55

impact on NEA members' collective consciousness, 1

impact on the NEA, 154

National Council of Urban Education Associations and, 52–53

North Carolina Teachers' Association involvement, 97–98

organizations and activities involved with, 50

Virginia State College students and, 165–166

Weaver and, 203–205, 206–208

Civil War period

education of blacks and, 13

Clayton, Marian

first wave of NEA minority hires and, 142

Clinton, Gov. Bill

teacher certification and, 179–180

Cobb, Jewell

president of California State University at Fullerton, 157

Cogen, Charles

proposal for an AFT/NEA merger, 113

Coleman, Eleanor

views on Futrell, 191

views on Wynn, 138

Coleman, James D.

study on disadvantaged students and education, 175

Coleman, William

Cabinet-level position, 157

Collective bargaining

Florida teacher strike and, 73–78

Maryland v. Wirtz case and, 74–75

NEA membership growth and, 107–108

New York teachers strike, 51

teacher union influence and, 108

Commission on the Defense of Democracy through Education

Davis' chairmanship of, 46

Committee for Economic Development
  critical report on education, 177
Committee on Equal Opportunity
  anti-discrimination resolution, 38
Community-controlled schools issue,
  105–108
Connection for Learning (Bundy and
  Lindsay), 106
Conrad, Hannah DeWolfe
  National Teachers' Association
    founding and, 5, 9
Constans, Phil
  Florida teacher strike and, 76
Council of Chief State School Officers
  National Council for Accreditation
    of Teacher Education and, 187
Critical Issues in Education Conference,
  104–105, 107–110
Crummell, Alexander
  convention address, 14–15

~D~

Davis, Ann
  IEA president career, 211
  Illinois Education Association
    and, 210
  NEA's minority inclusion and, 155
  relationship with Weaver, 205, 208
  teaching career, 208
Davis, Col. Benjamin O.
  Harris's meeting with, 130
Davis, John W.
  Commission on the Defense of
    Democracy through Education
    and, 46
Dean, Janet
  NEA convention resolution on
    strikes and, 79
Death at an Early Age (Kozol), 110
Delaney, Martin
  Back-to-Africa Movement and, 10–11
Delgado, Carmen
  Project Urban Education Neglect
    and, 145

Devlin, Father Joseph
  Urban Task Force and, 111
Diaz, Adelfa (Bebe)
  marriage to Braulio Alonso, 67
Disadvantaged students
  debate on public education for, 175
Dole, Elizabeth
  eulogy for Elizabeth Duncan
    Koontz, 119
"Double V" campaign, 42–43, 129–130
Dozier, Lolita
  views on Weaver, 206
  Weaver's mentoring of, 209
Dred Scott decision, 4
Dropouts
  Futrell's views, 188–189
  Weaver's views, 224–226
Dryer, Eugene
  NEA's minority inclusion and, 142,
    155
Du Bois, W.E.B.
  criticism of the industrial education
    option for blacks, 31
  racial issue prediction, 29
Duncan, Joe
  Black Caucus and, 137
  Koontz's appointment to head the
    Women's Bureau and, 113
Duncan, Samuel
  backing of Lois Edinger for NEA
    president, 100
  career of, 92, 98
  Koontz's appointment to head the
    Women's Bureau and, 113
Dushane, Donald
  Kate Frank case and, 44

~E~

Early years
  characteristics of the year 1857, 3–4
  emancipation of slaves, 3–4
  National Teachers' Association
    founding and first meeting, 5–10

Edinger, Lois
   Koontz's appointment to head the
      Women's Bureau and, 114
   views on Alonso, 71
   views on Koontz, 92, 100, 117
Edmonds, Ron
   Effective Schools Movement, 95
EDUCATE. *See* Educators Deployed to
   Underdeveloped Countries Affecting
   Total Education
"Education as an Element of
   Reconstruction" (Wickersham), 13–14
Education Association of Alexandria
   Futrell's service with, 169–170
Education Commission of the States
   critical report on education, 177
Educational support professionals
   Futrell's views, 189–190
   Weaver's views, 220–221
Educators Deployed to Underdeveloped
   Countries Affecting Total Education
   Harris and, 148
Ehringhaus, Gov. John
   appointment of an interracial
      committee to examine problems
      in North Carolina schools, 97
1865-1912
   black educational interests and, 12–
      13, 20–22
   black teachers' associations, 25–29
   convention of 1884, 15–19
   conventions between 1884 and 1900,
      19–25
   incorporation by an Act of Congress,
      11
   local- and state-level decisions on
      black education, 25–26
   local membership and, 12–13
   name change to National Education
      Association, 11
   "New South," 18–19
   Ohio Colored Teachers Association,
      26–27

perceived value of black teachers
   instructing black students, 13–15,
   19, 23–24
Eisenhower, Pres. Dwight D.
   "kissing case" and, 96
Embree, Edwin
   segregation issue, 37, 45
Equal Rights Amendment, 116
Ethridge, Sam
   NEA's Center for Human Relations
      and, 104–105
   NEA's first minority professional
      staff member, 142
   Project Urban Education Neglect
      and, 145
   relationship with Futrell, 172–173
Executive Committee
   Alonso's role, 71
   decision-making power, 72
   Mack's election to, 211
   minority representation, 141, 154, 234
   Weaver's role, 209, 212
   Wilson's election to, 99

~F~

Farmer, James
   Nixon's appointment to Assistant
      Secretary for HEW, 116
Fischer, George
   ATA/NEA merger and, 57
   educational background, 127
   Harris's Board of Directors career
      and, 134
   Harris's first campaign for NEA
      president and, 135
   Koontz's appointment to head the
      Women's Bureau and, 114
   memories of Harris, 128
   NEA president career, 123–124,
      155, 156
"Fit to Teach, Fit to Vote" voter
   registration campaign, 55

Fletcher, Arthur
Nixon's appointment to Assistant
Secretary for Labor, 116
Florida Education Association
Alonso's presidency, 70–71
post-strike chaos, 78
teacher strike, 73–78
Florida State Teachers Association
formation of, 28
resolution against segregated
accommodations at NEA-DCT's
Southeastern Regional meetings,
98
Floyd, Barbara
first wave of NEA minority hires
and, 142
Floyd, Jeremiah
Board of Directors and, 211
Ford, Pres. Gerald
blacks in Cabinet-level positions, 157
invitation to Harris to speak at
a White House conference on
inflation, 146
NEA Board meeting speech, 147
presentation of the American
Newspaper Women's club award
for distinguished service in
international affairs to Koontz, 118
Frank, Kate
NEA case in support of, 44
Frankfurter, Felix
Plessy v. Ferguson and, 41
Futrell, Mary Hatwood
black culture of Lynchburg and,
161–164
Board of Directors Minority-at-Large
representative career, 172–173
Brown v. Board of Education memories,
163
campaign for a seat on the Board
of the Virginia Education
Association, 170–171
Carnegie Forum on Education and
the Economy and, 178, 179, 227

childhood experiences, 157–158
Civil Rights Movement and, 165–166
description of NEA, 1
Education Association of Alexandria
service, 169–170
education reform issue and, 179–183,
189, 194
educational background, 160–167,
169–170, 203
honorary degrees, 194
Linda Pondexter-Chesterfield's
tribute to, 192–193
memory of Martin Luther King, Jr.'s
visit to Virginia State, 167–168
National Council for Accreditation
of Teacher Education and, 187–188
NEA members' appreciation of,
190–191
NEA president career, 154, 174–194,
193, 234, 235
NEA Secretary-Treasury campaign,
173–174
NEA Today columns, 188–190
parents' background, 158–159
personality and style of, 153–154,
174, 177, 183, 185, 186, 191
post-presidency career, 194
Pres. Reagan's policies and, 176,
184–185
protection of NEA's image, 177
re-election for a second term as NEA
president, 178, 193
relationship with Don Cameron, 156
relationship with Robinson, 177
relationship with Wynn, 191
study on public education and
Hispanics and, 186–187
teacher certification issue, 179–182
teaching career, 168–171, 172
teaching profession defense, 174–175,
176–179
U.S. Department of Housing and
Urban Development career, 168
VEA president career, 171–172

views on dropouts, 188–189
views on school support staff, 189
190
views on urban issues, 189
Virginia State College experience,
164–168

~G~

Gaines v. Missouri
segregation issue and, 41–42
Geiger, Keith
comments on Harris's second-term
election bid, 148
Futrell's speech on education reform
and, 182
NBPTS and, 227
Georgia Association of Educators
Tate's case against, 47
Georgia Negro Teachers Association
formation of, 28
Gibbs v. Board of Education
equal salaries for black and white
teachers, 42
Gilmore, Jackie
views on Futrell, 191
views on Wynn, 138
Givens, Willard
Committee to Select a conference site
for the RA and, 46–47
Grass Roots League
Brown v. Board of Education and, 49
Great Depression
effects of, 37
segregation and, 40
Greener, R.T., 20
*Guidelines for Local Associations of
Classroom Teachers*, 98

~H~

Hager, Daniel
National Teachers' Association
founding and first meeting, 7–9

Hansberry, Lorraine
A Raisin in the Sun, 205
Harris, James Alexander
attempt to win a second term, 148
bilingual education views, 147
Board of Directors career, 134–135,
140
childhood experiences, 124–126, 127,
158
compared with Koontz, 134
concerns about AFT, 142–143
"Double V" campaign and, 129
educational background, 126–128,
130–132
Educators Deployed to
Underdeveloped Countries
Affecting Total Education
and, 148
Johnny Bright football game incident
and, 132
local teachers' association president
campaign, 133–134
marriage of, 132
meeting with Col. Benjamin O.
Davis, 130
military career, 128–130
NEA committee work, 140
NEA president career, 123, 124, 135–
136, 143–148, 155, 156, 189, 234, 235
NEA president-elect year, 123, 140–
141, 142–143
NEA's Political Action Committee
and, 143
parents' background, 124–125
personal characteristics and style of,
124, 133, 139–140, 144, 149
personal reflections of, 149
Pres. Ford's invitation to speak at
a White House conference on
inflation, 146
Project Urban Education Neglect
and, 144–147
RA address theme, 144
relationship with Wynn, 139

reluctance of whites to endorse,
135–136
school lunch program and, 134–135
Selden's views on, 143
teaching career, 132–133
urban education conference keynote
speech, 145–146
Harris, Patricia
appointed to an ambassadorship, 89
Cabinet-level position, 157
Hastie, William
admission of a black student to
the University of Virginia and,
166–167
Plessy v. Ferguson and, 41, 93–94
Hatcher Richard
elected mayor of Gary, 88
Haynes, Felicia
first wave of NEA minority hires
and, 142
Haynes, LaMar
first wave of NEA minority hires
and, 142
Haynesworth, Clement
U.S. Supreme Court nomination, 57
HBCUs. *See* Historically Black Colleges
and Universities
Heinisch, Frank
National Council of Urban Education
Associations leadership, 52–53
Herndon, Terry
relationship with Futrell, 172–173
relationship with Koontz, 156
Hispanic, definition of, 61–62
Historical background
early years, 3–11
1865-1912, 11–29
1900-1959, 29–52
1950s, 46–52
1960s, 52–58
Historically Black Colleges and
Universities
number established by the early
1900s, 22

schools of education and, 33
teacher preparation and, 22
*History of the American Teachers
Association* (Perry), 28, 30
*A History of the Virginia Teachers
Association* (Picott), 171–172
Hocutt v. North Carolina
segregation issue and, 41–42, 93–94
Hope, John
criticism of the industrial education
option for blacks, 31
Spingarn Medal recipient, 32
Houston, Charles Hamilton
admission of a black student to
the University of Virginia and,
166–167
integration court case background,
38
Plessy v. Ferguson and, 40–42, 93–94
Hurricane Katrina
NEA's Hurricane Relief Fund,
226–227

~I~

IEA. *See* Illinois Education Association
Illinois
racism and, 207–208
Illinois Education Association
Black and Hispanic Caucus, 210
Weaver's experience with, 209–212
Industrial education *vs.* liberal
education option for blacks, 21–22,
27, 31
Inequality (Jencks), 175
Institute for Colored Youth, 5–6

~J~

Jablinski, Susie
NEA vice president campaign, 212
Jackson, Janice
first wave of NEA minority hires
and, 142

Jackson, Jesse
Project Urban Education Neglect
and, 145
Jencks, Christopher
Inequality, 175
Jim Crow laws
impact of, 26, 32–33
Johnson, Dr. Robert
residency in Lynchburg, 161
Johnson, F.J.
first wave of NEA minority hires
and, 142
Johnson, Mordecai
Spingarn Medal recipient, 32
Johnson, Pres. Lyndon Baines
appointment of Robert Weaver as
Secretary of Housing and Urban
Development, 88
civil rights progress under, 157
Kerner Commission and, 104
meetings with Alonso, 82
Johnson, Stan
views on Weaver, 211, 228, 230
Johnson, Willa
teachers rights case, 54
Joint Committee
accreditation of black schools and, 35
American Teachers Association and,
37–38
black affiliates' delegates to the
Representative Assembly, 46
Brown v. Board of Education and, 48
desegregation issue, 35–36
"Double V" campaign and, 44
Gibbs v. Board of Education case
and, 42
influence of, 38–39, 235
legitimization of NATCS priorities,
36
NATCS and NEA collaboration
and, 34–40
National Defense sub-committee,
42–43, 129

portrayal of blacks in textbooks
and, 35, 36
recommendation for an ATA/NEA
merger, 55
selection of members, 39–40
study of the effect of racism and the
Great Depression, 40
subcommittees, 39, 42–43, 129
Jones, George W.
first wave of NEA minority hires
and, 142
Task Force on Urban Education and,
105, 111
Jordan, Rep. Barbara
elected to the Texas state legislature,
88–89
Project Urban Education Neglect
and, 145

~K~

Kahlenberg, Richard
assaults on organized labor and, 108
Karpinski, Carol
observations of Carr, 53–54
Kate Frank/Dushane Fund for Teacher
Rights
origin of, 44
Kentucky Negro Education Association
formation of, 28
Kerner Commission
race riots and, 104
King, Martin Luther, Jr.
assassination of, 78–79
Cicero protest, 207
community-controlled schools issue
and, 108
Futrell's memory of his visit to
Virginia State, 167–168
NEA's suggestion for a national
holiday honoring, 57, 186
Nobel Peace Prize recipient, 88
philosophy on civil disobedience, 74

Southern Christian Leadership
   Conference leadership, 50
voter registration campaigns, 55
Kirk, Gov. Claude
   Florida's teacher strike and, 76–77
"Kissing case," 95–96
Koontz, Elizabeth Duncan (Libby)
   "An Agonizing Decision" article,
      115–116
   American Newspaper Women's club
      award for distinguished service in
      international affairs, 118
   appointment to head the Women's
      Bureau of the U.S. Department of
      Labor, 113–118
   Assistant State Superintendent for
      Teacher Education career, 118
   attendance at Martin Luther King,
      Jr.'s funeral, 79
   Black Caucus and, 109
   career as president of NCTA's
      division of classroom teachers,
      97–99
   childhood experiences, 90–91, 158
   College Board Medal for
      Distinguished Service to
      Education recipient, 118
   community-controlled schools
      views, 110–111
   compared with Harris, 134
   Critical Issues in Education
      Conference and, 104–105, 107–110
   death, 119
   decentralization efforts in New York
      City views, 110–111
   educational background, 94, 95
   family background, 90, 91–92, 93
   "kissing case" and, 95–96
   NEA president career, 87, 89, 99, 103–
      115, 123, 136, 156, 189, 234, 235
   NEA's Department of Classroom
      Teachers and, 98, 99, 100–101
   NEA's Teacher-in-Politics weekend
      and, 102–103

North Carolina State Department of
      Human Resources career, 118
   parents' background, 90, 96
   personal and leadership style, 94,
      99–101, 111–112
   president-elect year, 101–103
   proposal for an AFT/NEA merger
      and, 113
   relationship with Terry Herndon, 156
   retirement, 119
   special education views, 95
   state and local black teachers'
      organization involvement, 96–98
   symbolic importance of election to
      NEA president, 89
   teaching career, 94–95
   U.S. Delegate to the United Nations
      Commission on the Status of
      Women appointment, 116
   views on Alonso, 83
Kozol, Jonathan
   Death at an Early Age, 110

~L~

Lamb, Sandra
   recollection of racial relations in
      Illinois, 207–208
   relationship with Weaver, 206
Lambert, Sam
   convention address in 1968, 79
   relationship with Alonso, 156
   Task Force on Urban Education
      and, 105
League of United Latin American
      Citizens
   No Child Left Behind Act and, 214
Lee, J.R.E.
   National Association of Colored
      Teachers and, 29
Lindsay, Mayor John
   Connection for Learning, 106
Logan, Rayford
   racial issues in the South of the early
      1900s, 31

Love, Ruth
superintendent of Chicago schools,
157
Lucas, John
Black Caucus and, 137
committee to investigate Tate's
charges against the Georgia
Association of Educators, 47
Luty, Carl
relationship with Futrell, 177

~**M**~

Mack, Pearl
Board of Directors and, 211
Executive Committee and, 211
Illinois Education Association
and, 210
relationship with Weaver, 205, 208
teaching career, 208
March on Washington of 1963, 50
Marks, Michael
NEA's Hurricane Katrina relief
efforts and, 226
Marshall, Thurgood
admission of a black student to
the University of Virginia and,
166–167
appointment to the U.S. Supreme
Court, 88
integration court case background,
38
Plessy v. Ferguson and, 41–42
Martin, R.J.
merger of ATA and AFT and, 143
Martin, T.G.
NEA/AFT merger proposal and,
51–52
Maryland v. Wirtz
collective bargaining for public
employees and, 74–75
Mayo, Rev. A.D.
convention of 1884 address, 20

McClane, Curtis
National Council of Urban Education
Associations leadership, 52–53
McCoy, Cecil
Hocutt v. North Carolina and, 93–94
McCoy, Rhoda
Ocean Hill-Brownsville controversy
and, 106
McFarlane, Ray
first wave of NEA minority hires
and, 142
McGuire, Willard
NEA president career, 155
McSkimmon, Mary
NEA/NATCS Joint Committee
and, 35
Media
Alonso's relationship with, 77
Florida teacher strike and, 77, 78
Koontz's election to NEA president
and, 87–88
NEA's Teacher-in-Politics weekend
and, 102–103
Meins, Harriet
mentoring of Harris, 127, 128
Miles, Malinda
first wave of NEA minority hires
and, 142
Miller, Kelly
NEA membership, 20
Miller, Loren
"Double V" campaign comments,
129
Mineta, Rep. Norman Y.
Project Urban Education Neglect
and, 145
Mississippi Freedom Democratic
Party, 50
Mondale, Sen. Walter
Project Urban Education Neglect
and, 145
Montgomery County, MD
teacher strike, 80

Moore, Harry T.
    assassination of, 69
Morrison, Don
    Black Caucus and, 136–137
    conversation with Tate, 47
    NEA president career, 124, 136,
        155, 173
Morton, Robert R.
    NEA convention address, 36–37
Motley, Constance Baker
    appointed a federal judge, 89
Munoz, Bob
    views on Futrell, 191
Murray v. Maryland
    segregation issue and, 41–42
Muse, Jessie
    first wave of NEA minority hires
        and, 142

~**N**~

NAACP. *See* National Association for
    the Advancement of Colored People
NACT. *See* National Association of
    Colored Teachers
NATCS. *See* National Association of
    Teachers in Colored Schools
A Nation at Risk, 176–179
*A Nation Prepared: Teachers for the
    Twenty-First Century,* 180–181
National Association for Asian and
    Pacific American Education
    school dropout reduction plan,
        225–226
National Association for the
    Advancement of Colored People
    "Double V campaign," 42–43, 129
    Harris' local teachers' association
        president campaign and, 133–134
    Hocutt v. North Carolina and, 93–94
    identification of the ATA with, 41
    integration court case background, 38
    Legal Defense and Education
        Fund,42

    No Child Left Behind Act and, 214
    school dropout reduction plan,
        225–226
    teacher wage lawsuits, 42–43
National Association of Colored
    Teachers
    formation of, 29
    name change to National
        Association of Teachers in
        Colored Schools, 29
National Association of Land Grant
    College Presidents
    merger with the National
        Association of Teachers in
        Colored Schools, 30
National Association of Teachers in
    Colored Schools
    accreditation of black schools and,
        34–35
    achievements of presidents, 32
    attendance at national meetings, 30
    collaboration with the NEA, 34–40
    college instructors as members, 31
    expansion of membership, 33
    first meeting, 29
    impact of leadership, 32
    Jim Crow laws and, 32–33
    merger with the National
        Association of Land Grant College
        Presidents, 30
    name change from National
        Association of Colored Teachers,
        29
    name change to American Teachers
        Association, 37
National Association of the State
    Directors of Teacher Education and
    Certification
    National Council for Accreditation
        of Teacher Education and, 187
National Bar Association
    black professionals and, 33
National Board for Professional
    Teaching Standards
    background of, 181–182

NEA endorsement of, 227

National Business League
  black professionals and, 33

National Citizens Protective
  Association
  Brown v. Board of Education and, 49

National Commission on Excellence in
  Education
  A Nation at Risk study, 176–179

National Council for Accreditation of
  Teacher Education
  creation of, 187
  purpose of, 187–188

National Council of La Raza
  No Child Left Behind Act and, 214

National Council of Officers of State
  Teachers Associations
  NEA black leaders and, 137–138

National Council of Urban Education
  Associations
  addresses to NEA annual
    conventions, 74
  Alonso's support of, 76
  collective bargaining views, 74
  formation of, 52, 234
  leadership of, 52–53

National Education Association. *See
  also* Board of Directors; Executive
  Committee; Joint Committee;
  Representative Assembly; *specific
  presidents*
  accreditation of black schools and,
    34–35
  affiliation of black southern
    education associations, 45–48
  appeal of to blacks, 20
  Association of Classroom Teachers,
    136
  Bilingual Education Act lobbying
    effort, 75
  Black Caucus, 109, 136–140
  Brown v. Board of Education and,
    48–50, 99
  Center for Human Relations, 104–105

Citizenship Committee, 102–103

Civil Rights Movement and, 50–56,
  154

classroom teacher control of, 123–124

collective bargaining issues, 73–78

Commission on the Education of
  Disadvantaged Youth, 98

Committee on Equal Opportunity,
  38

Committee to Select a conference site
  for the RA, 46–47

competition with AFT and, 51–52, 72,
  78, 112–113

conference policies, 44–45, 46–47

constitutional changes, 101

Constitutional Convention, 124, 140–
  141, 154, 156, 183, 211, 234

convention attendance restrictions
  on blacks, 13

convention of 1884, 15–19

Critical Issues in Education
  Conference, 104–105, 107–110

defense of teachers dismissed
  without warning, 44

Department of Classroom Teachers,
  98, 100–101

Division of Classroom Teachers, 72

education reform and, 179–183

election of blacks to serve as officers
  at the local and state levels and,
  56–57

"Fit to Teach, Fit to Vote" voter
  registration campaign, 55

Florida teacher strike and, 73–78

growth of ethnic minorities on the
  national staff, 142

Health Information Network, 221–
  222

hiring of black staff members, 53

historical background, 3–58

Human and Civil Rights
  Department, 105

incorporation by an Act of
  Congress, 11

integration issue avoidance in
publications, 50
internal conflict between teachers
and administrators, 72–73, 76, 81
Kate Frank/Dushane Fund for
Teacher Rights, 44
Martin Luther King, Jr. national
holiday and, 57
merger with American Federation of
Teachers and, 51–52, 55, 112–113,
139, 154, 213
merger with American Teachers
Association, 1, 55–58, 71, 89, 109,
123, 234
Minority Affairs Committee, 155, 187
minority guarantees, 141, 154, 173,
184, 211, 234
minority inclusion and, 141, 154–156,
234, 235
Minority Leadership Training
Program, 137, 155
mission statement, 233
National Council for Accreditation
of Teacher Education and, 187
National Council of Officers of
State Teachers Associations and,
137–138
"new unionism" and, 227–228
1950s conservative nature of, 48–49,
50–51, 99
No Child Left Behind Act and,
213–219
one-year term limit of the
presidency, 72
organizational structure, 72
Paige's negative comments on,
217–218
plan to reduce school dropouts,
225–226
policy differences with AFT, 183–184
Political Action Committee and
lobbying efforts, 143
post-ATA merger changes, 136–140
presidential term extension, 124,
140–141

Prince Edward (VA) Free School
Association and, 54–55
Professional Rights and
Responsibilities Commission, 54
progressive and liberal tradition
and, 52, 55, 102
relationship with black educators
during the early 1900s, 30
Research Department, 38
Resolution 12 integration of all
affiliates, 55–56
*School Crisis Guide: Help and Healing
in a Time of Crisis*, 222
Staff Organization bargaining unit
for staff, 79–80
Task Force on Urban Education, 105
Teacher-in-Politics weekend, 102–103
universal education issue, 21–22, 27
views of the leadership on unionism,
50–51
women teachers' salaries and, 28
Women's Evening at the 1884
convention, 15
*The National Education Association: The
Power Base for Education* (West), 112
National Farm Workers Association
merger with the Agricultural
Workers Organizing Committee
to form the United Farm
Workers, 73
National Governors' Association
critical report on education, 177
National Indian Education Association
school dropout reduction plan,
225–226
National Medical Association
black professionals and, 33
National School Boards Association
National Council for Accreditation
of Teacher Education and, 187
National Teachers' Association
admission of women to, 9
Civil War and, 13
constitution of the organization, 6–7

democratic and progressive nature
of, 9, 52, 55
first meeting, 7–9
founding of, 2–11
name change to National Education
Association, 11
purpose of, 8
racial issues and, 10–11
second meeting, 9
universal education and, 9
women's issues and, 9
NBPTS. *See* National Board for
Professional Teaching Standards
NCAE. *See* North Carolina Association
of Educators
NCATE. *See* National Council for
Accreditation of Teacher Education
NCOSTA. *See* National Council
of Officers of State Teachers
Associations
NCTA. *See* North Carolina Teacher's
Association
NCUEA. *See* National Council of Urban
Education Associations
NEA: The First Hundred Years (Wesley),
16, 49
NEA Reporter
articles during the 1960s, 99
articles on black educators, 89
Koontz's "An Agonizing Decision"
article, 115–116
minority issues and, 235
Project Urban Education Neglect
special edition, 145
NEA Today
Futrell's columns, 188–190
teacher certification and, 179
Weaver's columns, 215–217, 219–229
New York
Ocean Hill-Brownsville controversy,
100, 105–108
teachers strike, 51, 76
Newbold, N.C.
Joint Committee and, 35–36

Nichols, Roy
A Historian's Progress, 235
1900-1959
American Federation of Teachers,
51–53, 55
American Teachers Association,
37–45, 48, 54–55, 56–57, 58
Joint Committee and, 34–40
"kissing case," 95–96
National Association of Teachers in
Colored Schools, 29–37
Representative Assembly and, 36
segregation issue, 31, 40–43, 45–51
World War II, 43–45
1960s
competition with AFT and, 51–52,
72, 78
National Council of Urban Education
Associations and, 52–53
progressive and liberal tradition
and, 52
summary of black "firsts," 88–89
Nixon, Pres. Richard M.
appointment of blacks to major
posts, 116
appointment of Koontz to head
the Women's Bureau of the U.S.
Department of Labor, 113
No Child Left Behind Act
"fix it and fund it" campaign, 218–
219
NEA and, 213–219
provisions, 213
Weaver's criticism of, 213–219
North Carolina Association of
Educators
Koontz's relationship with, 100
North Carolina State Teachers
Association for Negroes
uniform salary requirements for
black and white teachers, 28
North Carolina Teacher's Association
growth of membership, 98

Guidelines for Local Associations of Classroom Teachers, 98
Koontz's role, 96–98
presentation to the governor of a list of problems in black schools, 96–97
NTA. *See* National Teachers' Association

~O~

Ocean Hill-Brownsville controversy, 105–108, 110
Ohio Colored Teachers Association
"Address to the Friends of Colored Schools," 27
development of black leaders and, 27
formation of, 26
The Organization Man (Whyte), 204

~P~

Paige, Rod
negative comments on NEA, 217–218
Palmer, E.B.
ATA/NEA affiliates mergers and, 56
Black Caucus and, 137, 138, 139
focus on equity in the merger affiliates, 139
Harris's first campaign for NEA president and, 135
Koontz's appointment to head the Women's Bureau and, 113, 114–115
NEA's minority inclusion and, 156
teachers rights case, 54
views on Alonso, 71, 135
views on Futrell, 191
views on Harris, 139–140
views on Koontz, 101
Pan African Movement
Campbell's efforts, 10
Pendleton, Clarence
U.S. Civil Rights Commission and, 157

Pepper, Claude, 66
Perez, Patricio
first wave of NEA minority hires and, 142
IEA's Black and Hispanic Caucus and, 210
Perry, Thelma
History of the American Teachers Association, 28, 30
Person, Conrad
Hocutt v. North Carolina and, 93–94
Phillips, Craig
relationship with Elizabeth Duncan Koontz, 92, 118
Phillips, Guy
views on Elizabeth Duncan Koontz, 92, 118–119
Phillips, J.H.
"Negro Teachers in Negro Schools" address, 23–24
Picott, J. Rupert
attendance at Martin Luther King, Jr.'s funeral, 79
A History of the Virginia Teachers Association, 171–172
views on Futrell, 193
Pierce, Sam
Cabinet-level position, 157
A Pilgrimage to My Motherland (Campbell), 11
Pittman, Don
influence on Weaver, 203
Plessy v. Ferguson
black educators' objections to, 28
perceived vulnerability of, 41
segregation issue, 19, 20, 93
Pondexter-Chesterfield, Linda
tribute to Futrell, 192–193
Powell, W.B.
address to the convention of 1890, 21–22
Price, Joseph C.
address to the 1890 convention on segregation, 20

Livingstone College founding, 90, 96
Professional Rights and
   Responsibilities Commission
   responsibilities, 54
Project Urban Education Neglect,
   144–147
Public Education Network
   No Child Left Behind Act and, 214

~**R**~

RA. *See* Representative Assembly
Racial issues. *See also* Segregation
   issues
   National Teachers' Association and,
      10–11
   NEA conventions and, 13–22
A Raisin in the Sun (Hansbery), 205
Randolph, A. Phillip
   community-controlled schools issue
      and, 108
   discrimination against black porters
      and, 45
Ray, James Earl
   assassination of Martin Luther King,
      Jr. and, 78–79
Reagan, Pres. Ronald
   address to AFT convention, 184
   blacks in Cabinet-level positions, 157
   criticism of NEA, 176, 184
   public education views, 176–179,
      184–185
Reconstruction
   condition of blacks and, 16–17
Reed, Joe
   ATA/NEA affiliates mergers and,
      56, 57
   Black Caucus and, 137
   Harris's first campaign for NEA
      president and, 135
   Koontz's appointment to head the
      Women's Bureau and, 114
   NEA's Hurricane Katrina relief
      efforts and, 226

NEA's minority inclusion and, 156
   views on Alonso, 71, 135
   views on Futrell, 191
   views on Weaver, 228–229
Representative Assembly
   black affiliates' delegates to, 46,
      47–48
   dual affiliates and, 47
   Equal Status for Women
      Amendment resolution, 49
   Koontz's election to NEA president,
      88, 89
   minority representation, 141, 154–
      155, 234
   mission statement, 233
   NEA's mission and, 1
   Newbold's speech to, 36
   recommendation for an ATA/NEA
      merger, 55
   school lunch program and, 134–135
Research Department
   difference in pupil expenditures
      between southern white and black
      schools, 38
Rich, Columbus
   first wave of NEA minority hires
      and, 142
Richards, Edna
   Koontz's appointment to head the
      Women's Bureau and, 113
Rickoff, Andrew J.
   convention address, 13
Ridley, Walter
   admission to the University of
      Virginia, 166–167
Robinson, Dale
   first wave of NEA minority hires
      and, 142
Robinson, Dewey General
   Reginald Weaver and, 204
Robinson, Jackie
   integration of major league baseball
      and, 45

Robinson, Lithangia
    ATA/NEA affiliates mergers and, 56
    Black Caucus and, 137
Robinson, Sharon
    relationship with Futrell, 177
Robinson, W.A.
    NATCS and NEA collaboration and,
        34–35
Roosevelt, Eleanor
    "kissing case" and, 96
Rustin, Bayard
    community-controlled schools issue
        and, 108
Ryor, John
    defeat of Harris, 172
    NEA president career, 148, 155, 183

~S~

SASC. *See* Southern Association of
    Schools and Colleges
Saunders, John
    influence on Weaver, 203
Schlagle, Frank
    Harris and, 133
*School Crisis Guide: Help and Healing in a
    Time of Crisis,* 222
School lunch program
    Harris's advocacy for, 134–135
Schultz, Michael John
    election of Koontz to NEA president,
        101
Seay, Clarence Williams
    high school educational programs
        and, 162
Segregation issues. *See also Brown
    v. Board of Education;* Civil Rights
    Movement; Racial issues
    "dangers" of educating blacks, 20
    Futrell's experiences, 157–158, 159–
        167
    Great Depression and, 40

1900-1959 period, 31, 36–37, 40–43,
    45–51
Plessy v. Ferguson, 19, 20
    race riots and, 103–104
    Reginald Weaver and, 203–205
    reversal of segregation policies at the
        universities of Georgia, Alabama,
        and Mississippi, 89
    "separate but equal" doctrine and, 28
    "sundown suburbs" and, 204–205
    "white flight" and, 174–175
Selden, David
    proposal for an AFT/NEA merger
        and, 113, 139
    The Teacher Rebellion, 143
    views on Harris, 143
Shanker, Albert
    AFT/NEA merger proposal and, 139
    meeting with Lauri Wynn, 138–139
    NEA's minority goals and, 141
    Ocean Hill-Brownsville conflict
        and, 139
    prominent position of, 183
Shepard, James
    Hocutt v. North Carolina and, 41, 94
Simonds, Arthur
    National Council of Urban Education
        Associations leadership, 52–53
Slavery
    Dred Scott decision and, 4
    emancipation of slaves, 3–4, 6
    historical background of the
        institution, 4
    limited range of occupations for
        blacks, 4
SNCC. *See* Student Non-Violent
    Coordinating Committee
Solomon, Walker
    ATA/NEA affiliates mergers and, 56
    Black Caucus and, 137
    Harris's first campaign for NEA
        president and, 135

Sosa, Mary
  first wave of NEA minority hires
    and, 142
South Carolina
  NAACP membership and, 43
  prospective black teacher applicants
    and, 43
Southern Association of Schools and
  Colleges
  accreditation of black schools, 34–35
Southern Christian Leadership
  Conference, 50
Southern states. *See also specific states
  and state teacher associations*
  difference in pupil expenditures
    between southern white and black
    schools, 38
  formation of teachers' association by
    black educators, 28
  lack of publicly-funded schools, 3
  minority inclusion and, 155–156
  NEA/ATA merger and, 55–56
  "New South," 18–19
  response to *Brown v. Board of
    Education,* 49–50
  restriction of NEA membership to
    whites, 12
  "Southern Manifesto" on school
    integration, 49–50, 163
Spencer, Ann
  residency in Lynchburg, 161
States' Rights Council of Georgia
  Brown v. Board of Education and, 49
Stevenson, Margaret
  recommendation that Koontz be a
    member of NEA-DCT's advisory
    board, 98
Stewart B. McKinney Homeless
  Assistance Act, 185
Stokes, Carl
  elected mayor of Cleveland, 88
Student Non-Violent Coordinating
  Committee, 50, 105
Sturm, Dorothy
  influence on Weaver, 203

Sykes, Eloise
  first wave of NEA minority hires
    and, 142

~T~

Taney, Roger B.
  Dred Scott decision and, 4
Tate, Horace
  ATA/NEA affiliates mergers and, 56
  Black Caucus and, 137, 139
  case against the Georgia Association
    of Educators, 47
  Harris's first campaign for NEA
    president and, 135
The Teacher Rebellion (Selden), 143
Temple, Evelyn
  first wave of NEA minority hires
    and, 142
Thomas, Clarence
  Equal Employment Opportunity
    Commission and, 157
Thomas, Franklin
  Ford Foundation president, 157
Till, Emmett
  abduction and murder of, 203–204
Time magazine
  Koontz's election to NEA president,
    87
Tornillo, Pat
  Florida teacher strike and, 76
Trenholm, H. Councill
  ATA leadership, 38–39
  biographical information, 38–39
  NATCS and NEA collaboration and,
    34–35, 38–39
Truman, Pres. Harry S
  civil rights issues and, 45
Tuskegee Airmen
  description, 45
  Harris's military career with, 129,
    130
Tuskegee Institute
  Harris's views on, 130

~U~

UFW. *See* United Farm Workers

UNESCO. *See* United Nation's Educational, Scientific, and Cultural Organization

United Farm Workers
    formation of, 73–74

United Nation's Educational, Scientific, and Cultural Organization
    campaign to reduce illiteracy, 190

Universal education
    National Teachers' Association and, 9
    NEA and, 21–22, 27
    public funding for schools and, 23

Urban, Wayne
    election of Koontz to NEA president, 101
    prominent position of, 183

U.S. Department of Education
    school lunch program and, 134–135

U.S. Department of Labor
    Nixon's appointment of Koontz to head the Women's Bureau, 113–118

U.S. Supreme Court. *See also specific cases and decisions*
    civil rights cases, 88
    Dred Scott decision, 4
    Maryland v. Wirtz ruling, 74–75
    prohibition of segregation on interstate bus travel, 45
    unconstitutionality of all-white political primaries, 45

~V~

Valentine, Thomas
    National Teachers' Association founding and first meeting, 7–9

Varela, Sal
    first wave of NEA minority hires and, 142

Vasquez, Tony
    IEA's Black and Hispanic Caucus and, 210

VEA. *See* Virginia Education Association

Viegas, Maria
    first wave of NEA minority hires and, 142

Virginia Education Association
    Futrell's role, 155, 170–172

Virginia League
    Brown v. Board of Education and, 49

Virginia State College
    Futrell's experiences at, 164–168

~W~

Walverton, Forrest
    National Council of Urban Education Associations leadership, 52–53

Warren, Earl
    Brown v. Board of Education opinion, 48

Washington, Booker T.
    address to the 1884 convention, 16–18, 19
    address to the 1896 convention, 20
    death of, 31
    endorsement of NATCS, 30

Watkins, Helen
    influence on Weaver, 203

Watson, Ellen
    ATA/NEA affiliates mergers and, 56

Wattleton, Faye
    Planned Parenthood president, 157

Watts, Gary
    relationship with Futrell, 177

Weaver, Reginald (Reg)
    Black and Hispanic Caucus and, 210
    childhood experiences, 201–202, 224, 225
    Civil Rights Movement and, 203–208

Danville High School Wall of Fame and, 230

Education International and, 230

educational background, 201–205

Executive Committee role, 209, 212

Hurricane Katrina relief fund and, 226–227

IEA president career, 211–212

Illinois Education Association and, 209–212

Joint Center for Political and Economic Studies and, 230

local association vice president career, 208

marriage of, 209

National Council for the Accreditation of Education and, 230

NBPTS and, 227–228, 230

NEA outreach programs and, 228–229

NEA president career, 197, 213–231, 234, 235

NEA Today columns, 215–217, 219–229

NEA vice president career, 212–213

NEA's endorsement of Barack Obama and, 231

No Child Left Behind Act and, 213–219

Paige's negative comments on NEA and, 218

parental involvement views, 222–223

parents' background, 201–202, 205

pay for performance views, 223–224

personality and style of, 208, 215, 229–230

relationship with Chase, 212–213

school dropouts views, 224–226

school safety views, 221–222

teacher salaries and, 219–220

teacher shortages views, 219–220

teaching career, 205–208

Weaver, Robert
appointed Secretary of Housing and Urban Development, 88

Webb, William B.
remarks on black education, 22

Wesley, Edgar
NEA: The First Hundred Years, 16, 49

West, Alan
election of Koontz to NEA president, 101
The National Education Association: The Power Base for Education, 112

Westbrook, Joe
ATA/NEA affiliates mergers and, 56

White Citizens Council
Brown v. Board of Education and, 49

Whyte, William H.
The Organization Man, 204

Wickersham, J.P.
"Education as an Element of Reconstruction" convention address, 13–14, 17

Wilderson, Frank
NEA restructuring and, 109

Wilfong, Ester
Black Caucus and, 137

Williams, Chuck
relationship with Futrell, 177
study of ethnic groups and, 187
views on Mary Hatwood Futrell, 154

Williams, Jimmy
attendance at Martin Luther King, Jr.'s funeral, 79

Williams, William Taylor
Spingarn Medal recipient, 32

Wilson, Wade
Black Caucus and, 137
NEA Executive Committee leadership, 53, 99, 154

Wise, Helen
Harris's speeches to affiliates about, 142
NEA president career, 124, 155

NEA's Political Action Committee
and, 143
views on Harris, 140
Women's issues
Equal Status for Women
Amendment resolution, 49
"gender conduct" and, 28
National Teachers' Association's
early years and, 9
Nixon's appointment of Koontz to
head the Women's Bureau of the
Department of Labor, 113–118
salaries for female teachers, 28
Women's Evening at the 1884
convention, 15
World War II
"Double V campaign," 42–43, 129–
130
internment of Japanese Americans,
44
Tuskegee Airmen, 45, 129, 130
Wright, Richard R.
biographical information, 30–31

segregation views, 31
Wynn, Lauri
Black Caucus and, 136–140
lawsuit against the Milwaukee
School District, 138
meeting with Al Shanker, 138
nomination of Harris for NEA
president, 140
personal style, 138
relationship with Futrell, 191
views on Harris, 124

~Y~

Young, Andrew
Ambassador to the United Nations,
157
Young, Ella Flagg
election to NEA president, 87
Young, Whitney
address to the Critical Issues in
Education Conference, 109